1987

The Vulnerable Text

The Vulnerable Text

ESSAYS ON RENAISSANCE LITERATURE

Thomas M. Greene

Columbia University Press

New York

1986

Columbia University Press
New York   Guildford, Surrey
Copyright © 1986 Columbia University Press
Printed in the United States of America

Library of Congress Cataloging-in Publication Data

Greene, Thomas M.
The vulnerable text.

Bibliography: p.
Includes index.
Contents: Erasmus' ''Festina lente''—Petrarch
Viator—Il cortegiano and the choice of a game—
[etc.]
    1. European literature—Renaissance, 1450–1600—
History and criticism——Addresses, essays, lectures,
I Title.
PN721.G73 1986   809'.031   85-27978
ISBN 0-231-06246-X

for A. Bartlett Giamatti

Contents

Acknowledgments

"Erasmus' 'Festina lente': Vulnerabilities of the Humanist Text" is reprinted from *Mimesis: From Mirror to Method, Augustine to Descartes*, edited by John D. Lyons and Stephen G. Nichols, Jr., by permission of University Press of New England. Copyright © 1982 by Trustees of Dartmouth College.

"Petrarch *Viator*" was originally published in a special issue on "Heroes and the Heroic" of the *Yearbook of English Studies* (1982), 12:35–57, and is reprinted here by permission.

"*Il Cortegiano* and the Choice of a Game" is reprinted from *Castiglione: The Ideal and the Real in Renaissance Culture*, edited by Robert W. Hanning and David Rosand, and is reprinted here by permission. Copyright © 1983 by Yale University Press.

"The End of Discourse in Machiavelli's *Prince*" appeared in *Yale French Studies* (1984), no. 67, pp. 57–71, and is reprinted here by permission. This essay later appeared in *Literary Theory and Renaissance Texts*, edited by David Quint and Patricia Parker, published in 1986 by the Johns Hopkins University Press.

"The Hair of the Dog That Bit You: Rabelais' Thirst" appeared in *The Incomparable Book: Rabelais and His Art*, edited by Raymond La Charité and published by French Forum Publishers in 1985. Reprinted here by permission.

"Rescue from the Abyss: Scève's Dizain 378" appeared in *Textual Analysis: Some Readers Reading*, edited by Mary Ann Caws and published by the Modern Language Association in 1986. Reprinted here by permission.

"Dangerous Parleys—Montaigne's *Essais* I:5 and 6" appeared in *Yale French Studies* (1983), no. 64, pp. 3–23, and is reprinted here by permission.

"*Love's Labour's Lost:* The Grace of Society" appeared in *Shakespeare Quarterly* (Autumn 1971), 22:315–28, and is reprinted here by permission.

"Anti-Hermeneutics: The Case of Shakespeare's Sonnet 129" appeared in *Poetic Traditions of the Renaissance*, edited by Maynard Mack and George Lord, and is reprinted here by permission. Copyright © 1982 by Yale University Press.

"Pitiful Thrivers: Failed Husbandry in the *Sonnets*" appeared in *Shakespeare and the Question of Theory*, edited by Geoffrey Hartman and Patricia Parker, and is reprinted here by permission. Copyright © 1985 by Methuen.

"Ben Jonson and the Centered Self" appeared in *Studies in English Literature* (Spring 1970), 10:325—48, and is reprinted here by permission.

"History and Anachronism" appeared in *Literature and History: Theoretical Problems and Russian Case Studies*, edited by Gary Saul Morson, and is reprinted here by permission of Stanford University Press. Copyright © 1986 by the Board of Trustees of the Leland Stanford Junior University.

A passage from W. B. Yeats' poem "The Black Tower," which appears on pp. 340—41 of his *Collected Poems*, has been reprinted here by permission of Macmillan. Copyright 1940 by Georgie Yeats and copyright © 1950 by Macmillan.

Introduction

The essays gathered in this volume have been written over a period of years in response to a number of promptings, internal and external. The inquisitions and engagements that provoked them into being were various, and my mind was innocent of any pretensions to a grand design. Though most were written in the early eighties, two essays (on *Love's Labour's Lost* and Ben Jonson) are somewhat older; even within the more recent group, individual pieces visibly respond to a range of pressures, just as the choice of subjects elicits a range of method. Nonetheless, certain angles of questioning will be recognized as continuous. Many essays return to a central cluster of themes. In an unsystematic way the collection reflects my own slants, myths, obsessions with the period and the civilization that the essays collectively circumscribe. The methodological slants necessarily have theoretical implications, so that implicitly or explicitly a polemical undercurrent runs spasmodically through the book. In my critical beginnings I was a child of the (Anglo-Saxon) New Criticism and continental historicism; later I was exposed to the values of Renaissance Humanism. The reader who cares to can trace the effort of that child, now older and scarred, to map out an evolving position amid a swirl of critical currents.

The word "vulnerable," to which the title gives prominence, turns up in a number of the more recent essays. A kind of preface to the analysis of Scève sets out most fully what I mean by the word, but that definition is not restrictive, and other nuances emerge in other usages elsewhere. These essays themselves are conspicuously vulnerable, since they rest on presuppositions many will not grant. They assume that one can speak meaningfully of a literary text, that such a text has a moral dimension, that its historicity is essential to it, that some readings are more appropriate to it than others, and perhaps more crucially that, in Ricoeur's terms, a hermeneutic of faith is not incompatible with a hermeneutic of suspicion. The latter tactic is most clearly at work in the essays on Petrarch, Castiglione, Machiavelli, Montaigne, and Shakespeare's sonnets ("Pitiful Thrivers"). But the collection as a whole sets limits and qualifications upon critical suspicion, and from these stem both the concept of vulnerability and my work's own particular vulnerability.

The imprint of Renaissance Humanism shows itself not least here in the grounding of the literary text in a specific culture. A culture supplies the text with symbols and metaphors that are commonly arbitrary, subject to skepticism and erosion, worn by convention, tarnished by tendentious manipulation. Yet it would be reductive to describe a culture's symbolic vocabulary as inert *doxa*, lifeless opinion, sterile received ideas. The literary text that merits our attention "invents" the symbols already accessible, discovers their potency and renders them productive. Part of the text's vulnerability lies in its dependence on secondhand signifiers, a vulnerability aggravated in a culture which does not yet fetishize originality. The triumph of the text lies in its power to discover or uncover the density of the signifier and the sedimented substance of a tradition that does not merely erode or debase.

"Suffer then the world to inioy," writes Samuel Daniel, clairvoyantly but not ironically:

> that which it knowes, and what it likes. . . . Seeing that whatsoever force of words doth moove, delight, and sway the affections of men, in what Scythian sorte soever it be disposed or uttered, that is true number, measure, eloquence, and the perfection of speach: which I said hath as many shapes as there be tongues or nations in the world.[1]

Daniel's cultural relativism, his awareness of multiple semiotic worlds, his admission of the "shapes" of cultural conventions, do not lead him to deny an authentic eloquence. "Perfection of speach" is compatible with the most Scythian particularities; words have an inherent "force" though they cannot, he goes on, "be governed otherwise then custome and present observation will allow." The force indeed seems to take its momentum, for Daniel, from the custom of provincial shapes. The custom of one culture may always look Scythian to another; that is its vulnerability. The world which enjoys what it likes is always exposed to potential sarcasm. But Daniel is not sarcastic; he sees the limitations of caprice as inherent in the force of language. Custom is not *doxa*, if this is defined as dead; custom and its traditional vocabulary contribute to verbal power.

One might in fact consider a text as the stylized version of a culture. Just as certain masques of Ben Jonson, however open to the charge of courtly narcissism, still try to stage radiant visions of an ideal civilization, dancing impossible communities, so any literary text can be regarded as organizing communal constructs microcosmically. The text tries to "purify" its inherited language, as Mallarmé saw; it tries to regulate cultural tensions and harmonize dissonances; it tries to reproduce those activities of assimilation and rejection, moral discrimination, mythic fabrication, symbolic reordering, that cultures typically perform. The text can be read as an idealized miniature culture, whether or not it allows the idealization to be perceived as a critique. But it plays this role only at a risk: it may fail to harmonize its dissonances but only succeed in exposing them; its mythic constructs may collapse; it may fail to cleanse adequately its soiled vocabulary; the tensions it wants to regulate may explode. The text at its most effective will never overcome the incompleteness of our humanity. It will never achieve absolute closure, freedom from deferral, perfect finality, those unreal dreams of the twentieth-century mind. But it may still attain a distinction of conative energy and refinement. The incompleteness of the human sets off the distinction; as Daniel implies, the Scythian idiosyncrasy underlies the creative force. A textual construct like a cultural construct is a leaning tower, artificial and precarious, that draws our eyes. Rilke, evoking the unwelcome possibility that the saltimbanques' skill might reach a mechanical flawlessness, refers to "the ineffable spot where the pure too-little / incomprehensibly changes,—springs round / into that empty too much."[2] But even in our supreme masters we never reach that "leere Zuviel," happily. The text does not exist which cannot be parodied, just as the culture does not exist which an alien cannot perceive as barbaric.

The literary text is doubly exposed to potential offense through its dependence on two kinds of rhetoric. It depends first on the structures of tropes that are constantly changing. The structure of the "metaphor" at any given moment in any given community is historically conditioned. The structure of the trope at the determinant moment of origin stems from intangible intuitions, beliefs, and intellectual habits that fade and cannot easily be recovered. Thus the trope is potentially subject to misreading at a radical, intuitive level. (See the essay on "Anti-Hermeneutics.") But in addition to this "hard" rhetoric, the literary text also depends on what Nietzsche dismissed deprecatingly as the "popular" version of rhetoric, the performative kind that aims at "eloquence." Hard rhetoric, as Paul de Man showed, can be confused with grammar; it drifts toward Saussure's *langue*.[3] "Popular" performative rhetoric belongs to *parole*. Performative rhetoric calls not only upon figural deformations of language but on inflection, tone, gesture, voice, moral style, which are unique to each utterance. They are as constitutive of the literary text as the tropes of hard rhetoric; the text individualizes itself through them and it could not escape them if it would. Post-structuralist analysis is strong on nouns but weak on adverbs; the balance will sooner or later have to be righted. But the presence of a unique tone itself widens the margin of legitimate interpretive debate, since nothing is less tangible. We can miss the tone and we can also abuse it. The speaker as performer is exposed as the hard rhetorician is not: he acts to please, persuade, amuse, and affect us; he is naked on the stage; we can laugh with him or at him or we can hiss. This is the risk that a text assumes insofar as it makes a claim to be literary; it adopts a haecceity of inflection.

The text is exposed but it also conceals; there are cards the performer doesn't show us. It remains a bit of a riddle, inviting our own conative, incomplete inquisition, disappointing ultimately what Kermode calls the *spes hermeneutica*. Charles d'Orléans might be speaking for all poets.

Ma plus chier tenue richesse
Ou parfont tresor de Pensee
Est soubz clef, seurement gardee,
Par Esperance, ma Deesse.[4]

The poet's goddess Esperance is also the reader's, but the goddess-guardian keeps the lid on the treasure. In this respect the textual construct diverges from the cultural, which is intended to be grasped. The text we might say tends to *thicken* an inherited symbol into something more dense, opaque, complicated, mysterious, explosive, uncanny. Thus Petrarch thickens the symbol of the wayfarer, which in his canon becomes more matted and temperamental, also more revelatory of private guilt but not thereby more pervious. The exposure of guilt feelings by analysis does not reduce the core of poetic resistance to explanation, or if it does, the literary pretense stands betrayed as inauthentic. Machiavelli's shifting use of the term *virtù* is most aptly understood not as a vortex of semantic circularity but as a thickened, obscure, dynamic node of bursting energy, reified but not rigidified. The vulnerability of Machiavelli's usage, the semantic instability and opacity, constitute the price we pay for the newly created, uncanny thing.

Petrarch's and Machiavelli's books are literary insofar as they present densities that invite analysis. At this writing, much of the most rigorous contemporary analysis tends to be suspicious, and the major critical schools—Freudian, deconstructive, Marxist, feminist, reader response, among others—tend to converge in a common effort of demystification. This effort is open to readerly suspicion only if it is blind to the insidious ways in which demystification produces remystification. The risk of this blindness seems to me the only caution necessary to the gifted school in English Renaissance studies which has come to be called the New Historicism. The conceptual instrument used to demystify—say, the concept of "Power"—always needs to be examined for its own hidden and tendentious presuppositions. The text under study, if it is worth studying, will in its own turn remystify itself, positively, productively, after its dissection. The careful separation of elements leads to an abrupt recombination; the new totality will be vulnerable once again, will invite once again a dismantling, but it has recovered, as it will again recover, its provisional and insecure coherence. Thus the exposure of containment as the unacknowledged goal of Castiglione's courtiers does not ultimately reduce the center of semantic density within the *Cortegiano*.

This capacity for automatic recombination, like the reforming of scattered bodies when the last trump sounds, is as reliable a criterion as any of the literariness of a text. The literary text is that organization of verbal signifiers perennially subject to interpretation and misinterpretation, historical erosion, exposure, inversion, decentering, ingurgitation by the aporetic abyss—that organization that perennially regains a provisional, still questionable, uncanny gathering of force. This recovery is precarious; its very assertion is vulnerable, since a hermeneutic of faith will always appear less rigorous than its opposite. But the instability of the text is of a piece with its endurance. Hope may seem an unlikely guardian of that most secret and precious treasure of thought, but the treasure remains, "seurement gardee."

"Wit has his dregs as well as wine," writes Thomas Nashe, "words their waste, ink his blots, every speech his parenthesis."[5] That is as good a formulation of the vulnerable text as any, placed as it is concessively in an epilogue asking for applause. What does Nashe mean by "parenthesis"? Is that slightly puzzling metaphor a blot of *his* ink? Perhaps he means that every speech needs, ought to have, a parenthesis that explains what the speech will inevitably leave unstated. Or he may mean that the speech does in some way interrupt itself, digress, interpose extraneous material, intrude upon us the "waste" of its words. Or he may mean that a supplementary meaning will always impede the pure flow of language, checking its rhythm and hobbling its felicity. All these concessions are conceivably present, but there is no denial that wit has its wine as well as its dregs, or that wit makes use of ink, however blotted.

Nashe was a writer we assign to the "Renaissance," a cultural construct of the last century which resuscitates a cultural construct of the period designated. The Renaissance can be described as that stretch of history which wanted to act out a renascence, even if its desire was ambivalent. The mimesis of the Renaissance Humanist text, as the Erasmus essay argues, was a simplified imitation of historical process, and this mimesis had been arguably unknown for a millennium. The history imitated always ended with a figurative rebirth. This meant among other things that most Renaissance signifiers tended to be grounded in the "original" texts of a remote era or in the praxis of a modern culture self-consciously emerging from a more or less discredited past. Even when, as was often the case, the signifiers derived directly from that past regarded as outmoded, they tended to appear displaced. Rabelais' name "Pantagruel" derives from the mystery plays of the fifteenth century but its associations are radically redefined. The owl and the cuckoo of *Love's Labour's Lost* continue an old debate that is altered by its context. Erasmus in a colloquy *(Convivium religiosum)* restages the sacrament of the Eucharist at a luncheon for laymen. The reborn civilization was actually a displaced civilization, typically improvising forms, symbols, and rituals less firmly grounded than their medieval counterparts. Displacement creates the kind of anxiety visible on the pages of Petrarch, or the controlled threat overshadowing Castiglione's court, or the anguish that besets Shakespeare's lyric redefinition of love.

The fiction of rebirth produced both release and insecurity, and both will be found in the essays that follow. But if I have chosen to underscore the vulnerable character of the literary text, a character presented as universal, this choice is doubtless related to the peculiar displacement of the Renaissance text. I have quoted elsewhere Nietzsche's remarks on the danger of willfully cutting down an inherited tradition and have applied them to the Renaissance.[6] The danger is writ large in the books that era produced, including the most remarkable. Thus the drama of exposure, erosion, dismantling, and reformation appears especially acute and visible in the texts studied here.

Again in this anxiety of displacement the microcosmic text can be shown to mirror the macrocosmic culture. What is extraordinary in retrospect is the fecundity of the culture, or rather a series of vaguely kindred cultures strung across several centuries in several countries, each superbly pluralistic, each witnessing the creation of radically various currents, schools, genres, and individual geniuses. A culture begins to distort at its origin the work it has helped to nourish. A culture can bury a work as it buried Scève's, or it can disfigure a work as the Counter-Reformation disfigured Ariosto's. The institutions, codes, faiths, fictions, and symbols culture provides are riddled with its arbitrary and irregular incompleteness. Yet culture does foster maieutically the work that at once reflects its limits and myths while preserving a secret *tresor* against it. During the long period circumscribed by the following essays, each distinct culture did not inhibit intolerably the power of a work to reshape constructs, to modify its semiotic world, and to fabricate its brilliant unsteady towers resting on shallow basements.

Marcus Aurelius began his book by paying homage at length to each of his preceptors. This book is dwarfed by his, but commensurate homage to my teachers of three generations would, I suspect, properly amount to a still longer introduction. The reader will be spared a complete account of my debts, but I am unwilling to leave them altogether unacknowledged. During my years of formal study at Yale, I was fortunate enough to learn from a brilliant Pléiade of distinguished critical minds. There is no space here for all the names, but I feel obliged to mention William K. Wimsatt, Jr., Cleanth Brooks, René Wellek, Erich Auerbach, John Pope, and Henri Peyre. Courses with Eugene Waith and Louis Martz cemented my attachment to the Renaissance. Later as a novice teacher I would learn more from Maynard Mack than I might have from half a dozen lesser men. The voices and examples of my teachers at Yale have come together to shape my fundamental response to literature. Two ghosts in particular, Wimsatt's and Auerbach's, haunt my desk as I struggle to diminish my fear of betrayal. I might say of my masters collectively as Ariosto wrote of his, Gregorio da Spoleto, that they are men I have reason always to bless: "che ragion vuol ch'io sempre benedica."[7]

It was my continued good fortune to number among

my colleagues at Yale many gifted men and women whose friendship has been precious and whose attainments are rare. They included among them critics no less brilliant than my teachers, and from them too I have learned, in some cases through mutual discovery and in others through amicable dialectic and debate. Sometimes I have been required to articulate with some pretense of logic differences that might otherwise have remained unexamined prejudices. If I believed in history in an ambience not unanimously drawn to it, I was forced to find compelling support for my belief. I was awed by the power of the minds I wanted to engage, but I would like to hope that I grew from the challenge they represented. This has been chiefly possible because intellectual difference has been so markedly distinct from personal acrimony. Paul de Man, whose challenge I felt as most formidable, was a man of incomparable magnetism and generosity; his humanity and charm helped to preserve our academic community.

I should like to mention here as well a scholar-critic of wide and deserved influence in the field of Renaissance studies, Terence Cave, a critic not on our local scene but one who has played unwittingly a provocative role in determining the direction of my work. Two of the essays in this book take issue with him; a third ("Rabelais' Thirst") fails to mention his name but moves slantwise against his thought. Yet it is my belief that these and other essays would be slacker and thinner had Cave never written *The Cornucopian Text,* whose more or less deconstructive readings of Renaissance authors are formulated with admirable subtlety and insight. For a dissenter to wrestle with Cave is a wry and humbling education. Whitman writes, "Have you not learn'd great lessons from those who . . . brace themselves against you? . . . or dispute the passage with you?"[8] This has been my experience, although not all of those who braced themselves against me were even aware at the outset that our dispute had begun.

Most of the energy in my academic career has gone not into writing but into graduate teaching. My students have constituted a third pool of brilliant minds forming a third generation, and from them too I have learned more than I can measure. In my memory some inevitably stand out more than others, but the level of excellence has remained very high. Like all graduate teachers, I have watched with pride my junior collaborators go out to infiltrate institutions across the country. In looking back I think of my students in the terms Cicero reserved for those of Isocrates: from his school, as from the Trojan horse, emerged only princes—*meri principes*. To one of the first of these this book is dedicated.

Rewarded as I have been by contact with three—or as the years pass, four—generations of remarkable spirits, I sometimes ask myself in all seriousness if any single individual has ever been privileged by intimate interchange with a more gifted succession of literary minds. And I cannot easily answer that there has ever been such a one.

The Vulnerable Text

1
Erasmus' "Festina lente":
Vulnerabilities of the Humanist Text

The term "vulnerabilities" in my title may well appear perverse in connection with one of Erasmus' *Adagia*, the most notorious of all Renaissance *florilegia*, a vast, baggy, shapeless hulk of a book, its 4,000-odd entries apparently innocent of organization and proof against all its indexes, unread today for the most part and perhaps in its entirety unreadable. To deliver a wound, even to strike a blow, one wants to know where one is aiming, but this interminable leviathan—literally interminable—presents us no fore or aft. One might lop off a decade of entries here, a century there; no sequence would be interrupted. To assault this amorphous monster, even to talk about it, seems nothing if not quixotic; "Fluvius cum mari certas"—being no more than a river, you contend with the sea. Yet for all its formidable, swollen, and treacherous mass, one can discern a kind of structure organizing individual entries; one can also appropriately describe certain features of the *Adagia* as vulnerable, features that are endemic to the Humanist enterprise and inseparable from the peculiar type of Humanist mimesis.

The rough history of the *Adagia* is well known: its modest beginning with a paltry 800-plus entries in 1500, near the opening of Erasmus' literary career; its first large edition in 1508 with over 3,200 entries, nourished by its author's improving Greek as well as his access to Italian libraries and to the press of Aldus Manutius; then its frequent reeditions throughout the remainder of its author's life, each new edition containing more entries and interpolations inserted in the older ones, more autobiography and more polemic as the author discovered his book's potentialities. Each entry includes a proverb, a figure of speech, an enigmatic cliché familiar in antiquity, followed by a commentary that is primarily, ostensibly philological, citing the passages or authors where the phrase can be found and indicating its ancient meaning and evolving range of meanings. In some cases this purely philological commentary fades into a discussion of potential applications within Erasmus' contemporary world. In roughly 20 cases, this in turn leads to a longish essay capable of introducing almost anything Erasmus cared about. Thus any entry consists of two unequal parts—the original adage proper, inherited from antiquity, and its unfolding, its explication, at greater or lesser length, with greater or lesser inventive freedom, always subject to expansion.

Seemingly one of the freest of all the adage-commentaries is that produced by the little oxymoronic injunction "Speūde bradéos," "Festina lente," "Make haste slowly," which first appeared in the big Aldine edition of 1508. Erasmus privileges this adage not only by the length and range of his commentary but also by his enthusiasm. He writes that no other proverb is as worthy as this one, so absolutely concise, so fertile, so gemlike, so applicable to every situation in life. In fact, he writes, it deserves to be called "royal," *regius,* partly because its wisdom is needed by kings, but also, one gathers, because this is the king of all the adages. We observe, however, that the genealogy of this royalty is more obscure than befits most kings. Erasmus cites an expression from Aristophanes, "Make haste hastily," and conjectures that somebody later wittily reversed the adverb. At any rate, Octavious Caesar is known to have used the phrase repeatedly, and the emperor Titus had a coin stamped bearing a dolphin and an anchor to express the same thought.

The mention of this medal opens up alternative, older, and mistier genealogical reaches, back into the hermetic lore, the *prisca theologia* of the ancient Egyptians, who according to Plutarch and "Suidas" produced a so-called hieroglyphic wherein a circle enclosed a dolphin entwined around an anchor. Since a circle symbolized eternity (this symbolization permits a digression on the metaphysics of finite and infinite lines), since a dolphin symbolized speed and an anchor delay, the hieroglyphic is to be read:

"Always hasten slowly." After elaborating on each of these mystic meanings in turn, Erasmus modernizes hieroglyph and adage by referring to his printer, Aldus Manutius, who has made the anchor and dolphin his trademark. Nor, writes Erasmus, is there any falling off from the imperial coin to the printer's page, since this particular printer seems born to restore true ancient learning. Aldus typifies the Humanist hero-archaeologist-necromancer who restores the ruinous and the dead to life. No nobler work can be imagined.

> It is indeed a Herculean task, and worthy of a kingly spirit, to restore to the world so divine a thing, out of such complete ruin; to investigate what lay hidden, to bring to light what was concealed, to call to life what had perished, to fill up gaps and emend a text corrupted in so many ways.[1]

In conclusion Erasmus offers three overlapping interpretations of this royal adage: first, "It would be better to wait a little before tackling a matter; when a decision has been reached, then swift action can be taken"; second, "The passions of the mind should be reined in by reason"; third, "Precipitate action should be avoided in everything." Erasmus ends his commentary by expatiating on each of these sententious truisms.

This sketchy summary of mine recompresses a text that presents itself as a decompression and that underscores its own leisurely, digressive, serpentine progress, pulling in allusions, quotations, erudite bric-a-brac, souvenirs, and anecdotes to enlarge its substance and lengthen its course. How are we to understand the relationship of this garrulous paraphrase to the tiny urphrase which instigated it? What is the logic of this fusion of copia and brevity, and what structural principle, if any, orders it? The impulse, whatever it was, that produced this text and its thousands of companions has to be regarded with some curiosity, since the *Adagia* stands, whether or not we read it, as one of the fountainheads of Humanism. In fact, each paraphrastic, dilative unfolding can be considered as a microcosm of the Humanist enterprise.

The search for an organizational center should properly begin with Erasmus' love of verbal jewelry. At the opening

of the "Festina lente" essay, he says that proverbs in their conci-
sion and brilliance should be as clear-cut as gems *(gemmae)*. This
particular adage he finds especially gemlike. The analogy recurs
frequently. We meet it again in the adage-essay "Herculei labores": "Proverbs are like gems, so small they often escape the
searcher's eye unless you look very carefully. They are not ready
to hand but lie hidden, and it is a matter of digging them out
rather than collecting them" (p. 196). To search out these tiny
stones of meaning is for Erasmus precisely a Herculean labor, and
we can guess which one when he compares the ignorance and
laziness of commentators to dung concealing gold. In the prefatory
epistle to the *Parabolae*, which itself amounts to a book-length
catalogue of similes, the same metaphor returns.

> I have not chosen what was ready to hand, nor picked up pebbles
> on the beach; I have brought forth precious stones from the inner
> treasure-house of the Muses. The barber's shop, the tawdry con-
> versation of the marketplace are no source for what is to be worth
> the attention of the ears and eyes of educated men. Such things
> must be unearthed in the innermost secrets of nature, in the inner
> shrine of the arts and sciences.

This unearthing is worth the labor, writes Erasmus somewhat
surprisingly, since "almost all the dignity of language stems from
its metaphors."[2] In his fascination with the hard, secret, precious,
time-resistant capsule of signification, Erasmus seems to attribute
to it something theurgic, mysteriously and uncannily powerful.
The amulet of meaning carries an aura of potency all the stronger
if the meaning is enigmatic or figurative or paradoxical. Thus in
"Festina lente," what Erasmus calls the force and fecundity of the
words lies in their oxymoronic conflict: "verbis inter se pugnan-
tibus." The absolute brevity of the paradox produces its "precii
miraculum," and we should not, I think, try to diminish the
wonder of the writer before the *miraculum*, this talismanic marvel.
   The same fascination with the apparently irreducible
kernel can be found in Erasmus' devotional writing. The Christian,
like the Humanist, betrays this wonder, although he adjusts his
metaphors. In the adage-essay "Sileni Alcibiadis," he writes:

The parables of the Gospel, if you take them at face value—who would not think that they came from a simple ignorant man? And yet if you crack the nut, you find inside that profound wisdom, truly divine, a touch of something which is clearly like Christ himself. . . . The real truth always lies deeply hidden, not to be understood easily or by many people. (P. 276)

This principle of verbal expression is also the principle of biology, even of what we might call human ontology.

In trees, it is the flowers and leaves which are beautiful to the eye: their spreading bulk is visible far and wide. But the seed, in which lies the power of it all, how tiny a thing it is! how secret, how far from flattering the sight or showing itself off! Gold and gems are hidden by nature in the deepest recesses of the earth. Among what they call the elements, the most important are those furthest removed from the senses, like air and fire. In living things, what is best and most vital is secreted in the inward parts. In man, what is most divine and immortal is what cannot be seen. (Pp. 274–275)

This secret ontology of man is also the ontology of the kingdom of heaven, which "has as its symbol a grain of mustard seed, small and contemptible in appearance, mighty in power" (p. 273). That principle must be kept in mind by the interpreter of Scripture. The *Enchiridion* compares God's secret law to manna. "The fact that it was only a small thing signifies the paltriness of language, the vast mysteries contained in words which are, so to speak, crude and inadequate." Later Erasmus invites the reader to "break through the husk and find the kernel."[3] It is hard to resist pairing this sacred kernel of the *Enchiridion* with the potent gem of the *Adagia*: both are verbal Silenus boxes whose resistance to understanding has to be pierced for the initiate to participate in their latent semiotic infinitude.

Yet the "Festina lente" essay reminds us that this absolute brevity, "absoluta brevitas," is not absolute; the irreducible gem is further reducible, since the essay alludes to that pseudo-code that the Renaissance called "hieroglyphics" and that, following Plutarch's example, it credulously attributed to ancient Egypt.

[Hieroglyphics] is the word for the enigmatic carvings which were so much used in early times, especially among the Egyptian seers and theologians, who thought it wrong to exhibit the mysteries to the vulgar in open writing, as we do; but they expressed what they thought worthy to be known by various symbols, things or animals, so that not everyone could readily interpret them. But if anyone deeply studies the qualities of each object, and the special nature and power of each creature, he would at length . . . understand the meaning of the riddle. (P. 175)

From this passage it is clear that the hieroglyphic is superior to the adage on three counts: first, it is even more compressed; second, it does not signify idiosyncratically—its meaning is not dependent on historical accident but remains perennial; third, it points directly to the essence of its referent. In this account of the hieroglyphic, we can discern a kind of nostalgia or envy of a semiotic gem more durable, economical, powerful, and hermetic than the adage.

The hieroglyphic, as we meet it here, is the absolute signifier; the adage is a creature of history, subject to debate, to interpretation, to a variety of uses—the coin of the emperor Titus, the trademark of Aldus, the essay of Erasmus. The Aldine edition contains for the first time a preface that defines the adage or "paroemia" as a proverb adapted to certain times and circumstances ("accomodatum rebus, temporibusque proverbium");[4] thus the time-bound character of the adage is for Erasmus a part of its definition. Its meaning is not available, without special help, to all ages. Hieroglyphics represent semiotic perfection; they present the ultimate code, and thus they dramatize the imperfection, the vulnerability of language. It is clear that for Erasmus their perfection is related to the restriction of their use; their purity remained pristine because the Egyptian seers thought it a crime or sacrilege, *nefas,* to expose their age-old wisdom to the crowd. Erasmus indeed adds a revealing parenthetical clause: "to expose the mysteries to the crowd in ordinary writing, as we do" ("quemadmodum nos facimus"). The "we" of this clause, the "nos," can refer to the members of the Christian church; or it can refer to those contemporaries we would call Humanists, who taught and interpreted the wisdom of antiquity, whose profession was divulgation; or this "nos" could be read as an authorial "we," referring precisely to the writer compiling the *Adagia*, exposing all these precious stones to public view. Judged by the conduct of Egyptian seers, Erasmus writes his book, as the adage has it, "illotis manibus," with unclean hands. Erasmus' divulgation, like all Humanist divulgation, would be a kind of pollution.

Because, for better or for worse, he is not a guardian of hieroglyphics, because with clean or dirty hands he is involved in a massive, historic dissemination, because he depends on that everyday writing, *literis communibus*, which is vulnerable to historical contingency, Erasmus cannot leave his amulets pristine and hidden. He must, on the contrary, dilate his metaphors and oxymorons with commentary and interpretation. In this respect he plays the role of the antipriest, and he makes no attempt to conceal this role; the imagery of dilation, expansion, diffusion, is very common in the *Adagia* and especially prominent in the "Festina lente" essay. Expansion, of course, is the foremost activity in the *Adagia*. Not only is each entry the expanded explication of a single phrase, but this entry is likely to be lengthened in later editions as the number of entries is also tirelessly, heroically, pitilessly increased. The "Festina lente" essay itself is expanded by a long digression added in 1526 that I have yet to discuss. In a less concrete sense, the announced aim of the work is a widening of knowledge, a literal dissemination that was part of the Humanist mission. The opening page of "Festina lente" concretizes this disseminative impulse. These words, writes Erasmus,

> should be cut on every pillar and written over every temple porch, inscribed in gold on the double doors of princely halls, chased on episcopal rings, engraved on royal sceptres; . . . they should recur on every monument everywhere and be spread abroad and celebrated, so that such an important thing should be so much under the public eye that no single mortal could avoid acting on it. (Pp. 171–72)

Erasmus' enthusiasm leads him to vast fantasies of planetary dissemination: "Happiness like this far outflows the boundaries of empire, and is spread about throughout the most far-flung peoples of the world" (p. 172). Expansion like this can of course only be accomplished by the printing press, the instrument of the essay's hero, Aldus Manutius. Aldus, we learn, "is building up a sacred and immortal thing, and serving not one alone but all peoples and all generations. . . . [He] is building up a library which has no other limits than the world itself" (pp. 180–81). Aldus' library, extended immeasurably, becomes analogous to the verbal core of the essay, the two words paraphrased and dilated by Erasmus' spiraling commentary. The centripetal nostalgia for the absolute, hermetic, closed point is thwarted, but a centrifugal alternative emerges that is at once textual, semantic, sociological, and geographic. Never is Erasmus more quintessentially Humanist than in this paraphrase, dilation, dissemination perceived to be faithful to an origin, which is to say not, in our terms, Derridean.

It would be tempting to find in this movement outward the structural principle we were looking for. Expansion in all its various meanings is celebrated in the 1508 essay as a healthy exercise of power. Even the somewhat sententious close is quickened by an image of dynamic growth from Pindar. But in the late edition of 1526 a long addition makes its appearance in the "Festina lente" essay, roughly half as long as the original version. This addition is devoted to the risks of divulgation, which according to the aging Erasmus has been overtaken by disaster. This is due in part to the avarice of collectors but chiefly to the greed of the disseminators. The heroism of an Aldus has been debased and travestied by a swarm of lesser printers, thriving particularly in Germany, who care nothing for textual accuracy, who are lazy, unscrupulous, even illiterate, who print and circulate anything. Now the wave of centrifugal worldwide diffusion becomes an abominable danger. "To what corner of the world do they not fly, these swarms of new books?" (p. 182). These cursed printers "fill the world with books, not just trifling things (such as I write, perhaps), but stupid, ignorant, slanderous, scandalous, raving, irreligious and seditious books" (p. 184). Only in a passage such as this can one fully gauge how much power Erasmus and his world attributed to the written and printed word. The vision in fact becomes apocalyptic. The meretricious printer becomes the agent and the synecdoche for universal chaos.

> If things go on as they have begun, the result will be that supreme power will be concentrated in the hands of a few, and we shall have as barbaric a tyranny among us as there is among the Turks. Everything will give way to the appetites of one man or of a few, and there will not remain the slightest vestige of civilized society, but all will be under the rule of military force. All noble disciplines will wither away, one law alone will operate. (P. 183)

The church is threatened with impotence, the family with dispersal. And much of the mischief comes from the printers' "unbridled license." The press, once an instrument of enlightenment, threatens the globe with Armageddon.

Thus the process of sociologic and geographic expansion lies open at once to the sacred and the sacrilegious. It is both Herculean and vulnerable. But in a different sphere one can say the same for the textual, semantic expansion enacted by the text before us. As the adage-commentary grows into the adage-essay, its relation to the tiny, verbal gem presented as its center becomes more problematic. Here too the process of indefinite widening involves the threat of chaos, and not least in this meandering divagation away from the most royal and most privileged of all the adages. The commentary presents itself throughout the volume as a faithful unpacking of compressed but determinate meaning, as the translation of a trope, a paradox, ostensible nonsense, into the discursive, lucid sense of the nonfigurative. The commentary supposedly supplies the solution to the miniature problem posed by the verbal kernel; it proposes to fill in the signification, smooth over the paradox, by means of dilation, thus transforming mystery into wisdom.

But as the dilation proceeds further and further, as it reveals all the abundance, the copia, of the adage proper, the kernel becomes progressively indeterminate; it fails to center the essay. The act of spinning out meaning begins to look arbitrary and subjective. We come to realize that each writer might provide his own particular enlargement, just as each historical age would provide its own particular counterparts to ancient experience. The original trope begins to look utterly protean, to the point where the plenum of meaning may be indistinguishable from a void of meaning. Perhaps the adage proper is only an inkblot test, a starting place for random association. Failing to be a hieroglyphic, failing to possess that absolute, essential, perennial meaning that history cannot erode, perhaps the adage reveals only a pretense of meaning. According to this view, its dissemination *would* be Derridean. In the Erasmian terms employed by Terence Cave, this cornucopian text would betray its poverty of nourishing substance in its very cancerous growth, its failure to be *uber* as it becomes more visibly a *tuber*.

This risk is undoubtedly present in the adage, and it is all the more threatening in the shifts of perspective and moral emphasis that divide it. On one page a hymn to the dolphin, with its "almost incredible energy of movement," becomes a hymn to what the dolphin is said to symbolize, the ardent and dauntless vigor of the (human) mind ("acrem illum et indomitum animi impetum"). But on another page, the last, the dolphin is taken to symbolize the folly and ungovernable impulse of the mind ("socordia . . . vel immoderato impetu"). The adage-essay shifts its terms and values like an essay by Montaigne, but it lacks the putative center of those later wandering texts, a changeable yet knowable self. Thus we are left to ask if there is any way at all to recuperate some structural firmness for the adage, for this particular, exemplary adage or for all the others in this endless, Borgesian library of a book. The answer, if it exists, will concern not only this work but the intellectual and cultural movement for which it speaks.

One response to this structural question, one fashionable response, would point to the way many of the adages can be read as self-referential. We have already met explicit self-referentiality in the adages "Herculei labores" and "Sileni Alcibiadis." If "Festina lente" combines awe for the mind and fear of the mind, a celebration of the press with horror of the press, it is, arguably, merely acting out its originating oxymoron. Any number of other adages might be read, with only a minimal amount of nudging, as metaphors for their own compilation. To compose the *Adagia* may require the writer "cum larvis luctari," "to struggle with ghosts," or "a mortuo tribuum exigere," "to demand tribute from the dead." To compose the work may be a privilege, since "non cuivis homini contingit adire Corinthum," "not everybody is lucky enough to visit Corinth." But the work is also burdensome, since it deals with "difficilia quae pulchra," "things beautiful because difficult." Perhaps the writing of the book is essentially futile, as futile as transplanting an old tree: "Annosam arborem transplantare." With this thought, in fact, a host of monitory adages present themselves: "thesaurus carbones erant"—"charcoal instead of treasure"; "catulae dominas imitantes"—whelps aping their elders"; "Ne sutor ultra crepidam"—"The cobbler shouldn't aspire beyond his last"; "Felix qui nihil debet"—"Happy is he who owes nothing." It would be an instructive game to work through a century of adages, interpreting each as auto-descriptive or more frequently auto-refuting. Perhaps a scorpion sleeps under every stone ("sub omni lapide scorpius dormit"), even if the stone is precious. But ultimately this game would pall, and some of the 4,000 entries doubtless would resist even the ardent and dauntless vigor of the most ingenious interpreter.

This leaves us still without a structural center. But I want to argue that each adage does contain a center of sorts, and in coming to recognize it we will be in a position to recognize Humanist mimesis. This center will prove to be wobbly; as an organizing principle it will be vulnerable, but it will serve, in a rough way, to protect most Humanist texts from cancer. Margaret Mann Phillips, the best-informed student and translator of the *Adagia,* writes of it: "The aim . . . is to give [the proverb's] whole pedigree, to show it living a continuous life from one author to another, changing in scope and meaning" (p. 77). What Phillips calls a pedigree lies at the beginning of every adage-commentary; it offers a crude basis for structure that is philological. Each commentary, each essay, is arranged around a history of its concrete usages and applications, a history in which the modern instance takes its place, or rather a history from which this new usage, with all its congeries of associations, is in the process of emerging. The real center is not the static gem but rather the dynamic, wavering, but persistent continuity through history. The adage turns, like most Humanist texts, upon an uncertain, unsteady axis stretched backward through time, an axis that is anything but straight, that excludes long periods of history, that combines divination with science, but that allows the modern text to situate itself with all the limitations and the actuality of its own historical moment. Thus the "Festina lente" essay draws its own axis from the ancient theology of Egypt, from Aristophanes, from the emperor Augustus and the emperor Titus, down to Aldus and finally to its own successive, agglutinative incarnations. Following Phillips, one can call this succession a pedigree or genealogy; I prefer to call it an etiology, by which I mean a retrospective explanation of a textual coming-into-being, a process of accumulated significations through time (which does not of course exclude a concurrent loss of signification).

To see this wobbly axis as an organizing element is not to deny Erasmus' historical separation from his imputed origins, or to deny his own, individual eccentricity in the unfolding chronology. His essay is his own; no other contemporary would have written it as he did; doubtless no other contemporary would have made out precisely the same etiology. Later ages, including ours, would bend the axis in new directions. But one can recognize this separation and this eccentricity without accepting a purely random dissemination. The line from the supposed ancient seers to the Erasmus of 1526 is not a straight line, but its curves and shifts of direction are more or less contained by cultural history. Culture always presses the mind to moderate its haste, always wants to guide and limit intellectual change, which is semiotic change. The given trope, like all Humanist topoi, carries a past with it that it violates only within given parameters. The adage-essay is really about an emergence from a fragile, constructed line of continuity informed with retrospective awareness. Although Erasmus' metaphysics of the line includes only two kinds, the finite straight line and the infinite circle, his essay really adumbrates a third kind—incomplete, meandering, perpetually becoming.

Thus the adage-essay acts out a version of history; it

supplies an imitation, a mimesis of history. This version is of course grotesquely foreshortened; it may also be inaccurate, as we know the myth of hermetic theology to be inaccurate. The text offers us at best a stylization of history. But it does cast back into time its etiological umbilical cord, whose curves lie within the boundaries of cultural change. Other Renaissance texts are less explicitly informative; one has to subread their etiologies; they allude rather than name, imitate rather than cite, but they also ask to be understood in terms of an emergence out from a long line of development. Each line is a special representation, epitomizing and interpreting history, and therein lies the mimesis. That is the peculiar technique of Humanist reference. It bears roughly the resemblance to the actual course of history that the stylized world of a novel bears to an actual society. "Festina lente" posits an original era of hermetic wisdom, a practical wisdom in imperial Rome, a void of wisdom during the Gothic darkness, a new heroic necromancy in the age of Aldus threatened finally by imminent apocalyptic chaos. Within that construction it dramatizes its own appearance, which contributes at least one fact to the story. The story becomes a metaphor or synecdoche for the vast, confusing movement of crude history. The one story maintains a rough parallelism with the other, and in that wavering parallel lies whatever mimesis Humanism could produce. The *Adagia* as a whole consists of several thousand mimetic histories.

The retrospective sketch of a past such as Renaissance texts contain remains, in a sense, a fiction. It is constructed on insufficient knowledge, and therein lies part of its vulnerability. Its version of history stems from a union of philology and invention. It suffers from all the confusions and errors of history, both the kind that is written and the kind that is enacted. It is also exposing its own enterprise to potential criticism, including the criticism of its named predecessors. By continuing the life of the adage down to his own moment, his own scope, his own moral style and expansive interpretations, Erasmus was taking a risk. He was wagering that his own moment and his own prolongation would not diminish the tradition, that they would not pollute it with unwitting parody or bathetic anachronism.

The Humanist text that imitates or paraphrases an ancient model or topos assumes deliberately its own concrete historicity, the perspectives, the prejudices, the semiotic vocabulary, of its age, "accommodated to times and circumstances." This again involves a vulnerability. The text accepts the particularity, which is to say the limitations, of its historical situation. Erasmus accepts the printing press, which enlightens and vulgarizes, instructs and corrupts. More important, he reflects ways of understanding, interpreting, and symbolizing that are not those of his masters; if they were, there would be no history. This assumption of a difference is the admission of a risk, the risk of being smaller, of appearing blind, of betraying a degeneration, of falling into travesty or pollution. We don't have to look far to find Renaissance texts that lost their wager and that did betray helplessly their own inequality to their models or subtexts. But in those Renaissance works that bring the wager off, the vulnerability proves to be a source of strength. The concrete historicity reveals its fertility. "Virescit vulnere virtus."[5] Stength is renewed by a wound.

The constructed etiology of the Humanist text provides at best a simulacrum of order, a flexible, shaky order that remains in the realm of becoming. (This is especially true of the writing of Erasmus, who was skeptical of historical patterns and who tended to ignore theories of circular *chronos* for spontaneous occurrences of specific *kairoi*.) But the etiology serves in any case to contain any drift toward purely haphazard dissemination. And by presenting the emergence of modern meaning as a progressive exfoliation, it responds to the charge of perpetual deferral. This is the charge that Professor Cave has brought, with great learning and skill, against Erasmus' writing along with other writing of the Renaissance.

> The perpetual deferment of sense encourages—even constitutes—
> *copia*, defined as the ability of language to generate detours and
> deflections. Textual abundance (the extension of the surface) opens
> up in its turn an indefinite plurality of possible senses. The intention
> (will, *sententia*) which was supposed to inform the origin of a text
> and to guarantee the ultimate resolution of its *sensus* remains for
> ever suspended, or submerged, in the flow of words.[6]

The perspective changes if one shifts the origin of the text to a wavering line of succession in which the authorial will takes its place. The text can then be read as a progressive realization of modern meaning defining itself as it becomes present. This coming into being is never properly completed, which is to say the final word is never written; no ultimate closure is ever imposed. But the requirement of some ultimate closure, some switching off of textual generation, reflects a rigidity of the twentieth-century mind. It isn't clear why we should want that utopian "ultimate resolution" that contemporary readers miss; it isn't clear how we would recognize it if we found it; it isn't clear why its absence should be a symptom of cancer. To embrace history is to embrace contingency, incompleteness, the vulnerability of the contingent. But it is not to succumb to an incurable disease.

The *Adagia*, of course, present a double orientation— toward the modern variation and toward the beginning of the etiological line. The "Festina lente" essay begins with its conjectural speculation about a phrase from Aristophanes and later reaches further back into pre-Roman Egypt. Most of the adages supply firmer beginnings. But the quest for one is a constituent element. Phillips writes: "The important thing is the correlation of the proverb with the event or point of view which gave it birth, finding 'fabulam proverbii parentem' (III, x, 98)" (pp. 13–14). We are free to consider this quest misguided; we are free to quote the adage "Facilius sit Nili caput invenire"—it would be easier to find the source of the Nile. The source or the parent-fable of the adage may be another construct, another fiction. But it reflects an enduring impulse of Humanism that deserves our attention.

We might indeed learn from the Humanists the crucial role of "the point of view which gave [the text] birth," if by "point of view" we understand the entire, specific, semiotic world, the specific habits of attributing meaning peculiar to a given historical moment. Every literary work bears the imprint of that given formative moment, and it asks to be read according to those habits; it asks to be read appropriately. Thus the reader is obliged to seek to recapture the presuppositions, the signifying habits, of the text's origin; they are not always as imprecise as are a proverb's. Thus the "Festina lente" essay records its era's love of compression and its will to diffusion; these and other features help us to date the essay, and they oblige us to recognize its diachronic specificity. The text asks to be read with a sensitivity to its origin, which is to say with the historical imagination. The reader who abandons that task is guilty of hermeneutic narcissism, even though admittedly the task will never fully be accomplished. The exemplary heroes of this effort of historical understanding are Erasmus and his fellow Humanists.

Thus, in opposition to Derridean dissemination, with its deteriorating dispersal, diaspora, metempsychosis, oriented toward a destructuring future, might be set the orientation of an Otto Rank toward the trauma of birth, a textual birth whose marks, scars, circumstances, help to determine textual destiny. Rank argues that all psychic experience and all culture constitute a series of responses, displacements, sublimations, symbolizations, of the trauma of individual, biological birth. One can appropriate that psychoanalytic theory, right or wrong, as a metaphor for the determinacy each text receives, not from conscious authorial intention, but from the conditions of its origin. The text bears the inscriptions of a particular historicity and a particular semiotic world, and these inscriptions, however obscured by the text's passage through history, remain constitutive. Erasmus assumed with his fellow Humanists the determinate power of its beginning. It is this determinacy that shields it from uninformed, irresponsible, whimsical readings, Cave's "indefinite plurality of possible senses." The meaning of the text is available for new reflection, fresh updating, enlarged significance, but this is only possible because the text possesses an inherent quality, knowable or unknowable, because it has had a certain origin, knowable or unknowable. Its history is a function of that determination. Even if, in the case of an adage, the will to reach the beginning leads to mythology, this failure need not be absolute and universal. Without a theoretical essence, the essence of origin, there can be no displacement or dispersal; even a destructuring dissemination must assume some seminality.

For Rank's human being, the concealed burden is the

birth trauma. For the inherited text, the concealed burden is the remoteness of birth, a mystery of a birth that remains nonetheless decisive. We can never know fully the product of another semiotic world. Every text aspires to be a utopia of perennial meaning; to some degree it always fails. Humanism, like modern scholarship, was dedicated to mitigating the textual burden, to protect us from the difficulty of understanding, without narcissism, texts whose origins are remote. We need that philological protection, even if it is never altogether successful. Some texts and some critical schools presuppose utopias of pure synchronism; they are misguided. It is the strength of so much Renaissance writing that it settles for less than the utopian. As we gauge the endeavor of the Renaissance to cope with its own separation from its imputed sources and masters, we can recognize its need and its courage in stringing up precarious lifelines, imitations of cultural sequence, defining each work, each essay, as a vulnerable extension out of the remote into a self-creating, self-vindicating present. "Vitiat lapidem longum tempus"—"Even stone is worn away by time;" that is the basis of Humanist pathos. The basis for hope is more tenuous but it remains available: "Viam qui nescit ad mare, eum oportet amnem quaerere"—"Whoever can't find a [straight] road to the sea should follow the [circuitous] river."

2

Petrarch *Viator*

66 "Sumus ... omnes qui hanc vitam agimus, viatores," wrote Petrarch to a correspondent.[1] Much of his immense corpus can be read as a kind of revitalization, redefinition, recomplication, of the worn metaphor. So of course can his restless peripatetic career, the endless shuttling, departing, and detouring which constitute the primary complication of this metaphor, its literalization in activity. Petrarch confessed in another letter that by nature he found confinement oppressive and movement restorative (*Familiares* XI.1), only to confess in still another (*Familiares* XV.4) that his restlessness contained an element of spiritual sickness. Thus there is a sense in which he lived the cliché as few of his contemporaries chose or were able to do, a sense which one can regard as separating him from all the merely figurative travelers, all the *omnes* of humanity, or contrariwise as sealing his humanity more visibly and profoundly. But whatever the complex interaction between Petrarch's compulsive action and his obsessive image, an interaction whose intricacy one can only conjecture, there remains in the written image alone as it recurs in the canon more than enough to arrest, instruct, and disturb the reader. The image of the wayfarer, mariner, crusader, pilgrim, conqueror, invader, transgressor, pervades all spheres of human effort in Petrarch's imagination: it truly describes "omnes qui hanc vitam agimus," and it particularly evokes those, including poets, whose effort is so strenuous, so ample and sustained, as to be considered "heroic."

The distinctive character of the Petrarchan journey is its radical ambivalence. The traveler wants to arrive at his destination, but he also fears to arrive. He admires those who achieve their quest, but he is wary of minds with too single a purpose, minds so unlike his own. He wants to cleave to a single path, but he is easily enticed into deviation; he is congenitally an "alma disviata" (*Canzoniere* 365), a *displaced* soul. He longs for the death he fears; the earthbound soul, imprisoned in the body, exiled in this world from its heavenly homeland, veers repeatedly from its goal. "Isn't man mad," he writes to his brother Gherardo, "to wish the journey to continue and never wish to reach the end, or—what amounts to the same thing—to wish simultaneously progress and immobility?" (*Familiares* X.5). Canzone 331 phrases this Augustinian paradox more succinctly: "Nebbia o polvere al vento, / fuggo per piú non esser pellegrino" ("A cloud or dust in the wind, I flee in order to be no longer a traveler").[2] This ambivalence of the existential wayfarer can be traced more precisely in the specific roles Petrarch chose for himself or for those who caught his imagination. Out of the multifarious instances of this image it is possible to discern roughly four major fields, four pursuits around which the instances tend to organize themselves, four distinct destinations toward which the traveler makes his way, even though each of these pursuits crosses and recrosses the others. Each will appear sooner or later as itself a displacement.

Of these four fields of effort, that which remains most mysterious is that which sustains the poet's popular reputation— the sentimental. The *Canzoniere* mingles images of love as deviation (as in the concluding prayer to the virgin: "la mia torta via drizzi a buon fine"—direct my twisted path to a good end) with images of love as helpless pursuit:

> Ai crudo Amor! ma tu allor piú m'informe
> a seguir d'una fera che mi strugge
> la voce e i passi e l'orme. (*Canzoniere* 50.40)

(Ah cruel Love! but you then most [provoke] me to pursue the voice and the steps and the footprints of a wild creature who destroys me.)

Each brief quotation illustrates the passivity of Petrarchan diversion, which is caused by one displacing agency and can only be rectified by a counteragent, both apparently beyond the speaker's will. What is most unclear in this poetry is the goal of the hunter's pursuit. It is not apparently sexual possession; there is little genuine eroticism in the *Canzoniere*. The goal is sometimes defined as pity:

> Poi che 'l cammin m' è chiuso di mercede,
> per desperata via son dilungato (*Canzoniere* 130.1)

(Since the road to mercy is closed to me, on a despairing way I have come)

and a few of the poems *in morte* suggest that shortly before Laura's death this goal was nearly reached.

> Tranquillo porto avea mostrato Amore
> a la mia lunga e torbida tempesta. (*Canzoniere* 317.1)

(Love had shown me a tranquil harbor from my long and turbid storm.)

But this latter sonnet lapses from an ostensible objective record into fantasies of what might have been. This lapse is so prototypical, so habitual, as to call into question the very status of "Laura." Poem after poem enacts what is effectively a lapse into solipsism, so that the goal of the lover's pursuit remains internal. This may be the basic displacement of the lover's quest: not so much the substitution of an unworthy object (Laura) for a worthy (salvation), but the internalization of the fleshly object into a mental phenomenon. Like the old man in poem 16 who leaves home to see Christ's face on Veronica's napkin, the poet seeks a "sembianza" (semblance).

Nonetheless, the private phantasm has a life of its own. The lines from poem 50 quoted above demonstrate a peculiarly Petrarchan eddy, a reversibility of direction. Who in these lines is the aggressor? The pursuit of a wild beast suggests a conventional hunt where the beast is object and victim, but here the creature which flees becomes the destroyer. It destroys apparently even though it remains intangible. It is known only through its metaphoric traces, a voice heard and footprints seen, and yet it appears as the aggressive agent. By a mysterious and inexplicable circularity, hunter becomes hunted.

An equally convoluted relationship appears in the *Se-*

cretum. At one point in their debate over the love of a woman, Augustinus cries out to Franciscus:

> Have you then for sixteen long years been feeding with false joys this flame of your heart? Of a truth not longer did Italy once suffer the assaults of her most famous enemy, the great Hannibal; nor did she then endure more frequent onsets of her would-be lover, nor was consumed with more furious fires. You today carry within you as hot a flame of passion. . . . Yet was there found one who forced him to retreat and, though late, to take his leave. But who shall expel this invader from your soul if you yourself forbid him to depart?[3]

In Augustinus' extraordinary simile, Italy is the feminine figure assaulted by the male suitor or rapist Hannibal. We would expect Italy to correspond to Laura, whose angelic mind and form Franciscus has just been praising. But Augustinus seems to ignore this praise and indeed to ignore Laura; in his simile Italy corresponds to the lover's own mind assaulted by passion, only to be liberated by the hypothetical Scipio of Christian resolution. However, the question "Who shall expel this Hannibal from your breast?" ("Hannibalem tuum quis ab his unquam cervicibus avertet?") almost equates Laura with "your" Hannibal. Again there is an ambiguity of external and internal, again an essential passivity, again a reversal of roles and of the aggressive movement. To the degree that the objective Laura, possessing a certain kind of mind and appearance, becomes a subversive psychic force, we meet again a lapse into narcissism. Who or what is the principal enemy of the heroic internal Scipio?

The problematic journey of Petrarch as lover or pseudo-lover proves to be indistinguishable from his journey as errant Christian. If in one canzone the light emanating from Laura's eyes shows the way to heaven ("un dolce lume / che mi mostra la via ch' al ciel conduce," 72.2), another canzone presents his passion as a diversion from that right-hand path leading to heaven ("io lassai 'l viaggio / de la man destra, ch' a buon porto aggiunge," 264.120).[4] The path of the vagrant carries the stronger dramatic force. Petrarch's canon abounds in evocations of the Christian journey's harshness: "All of the roads are full of snares;

the branches of the trees are viscous with lime; the ground is everywhere strewn with brambles and thorns; the foot finds no place to step without danger'' (*Familiares* XVI.6). This tortuous path could be avoided if only the will were firm. Did not Augustine write that willing to go is not only identical with the journey but even with the arrival (*Familiares* XVII.10)? But this writer is uncertain of his will. The manifold descriptions of his vagrancy can be contrasted with the extended metaphor toward the close of the *De otio religiosorum,* where the journey of the virtuous toward Sion is represented as delightful.[5] In most of that treatise, however, the metaphor is reversed: the Christian and, most notably, the monk are immobilized within a fortress besieged by demons. Even this metaphor is reversed when the demons prove to be plotting *inside* the fortress, like Catiline. The Carthusians whom Petrarch is addressing here led a retired life for which beleaguerment provides a more appropriate analogy than wayfaring. But one cannot say that the former analogy is made more appealing.

The conflict of the two metaphors and corresponding ways of life organizes the first eclogue of the *Bucolicum carmen.* Silvius (Petrarch) begins by drawing the contrast for Monicus (Gherardo, himself a Carthusian).

> Monice, tranquillo solus tibi conditus antro,
> Et gregis et ruris potuisti spernere curas;
> Ast ego dumosos colles silvasque pererro.

(Monicus, hidden away alone in your quiet cavern, / You have been free to ignore the cares of the flock and the pastures; / I hapless vagrant, go straying o'er thorny hills and through thickets.)[6]

As Petrarch interpreted the eclogue in a letter to his brother (*Familiares* X.4), the cavern represents Gherardo's monastery, the Charterhouse of Montrieux. In the course of the poem Silvius declines Monicus' invitation to linger there and be edified by the songs of a shepherd (David) praising the true God. He must leave to invite the inspiration of the Muses, wandering freely as he pursues his imitation of the two old shepherds (Homer and Virgil) of a different school. Silvius must leave, as the closing lines make clear, to write the *Africa,* celebrating a youthful hero (Scipio) who is said to have forced his way into the cavern (Carthage) of Polyphemus (Hannibal) ("Te, Polypheme, tuis iam vi stravisse sub antris / Dicitur," 1 .115). In another reversal, Hannibal the rapist-invader of the *Secretum* here becomes the defender against an invasion. In the last line, Monicus bids Silvius as *viator* a safe journey despite the hazards of the road ("I sospes, variosque vie circumspice casus," l. 124).

This is a poem explicitly ambivalent, where the poet's bad Christian conscience is balanced by the creator's Humanist pride. Silvius, facing the risks of road and thicket, becomes a heroic poet in two senses, without ostensibly disparaging the alternative role of his brother. But the interpretative letter does subtly reduce it, not only by its unmistakable condescension but by its allusions to the crude simplicity of the untutored Monicus. The interpretation in fact raises ulterior questions. Silvius, it explains, is so named because Francesco loves rural scenes; Monicus takes his name from a one-eyed Cyclops because Gherardo has closed that eye which looks on this world and has remained content with the other one turned toward heaven. This explanation is curious because, as we have seen, the eclogue's conclusion introduces another Cyclops, "Polyphemus" or Hannibal, who as a historical personage did lose the sight of one eye. The eclogue gives us two one-eyed "Cyclops" living in caverns. If the poet's hero storms into one by force, it is tempting to suspect an unavowed temptation on the part of Scipio's bard to assault the other "cavern" at Montrieux. Perhaps by writing this eclogue, by asserting for once his vocation as wayfarer-Humanist-poet, he has exorcized momentarily the reproach of the single-minded saintly brother and his immobile community, obsessed as they are, mentally constricted just as Polyphemus-Hannibal was. The poet has in a sense canceled, destroyed, the inviting cavern, as a Scipio rather than a Catiline.

Such a reading would attribute more closure to this eclogue than it possesses for the naked eye. On a naive reading it is well balanced in its ambivalence, and this ambivalence remains the more constant principle throughout most of Petrarch's writing. He simultaneously wants the spiritual journey or voyage or flight

and he refuses it. As a Christian he deserves the rubric he quotes
(*Familiares* XXIII. 9) from that psalmist whom Silvius labels *raucus*
(hoarse): "O who will give me the wings of the dove, so that I
may fly to find my place of rest?" This is appropriate because the
psalmist himself has it both ways. In his savage invective against
a certain hapless physician, Petrarch pauses to remark that he
would travel anywhere to reach tranquillity of spirit. Yes, he
knows that this is only found in the mind, but perhaps certain
serene places . . .[7]

After the sentimental and religious pursuits, one must
consider the literal military enterprise from which both of these
spheres of effort draw many of their tropes. Typically for Petrarch
a battle involved a crusade. He loved the idea of a crusade and
used his pen to promote one or another. The crusade proclaimed
though never carried out by Philip VI of France is the subject of
Canzoniere 27, a sonnet, and 28, a canzone. The expedition to enter
and govern Italy which Petrarch tirelessly urged on the emperor
Charles IV assumed in the writer's eyes the precise character of a
crusade. So did the enterprise of driving out the invading barbarians to which the Italian nobility is summoned by the canzone
"Italia mia" (128). A crusade of course is an invasion turned inside
out, in still another Petrarchan reversal. It is not too much to say
that heroism for Petrarch was bound up with the forceful crossing
of a boundary, with some violent movement across frontiers,
thresholds, lines of demarcation. The heroic action might be such
an incursion (as in a crusade) or it could be a response to an
incursion (as in "Italia mia") or in Cola di Rienzo's liberation of
Rome from its desecration by barbarian aliens. Worthiest of all,
though not free from suspicion, would seem to be the invasion
which responds to an invasion, as when Scipio's expedition to
Africa responds to Hannibal's penetration of Italy. Were the emperor Charles to enter modern Italy, his exploit would resemble
Scipio's (*Familiares* X.1)

Thus heroic activity partakes not only of combat but
of significant motion; it is pilgrimage or transgression; the movement that leads to bloodshed acquires an apocalyptic aura. In
Canzoniere 28, a canzone addressed to Giacomo Colonna, the "ve-

race oriente" of heavenly paradise is conflated with the oriental goal (Jerusalem) of the crusade. Here the crusade is represented, somewhat oddly, as a retribution for the Persian invasions of ancient Greece, when Xerxes committed an outrage upon the Hellespont by inventing a new kind of bridge. *Canzoniere* 53 ("Spirto gentil") celebrates an anonymous hero who is about to redeem Rome from the civil strife which has led to pillaged churches and outraged shrines, symbols of criminal transgression. Eclogue 12 condemns Pan (the king of France) for perjury and greed like that of Crassus, who scorned a just treaty, violated his neighbors' frontiers, and justly died (ll. 92–95). This damning analogy is drawn by Arthicus (the king of England) as he himself invades French territory, whereupon Pan invokes the counterexample of Cyrus, who also met death at the hands of Tomyris for crossing unguarded boundaries. Both examples employ the same verb, *transcendere*, "to step over" or "to transgress."

Invasion is thus in its negative aspect among the most impious of crimes, a sacrilege or rape: the ironic praise for the papal invasion of Milan as "sacred and pious" is peculiarly withering.[8] But invasion in its positive aspect bears a halo of divine glory. In fact Petrarch's evocation of his own high (literary) endeavor in the canzone on glory (*Canzoniere* 119) uses language that recalls the language of his crusade poetry.

> per suo amor m' er' io messo
> a faticosa impresa assai per tempo;
> tal che s' i' arrivo al disiato porto,
> spero per lei gran tempo
> viver. (l. 11)

(For her I put myself early to difficult undertakings; so that if I reach the port I desire, I hope through her to live a long time.)

Here the desired port is probably literary achievement, but the phrase "faticosa impresa" echoes the "alta impresa" of the crusading canzone 28 (l. 42.).[9] Thus the strictly private ambition of the writer seems naturally to assume the garb of the soldier and traveler, traversing space no longer sacrosanct to reduce his own personal Jerusalem. The central imagery of the *Trionfi* betrays this fascination with irresistible forward movement. And a remarkable passage in the correspondence offers a fantasy of ancient Roman heroism as pure forward momentum, a mass rush of a single will against the enemy. "The trumpets sounded the call to battle or assembly and none was so deaf he failed to hear, none so dull he failed to understand, none so sluggish or fearful he failed to obey more quickly than I speak; together they rushed against the enemy; together they halted; together they struck" (*Familiares* XXII.14). In this fantasy there is no ambivalence; this irresistible onset of violence defines the greatness of Roman arms and defines by its absence the ineffectual waverings of the present.

The heroism of the poet and in particular the Humanist poet, the fourth and last pursuit to concern us, is also reflected in the image of the traveler. The *Invective contra medicum* points to the association of rhetoric and navigation in the cult of Mercury, patron of eloquence and commerce, as well as in the figure of the merchant-voyager. This human figure as Petrarch describes him (one who visits many shores, uses his power of persuasion, and shrewdly wins the minds of many people)[10] has an Odyssean character; elsewhere (*Familiares* XV.4) Petrarch confesses to a youthful desire to imitate Ulysses. The letter in which this confession appears constitutes a kind of apologia for the peripatetic life, which is chosen by the greatest poets for their heroes. Homer and Virgil, "whose insight into human nature no philosopher has surpassed, when they describe the character and conduct of a perfect man, have shown him learning something new everywhere by traveling throughout the world, nor did they think it possible to fashion such a man in language if he remained permanently confined to a single place." Heroism here has something to do with *paideia*, which in turn involves departure from the cavern of one's parochial native locale. In this defensive polemical text, the price paid for the peripatetic life, paid by the writer as well as the ancient hero, is suppressed.

The cramped corner to which fortune assigns one has to be left behind, has to be surmounted in time as well as space. Temporal distance is in fact repeatedly spatialized in Petrarch's imagery. There is a faint spatialization in the use of the verb *pervenire* as it appears twice in the opening sentences of the letter "To Posterity."

> Fuerit tibi forsan de me aliquid auditum; quanquam et hoc dubium sit: an exiguum et obscurum longe nomen seu locorum seu temporum perventurum sit. Et illud forsitan optabis nosse: quid hominis fuerim aut quis operum exitus meorum, eorum maxime quorum ad te fama pervenerit vel quorum tenue nomen audieris.

> (It is possible that some word of me may have come to you, though even this is doubtful, since an insignificant and obscure name will scarcely penetrate far in either time or space. If, however, you should have heard of me, you may desire to know what manner of man I was, or what was the outcome of my labors, especially those of which some memory or even a bare name may have reached you.)[11]

Petrarch as Humanist poet wants an *aditus,* an issue for his work; he wants to *arrive,* and the third book of the *Secretum* reflects his indecision over the possible vulgarity of this *parvenu* ambition. But of course as Humanist he also wants to move backward in time: *n'importe où hors du siècle.* The epistle to Horace (*Familiares* XXIV.10) reports that the modern poet has followed the ancient through the entire world in his fancy, and would follow him further to Antium or the citadels of Romulus or the Isles of the Blest. Movement in space and in time seem virtually to fuse through the ardor of the historical imagination. In his old age the poet is still writing: "If Livy were alive today, if my health were better, if the road were safe, I would go to visit him, not only at Rome but even in India" (*Seniles* XVI.7). If the serial conditional clauses betray the caution of advancing years, the centrifugal impulse remains unshaken.

In these Humanist fantasies the constrictions upon mortal men which limit their life span to a single era correspond to the boundaries and thresholds of other texts. To follow Horace, to meet Livy, is to accomplish the forbidden, to invade a world denied plodding mortality. If the path leads to the Isles of the Blest, then entering that privileged place would simply amount to an ulterior transgression. The opening sentence of the letter to posterity conveys at once the hope of reaching our notice and the unlikelihood, the overreaching boldness, of this hope. If Petrarch stopped dreaming of imitating Ulysses, this was doubtless because he dreamed of outdoing conventional heroism. In the tenth eclogue the creator himself of Ulysses guides Petrarch into the deepest recesses of his dwelling ("Attonitumque manu penetralibus intulit umbris," 1. 69), which is to say into the obscurities of his language and his fable. The modern interpreter penetrates the receptive cavern of the original heroic poet, and this very imaginative penetration (unjustified by the interpreter's actual Greekless experience) represents a kind of ultimate heroism. A revealing letter to Giovanni Colonna di San Vito clarifies the operation of this historical imagination.

> While I write I remain hungrily with our ancestors as best I can, and I gladly forget those contemporaries with whom an evil star has compelled me to live; I muster all the strength of my mind to flee the latter and follow the former. Just as the sight of my contemporaries displeases me, so the memory of the ancients, their magnificent deeds and famous names, brings me such incredible, inestimable joy that, if this were known to the world, many would wonder how I could find more pleasure with the dead than with the living. *(Familiares* VI.4)

This extraordinary avowal of pleasure in transgressing the boundaries of the dead authorizes us, I think, to scrutinize Petrarch's versions of ancient history with particular references to himself. If in fact the fantasizing or hallucinating power is so strong, the movement between living and dead so easy, then the stories about antiquity told in the *Africa* or the *De viris illustribus* or other texts become documents potentially revealing of the writer's sensibility. Whether or not it is legitimate routinely to read "history" for what it reaveals of the historian's desire, here if ever would seem to be an appropriate instance. The discussion of the *Africa* below will have to reckon with this possibility.

The correspondence contains marvelous manifestos of the freedom of the soaring creative faculty. In at least one letter the mind's sovereign disregard for all barriers reaches heroic dimensions. "The mind, noblest of all things and surpassing handiwork of nature, suffers no compulsion or constriction; it flies over mountains and seas, opens prisons, breaks locks, shatters bolts, stops at whatever place and time it wishes" *(Familiares* XXII.4). A comparable freedom is claimed for the Humanist writer in one of the two great letters to Boccaccio on imitation. The poet who follows another's guidance, writes Petrarch, is not so passive as to brook interference with his own capricious itinerary.

> I prefer a guide who goes before me to one who subdues me; even with a guide one may keep one's own eyes and judgment and freedom; I cannot be prevented from stepping where I choose, passing by what displeases me, and entering on the unexplored; I'm allowed to choose a shorter or smoother path, to hurry or stop or turn aside or turn back. *(Familiares* XX.2)

Here deviation in itself becomes a value, symbol of the author's unimpeachable will to which no path can be barred. The sovereign mind chooses its own routes and perspectives. To vindicate his right to select his own material as biographer, Petrarch includes the following anecdote in the preface to his *De viris illustribus*. Augustus Caesar, having entered the cavern at Alexandria where the ashes of Egyptian kings were contained in elaborate tombs, preferred to contemplate the corpse of Alexander. Asked if he wanted to visit the tomb of Ptolemy, Augustus replied that he wanted to see kings, not dead men. Augustus refuses the conventional guided tour and refuses the conventional title of king to the late Ptolemy. The true sovereign chooses to divert his attention to another true sovereign; his diversion or deviation demonstrates his distinction just as Petrarch's unconventional selection of materials in this book will demonstrate his own.[12]

Passages like these seem to betray no ambivalence or bad conscience in the double deviation of Humanist writing, from the Christian tradition and from the classical model. But other texts suggest a failure of assurance. The *epistola metrica* (II.1) which describes his worldly apotheosis, the coronation at Rome, opens the possibility of a violation in that ceremony. My oration was not long, writes the poet; custom forbids it, nor is it a small thing to violate the laws of the Muses. I led them from the peak of Cirrha to dwell briefly amid the crowd.

nec multa profatus;
nam neque mos vatum patitur, nec iura sacrarum
Pyeridum violasse leve est; de vertice Cirre
avulsas paulum mediis habitare coegi
urbibus ac populis. (l.47)

It is not quite clear whether the violation is hypothetical (the long oration avoided) or actual (the sullying of the Muses by exposing them to the city mob). The text seems to allow the force of the verb *violasse* to move both ways. If so, there *has* been a kind of desecration in the journey across time and space, a crossing of boundaries on this occasion not by the writer but by the Muses he has summoned and debased. The references to this coronation scattered endlessly through Petrarch's oeuvre cannot be explained simply as self-advertisements; they make better sense as obsessive returns to a source of insecure reinforcement. Did the laureate truly become a Roman that day on the Capitoline? Did he truly constrain the Muses to come? And in this constraining was there a desecration, an element of involuntary parody, about the whole affair? Is Humanist art itself essentially parodic? Even after the coronation, the journey to Rome never seemed to end: perhaps with the completion of the *Africa*, whose concluding scene leads Scipio up the Capitoline? But that poem, perhaps too burdened with psychic weight, never received its final form.

A letter to Gherardo lists the various allegorical roads men choose for themselves in this life, and then situates the poet in the shadows, avoiding the rest. "Some you see journeying in the open, others in secret, avoiding open ground and preferring shadows; they wish not to be sullied by contact nor to attract scorn by too loose familiarity, but rather to be seen by few and approached with difficulty" *(Familiares* X.5). The word *umbris* (shadows) refers among other things to the veil of fable employed by poets to cover their meanings, but it also has richer and vaguer implications that recall the polyvalence of the vernacular *ombra* in the *Canzoniere*. The furtiveness of the wayfaring poet may be due to the betrayal of poetry in the modern world, or it may be due to the inadequacies and deviations of that poetry. It is possible that for Petrarch the errancy, the vagrancy, of a Silvius, the digressions and transgressions which made poetry potentially "heroic", also made it suspect. Often, he writes, eloquence is frustrated; even a Virgil and a Cicero failed fully to voice their thoughts; the human mind tends to fall short at the middle of the journey toward expression *(Familiares* XII.5).[13] Language is shadowed both for the Augustinian Christian and the lonely proto-Humanist. If in the tenth eclogue the modern poet is admitted to Homer's penetralia, the epistle to Homer refuses to suppress its Humanist pathos: "Quam longe absis intelligo" (I realize how far from me you are) *(Familiares* XXIV.12). The shadow in which the poet journeys might be interpreted as the impotence of the fantasy to sustain its flight, its illusion of arrival.

As existential pilgrim, as troubled Christian, as arm-chair soldier, as proto-Humanist writer and actor, Petrarch combined many of his pursuits in the ascent of Mont Ventoux *(Familiares* IV.1). According to his account (which may or may not correspond to an actual experience), he was prompted to make the climb by reading Livy's relation of the ascent of Mount Haemus by Philip of Macedon with his troops (Livy, XL. 21.2–22.7). Petrarch suppresses the ridicule attached to this fumbled expedition in Livy's original. His description of the climb-proper focuses on his literal digressions from the straight and steep path upward, a description not lacking in allegorical overtones ill-fitted to an imitation of Livy. Thus the ascent is presented as an actual historical enterprise which is also a Humanist enterprise, an (allegorical) Christian enterprise, and the imitation of a military enterprise. Before reaching the summit, the climber nerves himself for the effort by auto-exhortations. "Having strayed far in error, you must either ascend to the summit of the blessed life . . . or lie prostrate in your slothfulness."[14] But once at the summit, in a predictable reversal the climber discovers that he is once again displaced. A passage from Saint Augustine read ostensibly at random shows him the folly of climbing mountains and neglecting himself, so that the hard ascent now proves to have been a detour. The imitation of Livy proves to have been a diversion from the imitation of Augustine, who himself underwent a spiritual redirection by opening a copy of Saint Paul.

As the climber descends, armed with determination to

battle his passions anew, he thinks, "How few will ever succeed in not diverging from this path." Upon his return below he already fears that his feelings may change along with the scene ("pro varietate locorum mutatis forsan affectibus"). By another reversal the summit experience appears retrospectively as a positive experience which the ensuing journey of life can only dissipate, lead away from. What was a threshold experience for Augustine may fail to be one for Petrarch. No wonder that the letter closes with a reference to wandering and inconstant thoughts ("cogitatus . . . vagi et instabiles"). This little narrative exemplifies the Petrarchan journey at its most deeply shadowed: a heroic ambition bewildered by an unshakable sense of evasion, aiming for a mirage, distracted from distractions, penetrating a world with centered egoism and decentering guilt.

II

We have seen how the experience of deviation in Petrarch is frequently doubled by transgression: a passing over in its original etymological sense with or without an explicit suggestion of wrongdoing. The chartless, formless space of errancy finds a focus in the boundary or threshold whose crossing situates a drama. A study of Petrarch as wayfarer is obliged to examine closely this crucial liminary act in its manifold versions since, whether the crossing is presented as courageous and constructive or profanatory and self-destructive, the meaning of movement tends to take its definition and intensity from the character of its "transgression." Petrarch in fact is a poet of thresholds.

The most intimate of these is the gateway of his consciousness, his inner selfhood. The letter which depicts poets as taking pleasure in shadows also represents them as reluctant to be sullied by the familiarity of other men. The initial sin of the physician who attracted the *Invective* was an act of aggressive invasion, rooting the poet out of his "Pierian penetralia" *(Pieriis penetralibus)* in the Vaucluse.[15] Laura, or her apparition, also violates his threshold.

> Sepe etiam, mirum dictu, ter limine clauso
> Irrumpit thalamos media sub nocte, reposcens
> Mancipium secura suum.[16]

(Often at midnight, O wonder! she forces the threshold of my bedroom, despite its three bolts, certain of finding her slave.

The slavery seems partly to consist in the inability to resist invasion not by Laura herself, whom the poetry almost never actualizes, but by the poet's image of her, felt as an invading intruder. Harassing images, conceived as originating outside the self, violate its gates just as, in the simile of the *Secretum*, Hannibal raped Italy. This sensitivity to the profanation of an inner threshold is then projected outward in increasingly wide concentric circles. Giovanni, the allegedly profligate son, is condemned never to place his foot on his father's threshold (*Familiares* XXII.7). The circle of the home gives way in any number of texts to the circle of the country. The scandal of civil conflict, denounced in the canzone "Italia mia," is the vicious employment of foreign mercenaries by the Italian nobility.

> Ben provide Natura al nostro stato,
> quando de l' Alpi schermo
> pose fra noi e la tedesca rabbia;
> ma 'l desir cieco e 'ncontra 'l suo ben fermo
> s' è poi tanto ingegnato,
> ch' al corpo sano à procurate scabbia. (*Canzoniere* 128.33)

(Nature provided well for our safety when she put the shield of the Alps between us and the Teutonic rage; but our blind desire, strong against our own good, has contrived to make this healthy body sick.)

Civil war in itself would not apparently be perceived as monstrous if the barbarians retired behind their natural boundary. Here the Alps constitute the threshold violated in self-destructive insanity by the native lords, thus infecting the body politic, and in this last metaphor, however conventional, one notes how easily the defensive fear of incursion narrows as well as widens.

The long letter to Cola di Rienzo and the Roman people (*Epistolae variae* XLVIII), written in the glow of hope sparked by the Tribune's initial coup, places its stress again on a sacrilegious invasion, but now the horror is balanced by enthusiasm over Cola's redeeming response. This letter can be regarded as a quintessential expression of Petrarchan heroism. In this Roman drama the city walls become the violated threshold, since the usurping nobility, treading on the ashes of the illustrious ancient dead, is of alien blood. Within the walls the nobles' crimes consist of countless ulterior desecrations—seizures of institutions, pillaging of churches, plundering of the very ancient ruins dismantled and sold for profit. "Many dangers beset him who travels this road." But Cola, if he perseveres, will be able to deal with them. What is needed is a furious rush of counteraggression, at the risk of life. This blind rush of force which we have already met is familiar to the reader of the *Africa*. In the letter as in the poem it has distinguished exemplars. "Rush fearlessly to the combat, inspired by the example of Brutus himself, who met in battle the son of the Proud King and slew him, though he himself fell covered with wounds. He thus pursued even into the regions of Tartarus him whom he had driven out from the city."[17]

In this reckless pursuit even into Tartarus we encounter a type of transgression outward, no longer the threatening centripetal invasion of an inner sanctuary but a centrifugal counterthrust which must match the invasion in force. The letter has pivoted from defensive shock to aggressive exhortation, even if the exhortation seems repeatedly to lead to self-destruction. "It was patriotism that compelled the Decii to offer their devoted lives to their country; that urged Marcus Curtius to leap, full-armed and mounted, into that yawning chasm in the earth; that urged Horatius Cocles to oppose his own body . . . to the Etruscan legions . . . then . . . to plunge headlong into the Tiber's tide" (p. 78). All these figures rush to death, but the crucial *exemplum* is Marcus Curtius. It is his story, more than any other, which dominates the survey of Roman history in the *Africa*. He crosses the most fearful threshold into the pure darkness of the chasm, which then closes upon him to seal his courage. If one looks for symbols of the proto-Humanist imagination in the classical legends favored by Petrarch, here doubtless is one of them. Marcus-Cola-Petrarch redeems the violation of the city by a heroic plunge into night. At the close of the long letter, the poet writes that he has seized his pen "that [he] too might perform [his] duty as a Roman citizen." In fact he is writing far from the scene in the Vaucluse. But his phrasing seems to suggest that for him too there is something bold, even risky, in this reenactment of the past.

For Petrarch the literal, symbolic, and creative wanderer there persists in any case the fear of crossing the wrong threshold. Monicus-Gherardo invites his brother Silvius to cross the stone threshold ("durum . . . limen," l. 46) into the former's cavern-monastery, but Silvius rejects the hardship of the cavern for the hardship of the road. In the "Trionfo d'Amore" the procession of souls in servitude of Love ends its march at a triumphal arch which seems to serve, a little confusingly, as the entrance to a dark and narrow prison ("tenebrosa e stretta gabbia"). The *Liber sine nomine* states that "whoever crosses the threshold of Avignon ceases to be his own man." In various symbolic ways one crosses a threshold into a trap, all the more sinister in the last instance since Avignon can be regarded as an emblem for what might be called the Petrarchan condition: a labyrinth without thread, without Ariadne or Daedalus. "There is no light anywhere, no one to lead you, no sign to guide you along its twisted paths."[18] The risk of crossing irremediably the wrong threshold heightens the courage of those who in other contexts choose more or less successfully to disregard boundaries. Bravery and folly, good and evil, seem almost to be reversed images of each other. Scipio like Hannibal was an invader. Transgression or intrusion or liminary freedom seems to involve in varying degrees heroic self-assertion, sacrilege, and self-destruction.

Destiny tends to reveal itself in terms of liminary experiences. *Canzoniere* 362 presents a fantasy whereby Laura and the poet beg God, unsuccessfully, to permit him entrance and residence in heaven. But in the third eclogue Stupeus, another surrogate for the poet, happens on the dance of the Muses and is invited to remain. "Dare to look on divine faces" ("Aude divinos cernere vultus," l. 94), Calliope tells him. This potentially dangerous intrusion proves to be inspirational. But it remains understood that confrontation with the Muses might have involved a risk. If we return to the private self in its chosen or reluctant withdrawal from the world, and if we think of a crossing no longer against the self but out from it, then we must think of language as the privileged liminary instrument. Language is a kind of extension of the self into all that is not the self; it crosses what for Petrarch, as doubtless for most of us, is the crucial threshold. One recalls the Homeric formula "What words have crossed the barrier of your teeth?" The danger of language is that it will fall into a void of deafness or oblivion; it requires a little of the bravery of Marcus Curtius. "It is no joke to go out to face the public" ("Non est ludus in publicum prodire," *Seniles* II.1), Petrarch wrote about the condition of authorship. Some of the *commiati* of the canzoni imply this bravery.

> Se tu avessi ornamenti quant' ài voglia,
> poresti arditamente
> uscir del bosco e gir infra le gente. (*Canzoniere* 126.66)

(If you had as many beauties as you have desire, you could boldy leave the wood and go among people.)

> Canzone, io t'ammonisco
> che tua ragion cortesemente dica
> perché tra gente altera ir ti convene. (*Canzoniere* 128.113)

(Song, I bid you to speak your message courteously, for you must go among a haughty people.)

The *Canzoniere* was produced by a consciousness as firmly cut off from external alterity as any we know, a consciousness responsive only to its own memories and phantasms, dreams and torments. The threshold of this ego's receptivity to the alien is so high as to be effectively exclusive. If the passage of language does achieve a crossing outward, it will not be without stress. The poem becomes a wayfarer itself, the most vulnerable extension of the ego. In the first, liminary sonnet of the *Canzoniere* the speaker refers to the poetry which follows as "il mio vaneggiar," my raving or my divagation, whose only fruit is shame. We need not take this as the whole truth about the author's feelings in order to perceive a genuine fear of exposure as the poetry crosses the fundamental threshold into the world and begins its detours toward posterity.

III

The road on which Silvius sets out as the first eclogue ends leads specifically to the *Africa*, the epic which represents Petrarch's major imitation of Virgil and what he knew of Homer. In that work one can study his most sustained effort to revive ancient heroism, as one can study those hazards or mishaps ("varios . . . casus") against which Monicus warns his brother. It is appropriate to recall the metaphor since it is reintroduced in the epic's dedicatory opening ("iter hoc ingressus agam," l. 57). In all the canon, the *Africa* offers the largest scope to an analysis of Petrarchan displacements.

A consciousness of deviation emerges already on the first page, where the poet invokes the assistance of Christ in apologetic accents. To compensate for his artistic digression from the Christian story, he promises to offer devotional poems as a kind of penance, or if these are unwelcome, then tears of repentance.

> Full many a reverent verse shall I bring back
> to Thee—if verses please Thee—from the crest
> of high Parnassus. If they please Thee not,
> then Thine shall be the guerdon of those tears
> which long since I might fittingly have shed.

> Tibi multa revertens
> Vertice Parnasi referam pia carmina, si te
> Carmina delectant; vel si minus illa placebunt,
> Forte etiam lacrimas, quas (sic mens fallitur) olim
> Fundendas longo demens tibi tempore servo. (I.14)[19]

Is there not in this particular context a failure of decorum in the reference to Parnassus, which qualifies the penance and shows the poet to be, like his allusion, out of place? There will be other passages which betray an uneasy Christian conscience.[20]

But this strain of Christian guilt is not a major theme in the *Africa*. What seems to me a much more pervasive source of anxiety is the transgression of the classical subject and style, the incursion into the ancient world of an interloper conscious of his alienation but choosing to use nonetheless the meter and rhetoric and mannerisms of ancient epic. It is true that a kind of precedent existed in such a poem as the twelfth-century *Alexandreis* by Walter of Chatillon. But Petrarch would scarcely have recognized that precedent; in his own eyes he was the first to make this incursion. And if one considers his acute sense of estrangement, if one considers, that is, his keener sense of distance from antiquity in comparison with that of twelfth-century Humanism, then he *was* the first to cross a boundary with a live sense of his action's significance. He was the first to feel an anxiety of intrusion.

It is notable that he continues to refer to this intrusion in the imagery of peregrination. The heroic poet travels backward against the current of time to find his original, as Ennius tracks Homer.

> I have traced back through ancient years,
> as best I might, the tenuous spoor of fame.
> At length, spurred on by my inquiring mind,
> I reached the furthest shades, the first of men,
> whom Time, grown weary of the lengthening road,
> had long abandoned to oblivion. (IX.183)

> Vestigia Fame
> Rara sequens, quantum licuit per secula retro
> Omnia pervigili studio vagus ipse cucurri,
> Donec ad extremas animo rapiente tenebras
> Perventum primosque viros, quos Fama perenni
> Fessa via longe ignotos post terga reliquit. (IX.133)

Or in search of a subject, the poet sends his muse back to wander ("erret") in the remote past.

in truth, the poets with such themes
as mine are wont to turn to times remote;
some send their Muse back o'er a thousand years
and others halt not at that ancient mark,
but none as yet has sung of his own age,
and thus the Muse, with no impediment,
wanders through old and unfamiliar years
in freedom. (I.62)

Namque solent, similis quos cura fatigat,
Longius isse retro: tenet hos millesimus annus
Solicitos; pudet hac alios consistere meta;
Nullus ad etatem propriam respexit, ut erret
Musa parum notos nullo prohibente per annos
Liberior. (I.45)

The assertion of freedom ("nullo prohibente") raises the question why there might be a prohibition, and the act of passing beyond the thousand-year *meta* (mark, goal, end, boundary) does suggest at least a kind of heady boldness. Even in this relatively bland formulation, the muse does take liberties. But it is hard not to juxtapose this passage with its mirror reversal near the bleak close of the poem: "It is impossible / to turn back on our path. Latecomers all, / this new age holds us fast" (IX.627). ("Non licet ire retro. Nos cunta novissima seros," IX.448.) *Non licet:* it is not possible but also, surely, it is not permitted, it is forbidden to travel backward in the mode of a heroic poet.

A few lines earlier, after the climactic coronation of Scipio and Ennius, the poet writes that he has tried to imitate them both.

I too . . . greatly strove . . .
to follow o'er the rough and thorny path
those precious traces and to imitate
with similar crown, like site, and glorious name,
the ancient heroes and their dignities
sublime. (IX.563)

Ipse ego ter centum labentibus ordine lustris
Dumosam tentare viam et vestigia rara
Viribus imparibus fidens utcumque peregi,

> Frondibus atque loco simul et cognomine claro
> Heroum veterum tantos imitatus honores. (IX.404)

The "crown" and "site" ("frondibus atque loco") allude to Petrarch's coronation, already mentioned before Scipio's, the coronation which constituted his best claim to see in himself an authentic Roman. But to read the desire to imitate only in terms of this ceremony, however portentous and fertile it had become in Petrarch's private mythology, would be to reduce the symbolic interplay between soldier and poet. Given the grounding of Petrarch's imaginative life in Roman history, one has the right to examine the particular history he privileged for its light on his imagination. His letter to Livy (*Familiares* XXIV.8) states that reading the historian's work introduces or transfers ("inseris") him to happier times. It is tempting to read this transfer as the kind of displacement performed by metaphor. A writer burdened with an anxiety of intrusion does not choose to narrate an invasion by coincidence. The narrative of the book may become a dim emblem of its composition.

What cannot be denied is that the *Africa* contains abundant imagery of despoilment, sacrilege, and desecration. It is true that these crimes are preeminently attributed to the Carthaginians. Hannibal is a defiler and polluter whose last act before leaving Italy, the profanation of the shrine at Croton with its attendant massacre, sums up his role. But Rome is by no means exempt from such acts. Julius Ceasar "will bring terror to the land of Gaul / and foul ["violabit"] its rivers with dark streams of blood" (II.289).[21] Rome as well as Carthage will show small respect for sanctuaries.

> The Caspian strand the conquerors will tread
> and penetrate to Saba, force the homes
> of incense-burning peoples, enter temples
> and peer into the holiest of shrines. (II.265–68)

> Caspia calcabunt victores claustra, Sabeam
> Turicremasque domos: intacti limina templi
> Intrabunt cernentque aditi penetralia sacri. (II.202)

More precisely they will cross the thresholds of unsullied temples ("intacti limina templi intrabunt"). Scipio hears from his father that Roman troops will lawfully violate the holy of holies in Jerusalem.[22] In this proleptic summary of the Roman future, the act of entering alien penetralia almost becomes the hallmark of greatness.

The latent sexual dimension of this act becomes explicit in the subplot centered on Massinissa, Scipio's African ally, and this general's demeaning affair with a married queen, Sophonisba. Massinissa's seduction of Sophonisba and their subsequent "marriage" is narrated in terms of crossed thresholds, from his first passage through the shattered walls of her beseiged city like a wolf entering a sheepfold (V.1ff.), to his meeting with his future lover on her threshold ("in limine," V.12), to his entrance into the citadel of her palace, to his movement still further inward: "Entering alone the high hall's inner chamber / beyond the secret threshold" ("secretaque limina," V.166). Later Scipio will upbraid his ally for a passion that invades all recesses.

> ruinous pleasure rages on
> through night and day; no rampart may avail
> to ward it off, past sentinels it sweeps,
> past faithful watchdogs to the inner chambers
> and through the armed gates ["ferrata . . . limina"] of the mightiest.
> (V.534)

> damnosa voluptas
> Nocte dieque furit; numquam tu menibus illam
> Arcebis: mediis veniet penetralibus inter
> Excubias vigilesque canes, ferrata potentum
> Limina transiliet. (V.407)

Still later we follow Sophonisba, a reluctant suicide, as she pauses on the "very sill" ("sub ipso limine," VI.51–52) of Hades. Sexual transgression emerges as a shamefully displaced version of that noble, military ardor that storms temples.

The retrospective sketch of Roman history given by Laelius in Book III brings both versions together in modified form. It concludes with the rape of Lucretia by Tarquin ("matrone limina caste intrat," III.686–87), narrated at considerable length. Among other legends the most prominent is that of Marcus Curtius, whose ride into the abyss we have already met in Petrarch's letter to Cola. Other prominent heroes are the Decii, three soldiers of three generations, each of whom wins fame by hurling himself suicidally but victoriously against the enemy. This blind rush forward characterizes archaic Roman heroism in the *Africa*. "Have we not often seen the legions charge / to meet sure death?" (III.798).[23] In this archaic, retrospective history, aggression has no fixed target and no boundaries to cross.

Scipio would appear to be the pivotal figure in Petrarch's version of Roman militarism. He too is represented as a little maddened at Zama, driving into the Punic army as a lion "falls on trees and beasts," with random force. But we see him, as well, struggling in situations where a threshold can at least be divined.[29] And we first see him at a natural barrier, the pillars of Hercules, a barrier which the invasion of Africa will lead him to transgress, not without hints of hubris.

> Here he stood
> where no resistant hand of man but Nature
> omnipotent herself has barred the way. (I.179)

> Hic ubi non vis ulla manu mortalis, at ipsa
> Omnipotens adversa aditum Natura negabat,
> Constitit. (I.131)

A minstrel at the African court of Syphax recalls how Hercules

> raised high—a wondrous feat—
> twin pillars o'er the turmoil of the deep,
> and thus decreed that here was fixed the end
> of human journeys. So it long remained.
> But newly, from the east, a savage youth
> has dared to spurn such limits ["metam"]. (III.497)

> alte
> Erexit geminas pelago turbante Columnas,
> Utque pererrati foret illic terminus Orbis
> Edixit; fueratque diu, sed nuper ab Ortu
> Vesanus veniens iuvenis convellere metam
> Est ausus. (III.397)

Thus the expedition into Africa involves a defiance of nature and legend, a provoked defiance, doubtless, but which betrays nonetheless a disregard for bounds. Analogously the dream whereby Scipio enters heaven to discourse with his father represents a concession by God, a permitted transgression ("stellantia celi / Limina—perrarum munus—patefecit," (I.173). A more astonishing implication glimmers in the curious comparison of Hannibal, after his defeat at Zama, to a raped matron.

> Wherefore in shame
> and sad dejection he at length comes forth,
> leaving his hiding place, in aspect like
> a high-born spouse who through no fault of hers
> has been defiled, and conscious of disgrace,
> utters no word and seeks to pass unseen. (VIII.376)

> Mestissimus ergo,
> Confususque pudore gravi ac merore, latebris
> Egreditur, qualis rapto matrona decore,
> Que quamvis culpa careat, sibi conscia tanti
> Dedecoris, silet ipsa tamen refugitque videri. (VIII.263)

Hannibal, beaten by Scipio, looks like Lucretia after Tarquin is through with her. Here the sexual and military pursuits, held apart elsewhere, are visibly allowed to come together.

In all this ambivalent play with the nature of invasion and aggression, seduction and rape, the morality of boundaries, the traps of heroism, one can sense a play at one remove with the morality of the historical imagination, penetrating a sacrosanct, supremely valorized world with the dubious motives of a scout or spy, and the potential fate of a Marcus Curtius. The *Africa* also wants to make a blind rush, according to an *epistola metrica* by its author (*Epistolae metricae* II.1).

> The little book itself, now growing bold,
> Burns with desire to run and cast itself
> Before those sacred feet, and day and night
> Pleads for release.[25]

But the book never reaches King Robert's sacred feet nor anyone else's during its author's lifetime; it never crosses into the public gaze. The *Africa* also recognizes the melancholy of illusory achievement; the regrets of Mago (VI.885ff.), the one famous anthology piece of the epic, are anticipated in Scipio's dream and echoed by Petrarch's bitter conclusion on his own fate as writer.[26] No one to my knowledge has remarked on the significant fact that Scipio is never shown to enter Carthage any more than Hannibal has entered Rome. Instead of reaching this preeminent goal, Scipio's destiny leads him to the Capitoline where, however, the dignity of his coronation is subverted by our knowledge of his future, unjust disgrace and exile.[27] This also, we learn, is to be the destiny of the poem he inspired.

"He who writes / will openly admit indebtedness / to him [Scipio] above all heroes of the past" (IX.358).[28] One common element between soldier, poem, and poet is homelessness, the aftermath of laureation. Petrarch on his last page warns his poem in a kind of epic envoi against the hazards of *its* route, not far from the meanest threshold.

> I bid you make your cautious way
> with careful step, revealing not your name,
> through the indifferent years that lie ahead.
> Few homes you'll find, alas, to shelter you,
> and rare infrequent welcome where you go
> throughout the universe. (IX.654)

> Interea tamen hec, iubeo, per inertia transi
> Agmina solicito populorum incognita passu,
> Vix procul extremo salutata a limine linquens,
> Heu paucas habitura domos et rara per Orbem
> Hospitia! (IX.466)

The poem becomes an outcast, like Hannibal and Scipio at the end of their careers. Hoarded as it was by its author, fragmentary and uneven, it can be read as a fable of failed power, like Roman eloquence in the time of Ennius, "lacking the strength to reach the goal it seeks" ("propositam . . . contingere metam," IX.46). Or it can be read as a fable of guilty power. The meditation after Zama on the destiny of pillaged wealth may be faintly self-referential. "What are the fruits of so much plunder? Nay, / one thief despoils another" (VIII.40)[29] The artistic doubt about this poem which Petrarch never circulated seems to have been mingled with a moral doubt as well as with the fear of exposure to indifferent malice.

> Seek but a corner of a poor man's hut—
> rather than wander lonely through the world,
> forever dogged by wickedness. (IX.662)

> secura repostum
> Angustumque precare locum sub paupere tecto,
> Atque ibi, sola quidem potius peregrinaque semper
> Quam comitata malis, annosa fronte senesces. (IX.471)

The doubts surrounding the *Africa,* the doubts enclosing it, refusing the release it pleads for, should perhaps be read as representative of the fundamental doubt concerning all emission of speech released from the self into homelessness: vulnerable, suspect, intrusive, vagrant, fallen.

Monicus then was surely right about the hazards of this unfinished journey. Still it is a significant journey, and not least at the close when the gloom of the near future is brightened by a fantasy of a distant posterity which might walk back spontaneously into a past bathed in radiance.

> Our posterity, perchance,
> when the dark clouds are lifted, may return
> once more to the radiance the ancients knew.
> Then shall you see on Helicon's green slope
> new growth arise, the sacred laurel bear
> new leaves. (IX.639).[30]

> Poterunt discussis forte tenebris
> Ad purum priscumque iubar remeare nepotes.
> Tunc Elicon nova revirentem stirpe videbis,
> Tunc lauros frondere sacras. (IX.456)

In this fantasy, realized or not according to one's reading of history, the ban would be lifted against returns to the source, and language presumably would have the strength to reach its goal. A writer might journey back into the ancient light, no longer as a pilgrim shadowed by centuries of guilt, but truly and profoundly free, the disencumbered traveler of a Renaissance.

3

Il Cortegiano
and the Choice of a Game

The narrative of the *Libro del Cortegiano* involves at once subdued drama and slightly risky play. It begins with a game whose purpose is to propose a second game that will occupy the company at Urbino for the rest of the evening. This elaborately two-tiered pastime suggests immediately the centrality and formality of play for this group and throws the dramatic focus on the question of a given proposal's suitability. The reader does not know what criteria will determine the excellence of the winning invitation, but he is allowed to participate in the consideration of each. Thus in this preliminary contest Gasparo Pallavicino makes a proposal, and then Cesare Gonzaga another; then the buffoon Fra Serafino and the poet, Unico Aretino, each makes a kind of nonproposal in bad faith, which has to be dealt with by the arbitress, Emilia Pia. Then the contest resumes with another proposal by Ottaviano Fregoso, and then another by Pietro Bembo. Each of the four legitimate proposals is ingenious and imaginative; each might be in fact amusing to play; most of them kindle some enthusiasm among the assembled company. Each game might, in another book, conceivably have furnished matter for a witty and revealing scene. But in this book the arbitress chooses none of them and simply turns in silence to the next speaker whose turn it is, Federico Fregoso, a gentleman who begins by saying that he would gladly approve any of the games already described, but if obliged to suggest another, he would propose forming in words a perfect courtier. Before he has finished defending this somewhat irregular idea, decidedly unlike all the others, Emilia interrupts to decree that this will indeed be the evening's recreation. "This, should it please the Duchess, shall be our game for the present" (1.12).

("Questo, . . . se alla signora Duchessa piace, sarà il gioco nostro per ora.")[1]

It might be said that this contrivance of a preliminary game before the principle one constitutes a leisurely and somewhat circuitous entry into the main business of the book. We have no way of knowing with assurance why Castiglione chose it, any more than we can know what motives led his creature Emilia to pass over those other amusing suggestions and to make the unconventional choice, loaded with hidden implications, that in fact she made. But as readers we can reflect on the character of the five proposals, four of them stillborn, barren of the ghostly gaiety they might have provoked, and the fifth so seminal, so contagious, so resistant to conclusion, that its enjoyment continues for at least five evenings and perhaps for many more. It is worthwhile reflecting on the loaded consequences of Emilia's impulsive decision because Castiglione did choose to begin with all five alternatives as well as those two nonproposals which he thought fit to introduce.

There are of course obvious narrative advantages in this particular kind of opening. It permits the writer to acquaint us with several of the most articulate members of his gathering; it permits him to establish from the start the complex and fascinating division of roles between the sexes in this community; it permits him to establish the special tone of its talk, the mingled banter and formality, the byplay that is almost ceremonial, the rituals of command and obedience which are both pretense and reality. But the rejected games are of interest in themselves.

The first, invented by Pallavicino, is about self-deception: since all lovers deceive themselves, he says, let each one say what special virtue he would wish to find in his beloved, and which fault; in this way the judgment of the lover is likely to be less beguiled. Gonzaga's game is about folly: since each of us perceives his neighbor's folly but not his own, let each examine himself and reveal what his own true folly is, thus gaining self-knowledge. Ottaviano's game is about anger and scorn: since some suffer and some find sweetness in their lady's displeasure, let each one say "in case she whom he loves must be angry with

him, what he would wish the cause of that anger to be" (1.10)
("avendo ad esser sdegnata seco quella persona ch'egli ama, qual
causa vorrebbe che fosse quella che la inducesse a tal sdegno"),
thus presumably coming better to understand her hostility and his
own response to it. Bembo's game finally is also about the lady's
anger, justly or unjustly based: "Each should tell, if she whom he
loves must be angry with him, where he would wish the cause of
her anger to lie, in her or in himself" (1.11). ("Che ciascun dicesse,
avendo ad esser sdegnata seco quella persona ch'egli ama, da chi
vorrebbe che nascesse la causa del sdegno, o da lei, o da se stesso.")
Thus one might learn whether giving or receiving displeasure
causes more suffering.

     These are all distinctly different inventions but they
bear a certain family resemblance; they all deal with the socially
aberrant, with private passions and imbalances and blindnesses
which could threaten the harmony of the group, that magic chain
which, we have been told, binds all members together in bonds
of love (1.4). The games suggest the presence of the potentially
dangerous (of self-deception, cruelty, folly, and hostility) just as
the pseudo-game proposed by Serafino hints at indecencies and
the pseudo-game proposed by Aretino reveals in him a self-ad-
vertising and manipulative affectation. All of this emerges from
the proposals, but what emerges with equal clarity is the therapeutic capacity of the group to cope with this potential venom.
All four original games are calculated to function as measures of
healing, to induce self-knowledge and understanding, to contain
the antisocial deviations that in the recurrent phrase "go beyond
bounds." Emilia's disposition of Aretino, here and elsewhere, is
itself a brilliant model of tactful containment in the subtlety of its
ironies and the indirection of its reproof. Thus at this early stage
of the book the drama of social cohesion appears already as a
testing of the company's *power of containment,* and this drama will
be sustained when the final game is approved and played to its
inconclusive ending.

     All four original games stem from a recognizable ge-
nealogy that is old and astonishingly stable, a tradition that strad-
dles literary and social history. The tradition has its source, as far

as we know, in the medieval *cours d'amour* and the Provençal *jocs partitz*, which latter institution confronted two poets arguing opposed solutions to a subtle question drawn from the codified doctrine of *fin amors*. The questions were chosen clearly to admit of no final judgment beyond appeal. Which are the greater, the joys or the sorrows of love? Must a lady do for her lover as much as he for her? Which is the most in love, the one who speaks of his lady everywhere or the one who remembers her in silence? Which lover shall a lady take, one who confesses his love or one who does not dare to?[2] Scores of similar teasers are extant from the refined casuistry of the Provençal intelligence, and many more from its Italian disciples. Trecento literary reflections of the tradition appear in Boccaccio's *Filocolo* and the *Paradiso degli Alberti* by Giovanni di Prato. It is no surprise to read that the courtiers at Urbino amuse themselves with *belle questioni*. Of the four original games proposed, the latter two are quite simply *questioni* in the medieval tradition and the first two merely variants.

This of course is not the case of the game that is chosen for play, and if we had any doubts about *its* provenience, the author's prefatory letter would remind us that its models are in Plato, Xenophon, and Cicero. The medieval *questione* is exchanged for the ancient dialogue, the Socratic or in this case the far more influential Ciceronian conversation about a hypothetical ideal. This gesture toward Cicero as the main authenticating model is sustained by the number of allusions and echoes that appear throughout the body of the *Cortegiano*, chiefly from the *De oratore*. Emilia Pia, in making the choice she does, rejects the familiar game of erotic litigation, a game that in Urbino seems to be contrived as personal and social therapy; she chooses in its place an unfamiliar game, rich in classical associations, a game whose limits and whose drift no one as yet can fully forsee. It commits the players to try to define the ideal that underlies their own approved conduct, the authorized version of behavior that has regulated their day-to-day activity but has heretofore regulated it tacitly. The choice to form a courtier commits them to examining their own values and norms, with the opportunity to criticize those norms and so acquire a self-consciousness as a community. This

Ciceronian game assumes a capacity for mature self-criticism as well as a firm, stable society capable of questioning its own foundations. If there is anything radically insecure or hypocritical, any area where norm and reality diverge too widely, it could be a destructive experience; it could confront the company with truths it might not be able to face. So the questions that hang over the drawing room as these elegant people begin to play are first, whether the game will actually lead to more self-understanding, but also whether it will lead to so much that it will destroy the delicate fabric of their social equilibrium.

Two structural oppositions underlie the distinction between "medieval" and "classical" game. First, the medieval *questione* is fundamentally deductive. One begins with certain norms, certain rules, which are taken for granted, and one then analyzes specific cases, specific problems or aberrations, in the light of these sacrosanct assumptions. In the classical game, one begins with a certain praxis, with what is done, and out of that praxis one elicits the norms, inductively; this constitutes the game. The second structural opposition stems from the first. The medieval game, because it rests on the sacrosanct, can never legitimately overflow its boundaries. Although in a juridical sense closure is difficult because there is always more to say, because the question is contrived to invent endless debate, nonetheless in a structural sense closure is tight because the debate proceeds within limits which by definition can never be called into question.

This however is not the case in the classical game, which is to say the game that more or less makes up Castiglione's book. There the boundary is vague between the area that is "serious," untouchable, outside the play, on the one hand, and on the other that area where the play can range freely. Because there is no code, traditionally defined, to focus and delimit the talk, this is a parlor game which can expand indefinitely, which can become coextensive with all that is normally nonplay. Indeed if it were permitted by its arbiters, this game could conceivably swallow up everything outside itself. We think normally of a game as a detached figure against a background of the serious, the nonludic, but in this case the ground becomes the content of the figure. In

Plato and Cicero this situation does not arise because the conversation in each case is not regarded as ludic, as enjoying that special isolation from context we attribute to games. But the *Libro del Cortegiano* insists on its ludic purpose, thus possibly risking the comment which the Grand Turk's brother makes on jousting: "too much if done in play and too little if done in earnest" (2.66) ("troppo per scherzare e poco per far da dovero"). It risks also that ambiguity which is said to arise when a prince masquerades as a prince: "If he were to perform in play what he must really do when the need arises, he would deprive what is real of its due authority, and it might appear that the reality were mere play" (2.11). ("Facendo nei giochi quel medesimo che dee far da dovero quando fosse bisogno, levaria l'autorità al vero e pareria quasi che ancor quello fosse gioco.") Because *bounds* matter so much at Urbino, one test of the players will be their ability to sustain the game as a game, to protect it from this ambiguity which might subvert play and reality alike.

It has been asserted of course that this ambiguity is fundamental to play. If, as was argued by Schiller and Huizinga and later by others, the play impulse lies at the root of human culture, then clearly the ludic is inseparable from all that we think of as most meaningful in civilization. Huizinga was in fact criticized with some justice by Jacques Ehrmann because Huizinga seemed always to maintain a category of nonludic seriousness while demonstrating simultaneously how deeply that serious activity was pervaded by the play element. Ehrmann's alternative is more radical.

> In an anthropology of play, play cannot be defined by isolating it on the basis of its relationship to an *a priori* reality and culture. To define play is *at the same time* and *in the same movement* to define reality and to define culture. As each term is a way to apprehend the two others, they are each elaborated, constructed through and on the basis of the two others.[3]

If Ehrmann was right, if play, culture, and reality are ultimately inextricable, then the particular game at Urbino will tax even more severely the power of its players to segregate it as a *diversion*.

To be sure, this segregation of the ludic is made easier by its physical disposition: everything that occurs is contained within four walls. We first meet the players in the flesh after they have taken their places in a certain drawing room, an actual room that still exists today, and we remain with them in that room, *only* in that room, until the conclusion. The last voices we hear on the last page belong to individuals who are just about to leave the room but have not yet done so. The sense of enclosure is strong, and this sense is only heightened by that magical and unexpected moment at the end when a window is opened. This sense of enclosure powerfully affects the reader's impression of the society and the game. Whether or not there is structural closure, there is strong physical containment.

This concrete delimitation of a play space is of course one of those essential elements stipulated by most theoreticians of play, a space that must be fixed and separate in order for the game to define itself. This separation exists at Urbino to a degree that might in another work almost become claustrophobic. All we know of the court, of the society, of the world at large beyond it, reaches us through this rigid and compressed mediation. And the very sharpness of this ludic circumscription reflects of course something significant about the group enclosed. The artistic sealing of this drawing room comes unavoidably to represent a community itself turned inward, flawless in the perfection of its withdrawal, protected momentarily by its mountains, its palace, its style, its harmony, from the violence and vulgarity beyond it. A chrysalis of a culture seems to exist in its own static, circumscribed self-sufficiency and proposes to mirror its contentment by a game of auto-contemplation.

We can measure that degree of enclosure by comparing the *Cortegiano* with a work far less substantial and complex written a century earlier: the *Ad Petrum Paulum Histrum Dialoghi* by Leonardo Bruni.[4] At the opening the narrator, Bruni, meets Niccolò Niccoli at an Easter service in Florence, and the two Humanists decide to pay a call on their revered chancellor Coluccio Salutati. On their way they meet a friend, Roberto Rossi, who joins them. During the talk that ensues, Salutati recalls the spontaneous visits *he* had paid as a younger man to the theologian Luigi Marsili. The four Florentines discuss the state of modern learning and agree to meet the next day at Rossi's villa beyond the Arno, where they will be joined by a fifth friend. Before recommencing the discussion at Rossi's, they take a turn in the villa's garden and pause to admire the dignity of their city in the distance. These indications of spontaneous movement by independent citizens through the streets and squares and faubourgs of Florence receive no special prominence in Bruni's little work, but they reflect all the more tellingly the open converse, the mobile liberty of the commune. They bespeak a different organization of space without circumscriptions or enclosures, a space actually closer than Urbino's to that of the *De oratore,* where recreation is not firmly segregated from the rest of experience. To draw this contrast is not to diminish the peculiar grace of the Urbinese court but rather to underscore its will or its compulsion to turn so insistently inward. Its play space is not a public space.

The drama of the game, as it is played out in this space, will be again a drama of containment but no longer the containment of passion or folly but rather the containment of insight. It is healthy doubtless for a community to confront itself, but when the community rests upon unsteady political and ethical props, too much illumination can be destructive as well as enlightening. This holds true even for so brilliant, so articulate, and so poised a set as these talkers of the *Cortegiano.* We can follow the progress of the game in terms of the potentially threatening or divisive issues it raises, in terms of the doubts it flirts with, the embarrassments it skirts, the social and political and moral abysses it almost stumbles into, the dark underside of the authorized truth it sometimes seems about to reveal. This threat is really double. There is an intellectual threat to the minds of the players, but there is also a social threat that the conversational surface might be ruffled irreparably; there is a threat that the talk might reach a point that would destroy its quality as game, as amusing conversation between ladies and gentlemen. So we can measure the resiliency of the group to these implied threats by the way it heads off the threatening while protecting its governing mythologies and its social tone. The game really becomes a contest between the community's will to understand itself, to examine and know itself, and conversely its will to protect itself from excessive knowledge in order to function politically and socially.

One way to gauge the threat to the social surface at any given moment is to note the presence or absence of laughter. It is extraordinary how many speeches are introduced with the participle *ridendo*. The presence of this participle is an indication that the playful dimension of the conversation is intact. Laughter proves that the discussion of norms and ideals can coexist with banter, that "serious" talk represents no danger to the social occasion. Laughter is a guarantee of the polish of the conversational surface, and when it is silenced for an immoderate time one can detect a tension; one should be alert to the potentially intrusive.

Count Ludovico da Canossa hits upon a potentially explosive issue at the outset by raising the question of the courtier's aristocratic birth. The courtier requires it because, says the count, birth acts as a spur to achievement, deters one from dishonor, and implants a hidden seed which lends distinction to an aristocrat's conduct. He speaks of aristocratic *grazia* almost as though it came through the genes. Whereupon Gasparo Pallavicino, who tends to play the role of demystifier throughout, asserts that many aristocrats are vicious while many people of humble birth have become illustrious; he also suggests that Fortune has as much to do with eminence as does Nature. Curiously and significantly, Ludovico in rebuttal fails to defend his earlier assertions but falls back on the pragmatic argument that the courtier will encounter less hostility and will make a stronger first impression if he is wellborn. This little difference of opinion, followed by a partial retreat, signals a soft spot in authorized opinion, a genuine rooted ambivalence which the dialogue structure reveals. The ambivalence is dangerous because it threatens one of the principles of selection on which this company has been assembled. It also clearly threatens the company's ostensible function. If in fact the alleged superiority of birth is only a myth, what is the rationale of a community serving a nobleman whose power is inherited? We are not surprised when the subject is dropped for other, less controversial gifts by which to adorn the court's hypothetical archetype. The subversion has been headed off and the group's resiliency, the game's resiliency, have been quietly vindicated.

But during the second evening another test arises, and this time the challenge is blunter and uglier. The younger Fregoso remarks that the courtier should devote "all his thought and strength of spirit to loving and almost adoring the prince he serves above all else, devoting his every desire and habit and manner to pleasing him" (2.18) ("si volti con tutti i pensieri e forze dell'animo suo ad amare e quasi adorare il principe a chi serve sopra ogni altra cosa; e le voglie sue e costumi e modi tutti indrizzi a compiacerlo"). But Fregoso is told that he has described nothing but a flatterer. A few minutes later he is told that his vision of a modest and retiring courtier falsifies reality; only presumptuous courtiers win advancement. Fregoso's reply concludes with the statement that the courtier must hold to what is good, only to meet further skepticism about the nature of princes, who look not for goodness but for willing instruments of their despotic wills. Should one obey a dishonorable command? No, says Fregoso, but some commands only appear dishonorable. Here the players almost expose themselves to a perception of the corruption endemic to the system they live by, the perception of a courtier essentially passive, dependent on the whim of a master who may be evil and is likely to be a despot. A vision almost takes shape of the very condition of courtiership as potentially and inherently corrupting. The vision flickers briefly and obliquely but unmistakably, and for a while there is no laughter. Mercifully the subject is changed to dress, but that too leads to a painful admission: Italians have given up their own styles, as though to symbolize their helplessness before foreign invasion. The talk remains dogged by the morally equivocal but finally will be saved by Bibbiena's discourse on jokes, by the return of that saving laughter which proves a game is still being played.

On the third evening a different kind of threat emerges, a threat to that balance between the sexes which has governed the decorum of the Urbinese social ritual. To denigrate the status of women in any group that contains them will clearly place a strain on its cohesion. But in this company the insult is more scandalous because the court takes its fundamental character from the dominant presence of women, and in particular one woman. The creative male figure, Federigo da Montefeltro, the founding father, is dead. In his place there exists a vacuum. Duke Guidobaldo, the putative male leader, is indisposed and absent. He never enters the stage, the game space of the drawing room, and he fails to play the centrifugal, out-thrusting role that his father had played and that would open up the rigid enclosure of the court's withdrawal. The distinction of this society, its felicity, its *dolcezza*, that which justifies its memorialization in a book, all stem from the radiating presence of the duchess Elisabetta. The author has told us this quite explicitly from the beginning, where he pays her a tribute of remarkable resonance: "It seemed that she tempered us all to her own quality and fashion, wherefore each one strove to imitate her style, deriving as it were a rule of fine manners from the presence of so great and virtuous a lady" (1.4). ("Parea che tutti alla qualità e forma di lei temperasse ; onde ciascuno questo stile imitare si sforzava, pigliando quasi una norma di bei costumi dalla presenzia d'una tanta e così virtuosa signora.") To deny the worth of women is to attack from another direction the foundations of this company's particular grace.

Yet in fact this attack on the feminine enclosing power never succeeds in suspending the laughter of the play spirit as had the attack on the masculine corrupting power. This is true despite the social injustices suffered by women which the discussion reveals, despite the double standard applied to sexual conduct, and despite the sexual hostility which surfaces repeatedly. Once this almost leads to blows: "At a sign from the Duchess, many of the ladies rose to their feet and all rushed laughing upon signor Gasparo as if to assail him with blows and treat him as the bacchantes treated Orpheus" (2.96). ("Una gran parte di quelle donne, ben per averle la signora Duchessa fatto così cenno, si levarono in piedi e ridendo tutte corsero verso il signor Gasparo, come per dargli delle busse, e farne come le Baccanti d'Orfeo.") There is plenty of hostility here, but again the key word is *ridendo*. Nobody among those present, including the women, wants the laughter to fade; nobody wants to pass that limit beyond which hostility would banish play, just as nobody expects a woman to take over the defense of her sex from the male champions who assume it so articulately. The women of Urbino do not want an interchangeability of social roles; what they want is respect for the distinct roles society has assigned them. And because ultimately their position in this faintly effete community is so strong, the challenge to their dignity is contained like the earlier challenges to the authorized version. But again, the insecurities and inconsistencies of that version have been exposed; the court and the game have been tested; the tension of containment has betrayed its strain.

The fourth book and fourth evening call into question much more visibly and explicitly not only the authorized version but the game that has reflected it. The elder Fregoso is in no playful mood, and he brands most of the ideal courtier's accomplishments, so carefully compiled, as nothing but "frivolities and vanities" (4.4) ("leggerezze e vanità"). Here is yet another subversion, the most systematic, the most articulate presented thus far, and it is hard to see how this dismissal of frivolity could fail to include the game, the diversion which is still going on and which frames the repudiation. Ottaviano's discourse represents an effort to salvage courtiership at a higher level of moral responsibility, but is not in its turn free from flaws of argument that might, once exposed, give away more than it gains. Ottaviano argues that the courtier's several accomplishments are justified only if they serve a higher end, namely, the moral and political education of the prince. He attempts to beat off the doubts raised concerning the prince's educability, and he evokes a quasi-divine portrait of the model prince to balance the more familiar portrait of the demonically cruel and rapacious tyrant. But he cannot deny that the tyrant is by far the more common figure, and later in his discourse he confesses that some princes are not in fact redeemable.

There is one especially telling Freudian slip when the duchess puts a hypothetical case to him. "Let us assume," says the duchess, "that you have won [your prince's] favor completely, so that you are free to tell him whatever comes to mind" (4.25).

("Presupponetevi d'avervi acquistato compitamente la grazia sua, tanto che vi sia licito dirgli liberamente ciò che vi viene in animo.") Whereupon Ottaviano laughs and replies: "If I had the favor of some of the princes I know, and I were to tell them freely what I think, I fear I should soon lose that favor" (4.26). ("S'io avessi la grazia di qualche principe ch'io conosco e gli dicessi liberamente il parer mio, dubito che presto la perderei.") That laughing remark in its context cancels out a good deal of Ottaviano's argument, and it leaves the courtier suspended between the frivolity of his style and the futility of his political vision. This long discourse repudiates the elegant dilettante of the drawing room without convincingly establishing the adviser of the council chamber. Thus it constitutes the most formidable threat we have seen to the court and its play. Yet it too is contained, doubtless because no one present is disposed to press the negative implications all the way, to go beyond bounds. The court chooses to accept what is palliative in the discourse, chooses to settle for the partial self-consciousness that will permit it to continue.

At one point Ottaviano retells the myth of Epimetheus he found in Plato's *Protagoras*. At the end of that myth Zeus takes pity on primitive men who are the victims of wild beasts because, lacking civic virtue, they do not congregate in cities. So he orders Hermes to bring justice and shame to all men in order that civic life will become possible. Fregoso's repetition of this myth betrays a nostalgia for that kind of community where the civic virtue of all citizens does determine its destiny—communities such as the Athenian *polis,* which inspired the myth, or the Roman republic Cicero defended, or the commune of Bruni's Florence. The Platonic myth is pathetically or tragically anachronistic at Guidobaldo's Urbino; it points precisely to what the little Urbinese state lacks, the creative interplay of free and equal men in shaping the policy of the city. Here in this brilliant and worthy company the one thing not obtainable is the civic virtue of the *polis* and the commune. For that to be present, the play space of the drawing room would have to yield to what Hannah Arendt called a "public space," that place where equal and distinct individuals create a shared tradition of integrity. "The *polis,*" writes Arendt, " . . . is the organization of the people as it arises out of acting and speaking together, and its true space lies between people living together for this purpose."[5] The courtiers of Urbino play but do not act together, in Arendt's sense, which is why the Platonic myth is cruelly inappropriate. But the will to self-consciousness which produced their game is not so strong as to confront that anachronism.

According to the psychiatrist D. W. Winnicott, there is an area of experience that mediates between the inner psychic world and the outer objective world. Winnicott calls this the area of play, which begins in infancy and "expands into creative living and into the whole cultural life of man."[6] He locates this area in the potential space between the individual and the environment; it is made possible, he argues, by the child's trust in its mother, which permits a distinction between the self and the nonself. The pain of the separation is averted by filling the potential space with creative play and that which will later become cultural life. For our purposes, the significant word in Winnicott's theory of development is the verb *expand*. As the experience of trust is confirmed, the area of creativity widens. This widening leaves the maternal space behind for a broader, agonistic public space. But in the *Cortegiano* the trust in a broader scope of activity is weak; the role of the soldier has become vestigial; each of the four prefaces bespeaks a helpless consciousness of mutability, loss, and death. Here the play space has failed to expand; the area for creation has remained constricted, dominated by a benevolent but authoritative woman.

It is precisely that sense of mutability, that unavailability of political interplay, that beleaguering force of enclosure, which defines the quality of the laughter in this book. The laughter is so perfect that it is poignant; it almost brings one close to tears. It has its own purity and its own courage even if that courage falls short of the full lucidity which would render this purity impossible. It remains to the last sentence. The final test of the court's resiliency is the rhapsodic hymn to love by Bembo, which brings to the book and the company a spiritual element they had conspicuously lacked. But in the privacy and intensity of its mysticism, it constitutes the supreme denial of the company, the game, and the society behind them. It is the extreme assault. When Bembo's eloquence finally pours out of him, he falls silent as though he were rapt. There is a moment of sublime silence that is a terrible silence, a moment when the collective heartbeat has stopped, when the game is no longer being played. No one has anything to say. The social surface that has withstood all other threats has finally been torn. It is only a moment, and then Emilia Pia leans forward and gently tugs Bembo's sleeve, saying, "Take care, messer Pietro" (4.71). ("Guardate, messer Pietro.") He replies to her, and the others then begin to speak and the crisis has passed. A moment later we hear Emilia laughing, and we hear plans for the discussion the following evening. The play and the society have absorbed this last accession of blinding light; the choice of the game has been vindicated; one can be confident that nothing will be said on the fifth evening which the resiliency of this circle will not contain.

4

The End of Discourse
in Machiavelli's *Prince*

Machiavelli was a writer preoccupied with the gravity of endings, oppressed even with the pathos of human terminations, but he was capable of discriminating between what might be called their degrees of decorum.

> Egli è cosa verissima come tutte le cose del mondo hanno il termine della vita loro; ma quelle vanno tutto il corso che è loro ordinato dal cielo, generalmente, che non disordinano il corpo loro, ma tengonlo in modo ordinato.

> There is nothing more true than that all the things of this world have a limit to their existence; but those only run the entire course ordained for them by Heaven that do not allow their body to become disorganized, but keep it unchanged in the manner ordained.[1]

This sentence moves, not uncharacteristically, from a universal fatality to a sense of human obligation to perpetuate things (most notably, political regimes and institutions) through their natural or prescribed career. Things which attain their destined end expire decorously as things do not which are botched by human misjudgment, neglected or aborted irresponsibly. Few things in fact do attain that decorum for Machiavelli; part of the oppression of human affairs lies in the interruptions, the truncations of natural curves, the human impotence or malignity that produces amputated history. It is the unique achievement of the Roman republic, as analyzed in the *Discourses on Livy*, to have sustained its own natural course for so many centuries, but the more common pattern is the uneven, jarring, indecorous rhythm of *The Prince*, *The History of Florence*, the *capitolo* "Di Fortuna." In *The Prince* endings

tend to be violent, disastrous, and simultaneous with fresh beginnings which are themselves shallowly founded and insecurely
extended. The kind of harmonious change which dovetails each
new structural addition (chapter 2) appears in the context of the
entire work as a rare exception.

The treatise indeed would have no reason for being
were this not the case. It assumes and addresses the indecorum of
contemporaneous Italy. It *assumes* the political muddle like a
weight to be carried and disposed of, and in so doing it abjures
the false decorum of *belles lettres*. The dedicatory epistle repudiates
rhetoric; the clipped opening chapter repudiates the graces of
Humanist elegance; from the beginning, the book refuses to be
literature, that most refined corrupter of communal discipline
(*History* 5.1) *The Prince* signals its willed estrangement from the
cultural processes it claims to analyze. It will not enjoy the ritual
comforts of the products of high culture, including the factitious
ending, the dialogue that fabricates consensus, the generous un-
realities and bland conclusions of fiction that pass for description.
It will remain outside all that, so that any closure it succeeds in
attaining will be the hard-won closure of the intelligence embedded in that actual history which frustrates natural endings. "Unlike
writing, life never finishes," wrote Robert Lowell. Machiavelli's
authorial stance as his book opens seems to reject that *textual*
conclusiveness and to promise only whatever *analytic* conclusiveness can be wrung from the perennially continuous. This honesty
of method is the honesty which would leave the *Discourses* essentially unfinished and the last sentence of the *History* opening onto
the ruin that continued to engulf Italy endlessly.

But the reader who begins *The Prince* is not discouraged
from presuming that a decorous analytic closure lies within its
author's power. What the reader first encounters are the curt
distinctions of a new, embracing political science. All states are
either republics or principalities. Principalities are either hereditary
or acquired. If acquired, they are either entirely new or grafted.
We appear to enter upon a total system, a Thomism of statecraft
which within its modest length will find a place for all possible
political conditions and define their constituent elements from a

position outside and above them. Yet in the following chapters devoted to successive individual cases, the reader receives rather the opposite impression: he or she is down on the ground of history, watching the author clear away limited areas of general truth, moving not inward from universal principles but outward from concrete events. This is the first shadow cast upon the presumption of analytic closure. The author's goal is to clear away a conceptual space uncluttered by prejudice or ethics or loyalty or myth, a space where the pure intelligence can operate freely to discover the laws of political behavior and precepts for political success. But this enterprise has no basis in axiomatic first truths; it is rigorously, bravely inductive.

The faculty engaged in clearing this space is elsewhere termed *discorso* by Machiavelli (*Discourses* 1, Proemio, 73), a term which might be glossed as the power of rational analysis. It begins with concrete experience and history, such as the debacle of Louis XII's Italian wars discussed in chapter 3, and its actual power can be measured in the tightness of the correspondence between example and generalization. The generalizations in chapter 3, "Composite Principalities," are based upon the negative examples of Louis' failures, but the failures have prescriptive value: they can be used to produce rules for success. Louis can be said to have made five errors, which historical analysis can isolate from his experience and others'. In the future a ruler who wishes to graft a new member upon an established state, as Louis did, can be taught how to proceed effectively. This is a small clearing of conceptual order, since it involves only one particular situation among many hypothetical situations confronting a prince. But in theory this clearing can be duplicated in the analyses of all other situations. When this has been accomplished, then a legitimate analytic closure would be reached.

In chapter 3 little is said of individual *virtù*, because *virtù* is an explosive, improvisatory, antisystematic capacity for which the emergent political science has no need nor indeed any place. It appears in the brief opening chapter as a kind of enabling talent which would permit the apprentice ruler to attain a position where scientific precept would be useful to him. But *virtù* only begins to emerge as a significant force in a chapter devoted to legendary legislator-founders, and then later, more dangerously, in Cesare Borgia's sanguinary epic. *Virtù* in these earlier chapters is not contained by analysis, but it does not threaten seriously to blunt analytic reason, *discorso*. It might be said merely to complicate that close correspondence between precept and event which is essential to the writer's method. Thus governments set up overnight "are destroyed in the first bad spell . . . unless those who have suddenly become princes are of such *virtù* that overnight they can learn how to preserve what fortune has suddenly tossed into their laps" (54).

> Se già quelli tali . . . che sì de repente sono diventati principi, non sono di tanta virtù, che quello che la fortuna ha messo loro in grembo e' sappino subito prepararsi a conservarlo. (19)

Already in this passage exceptions have to be made for genius, and in the very negative, concessive formulation the text admits an energy which gathers power from its semidismissal. Contrary to custom, contrary to precept, a wayward dynamism enters the text, is created by the text which seems to dismiss it. But it does not here threaten the very logic of the argument.

The conceptual space cleared by intellectual power is however progressively perceived as hemmed in by all the immense body of history that resists generalization. Every law is vulnerable to the exceptions, the qualifications and inconsistencies of political experience, just as the intellectual power is vulnerable to any internal inconsistencies or faulty logic. Because there are no transcendental principles, because the analytic movement always works from the specific case outward, *The Prince* reluctantly reveals its radically *conative* dimension; it is obliged to strive against the complexities that hedge its clearings. Its language betrays the traces of an academic *disputatio:* "If you advance this objection, then I reply thus. . . ." "*Disputerò* come questi principati si possino governare" (7) ("I shall debate how these principalities can be governed" [33]); the verb adumbrates an adversarial relationship. To extend the circumscribed area of truth requires a felt effort, a courage, a risk, as well as a violence upon convention and morality. Given the resistances, it becomes hard to believe that the extensions outward will come to control all the delimiting space. One suspects that something will always remain to be appropriated. Closure at best, it seems, will fence in a finite territory against the uncharted space always lying outside.

II.

Machiavelli's effort to clear a conceptual space resembles the prince's effort to clear a politico-geographical space on which to impose his will and his order. The metaphor commonly applied to the prince's activity, the imposition of form on matter, can equally be applied to the writer's activity. The writer employs a conceptual violence, a sacrifice of myth, of ethics, of "literature," and this violence is vulnerable to conventional judgment as is the physical violence of the ideally ruthless ruler. The writer of *The Prince*, like his creature, has to wrestle with Fortune, who can jumble *post hoc* analysis as she frustrates *ante hoc* calculations. Each space, the conceptual and concrete political, is threatened by an inherent principle of disorder which must be allowed for and which to a degree can be combated. Thus the hero of the book, the timeless hero with a hundred faces who battles and plots and kills to impose his discipline on a recalcitrant polity, is doubled by the thinker who in defining him has risked a murderous sacrifice of pieties in order to discipline the wayward details of history.

The common effort in which writer and statesman meet is termed "imitation." Imitation for Machiavelli as for many other Renaissance preceptors is an extension of reading, and in his specific extension writing and action come together. This duality is first suggested in chapter 6 of *The Prince*, and perhaps it is no accident that in this opening paragraph the word *virtù*, employed three times, makes its first important appearance in the treatise, as though through the pedagogy of imitation that antisystematic energy could be contained.

Non si maravigli alcuno se nel parlare che io farò de' principati al tutto nuovi e di principe e di stato, io addurrò grandissimi esempli; perché . . . debbe uno uomo prudente entrare sempre per vie battute da uomini grandi, e quelli che sono stati eccellentissimi imitare, acciò che, se la sua virtù non vi arriva, almeno ne renda qualche odore; e fare come gli arcieri prudenti, a' quali, parendo el loco dove disegnano ferire troppo lontano, e conoscendo fino a quanto va la virtù del loro arco, pongono la mira assai più alta che il loco destinato, non per aggiugnere con la loro freccia a tanta altezza, ma per potere, con lo aiuto di sì alta mira, pervenire al disegno loro. (16–17)

No one should be surprised if, in discussing states where both the prince and the constitution are new, I shall give the loftiest examples. . . . So a prudent man should always follow in the footsteps of great men and imitate those who have been outstanding. If his own *virtù* fails to compare with theirs, at least it has an air of greatness about it. He should behave like those archers who, if they are skilful, when the target seems too distant, know the capabilities *(virtù)* of their bow and aim a good deal higher than the objective, not in order to shoot so high but so that by aiming high they can reach the target. (49)

The writer implies that the prudent prince should imitate *him* in his own scrutiny of the most illustrious (ancient) examples; the writer and the prince are properly ranged side by side as they both put to use the book of the past. A later restatement of this theme will underscore the inseparability of reading and action.

Quanto allo esercizio della mente, debbe il principe leggere le istorie, e in quelle considerare le azioni delli uomini eccellenti; vedere come si sono governati nelle guerre; esaminare le cagioni delle vittorie e perdite loro, per potere queste fuggire e quelle imitare. (39)

As for intellectual training, the prince should read history, studying the actions of eminent men to see how they conducted themselves during war and to discover the reasons for their victories or their defeats, so that he can avoid the latter and imitate the former. (89–90)

The prince in other words should do what in fact Machiavelli is doing in the composition of this treatise. In the prince's conduct we can judge his skill as reader, the skill which renders this particular treatise unique. The wise prince will join Machiavelli in rejecting history as mere *belles lettres;* he will scorn Humanist reading for the creative, dynamic reading of history which acts upon the concrete present.

The fullest discussion of imitation appears in the "Proemio" to Book 1 of the *Discourses.* The neglect of the past by modern rulers, Machiavelli charges, is due to the lack of real knowledge of history ("vera cognizione delle storie"), which is read only for the pleasure afforded by its variety rather than for the purpose of active imitation, wrongly judged to be not only difficult but impossible. Machiavelli will study Livy so that his readers will be able to derive from it that utility in which true knowledge of history must be found. The author writes to perform ("operare") things desirable for the common good, and the content of his labor will be those achievements filled with *virtù,* those "virtuosissime operazioni" wrought ("operate") by ancient kingdoms and republics. The *Discourses* comprise an imitative *operazione* designed to inspire ulterior imitative *operazioni* on the part of the active, "virtuous" reader/ruler. Thus this Proemio draws a distinction implicit in *The Prince* between the Humanist/dilettante, the merely verbal imitator, and the true reader/knower/active imitator. The result of this distinction is to lump Machiavelli together with his ideal hero and his ideal reader, active imitators all.

This is the positive version of what Machiavelli is doing in writing as he does, but even in these optimistic formulations one discerns shadows of doubt. There is clearly doubt in the simile of the archer quoted above, who aims above his target in order to reach it. This tacit admission that the summits of ancient achievement will always prove superior to the modern reveals the intrinsic flaw in Machiavelli's imitative project. The affirmation of the unchanging character of man, made in the same Proemio in Book 1 of the *Discourses,* has to be balanced against the contrast between ancient *virtù* and modern vice which, he writes elsewhere, is "clearer than the sun" (Proemio to Book 2). Machiavelli's historicism and his doctrine of imitation have to be accommodated to these antithetical perceptions, each often repeated but never fully reconciled. If the ruler/imitator is inherently corrupted, then his "reading" will be continuously vitiated and the thought of the writer/imitator wasted. The rejection of textual, fictive, mythical conclusions for analytic, prescriptive, operative conclusions may entail a final result in botched and vicious parodies.

This likelihood is increased since modern decadence confronts both thinker and ruler with the common challenge of *extension*. There is a risk, we learn from the *Asino d'oro (Golden Ass)*, in the extension of power beyond the walls of the city-state. The appetite for extending dominion is there represented as self-destructive, whereas German cities, content with no more than a band of six miles surrounding them, live in security.

> A la nostra città non fe' paura
> Arrigo già con tutta la sua possa,
> Quando i confini avea presso alle mura;
> E or ch'ella ha sua potenza promossa
> Intorno, e diventata è grande e vasta,
> Teme ogni cosa, non che gente grossa.

(Formerly [the emperor] Henry VII with all his might aroused no fear in our city, when her boundaries were near the walls, but now that she has extended her power round about and become large and vast, she fears everything, not only the strong.)[2]

Florence's spatial expansion is a cause of insecurity although, as the *Discourses* suggest, a city like Rome might feel a compulsion to expand in order to preserve internal equilibrium. A still more serious challenge lies in temporal extension. Because Fortune operates in time, time itself is dangerous. A legislator may found a healthy state, but his laws and institutions may be subverted before they have time to root themselves. If a state attempts to reform itself (Florence in 1502 under the Soderini republic), it may be crushed before it has time to conclude (Florence, 1512, after the return of the Medici). But if Fortune favors the state with victory and prosperity, these may lead in time to softness and corruption (*History* 5.1). The paradigmatic story of Borgia is the story of a clever antagonist of time, who staves off ruin for a while through a protracted series of expedients. Even Cosimo de' Medici, the most successful single figure of the *History,* sees his public and private affairs "going to ruin" at the end of his life (7.6). Real duration in Machiavelli represents a (perhaps unknowing) concession to myth, since the true founders of enduring states— Moses, Theseus, Romulus, Cryrus—were all to some degree legendary. The modern archer cannot shoot so high; he must aim for narrower expansions, indecorous endings, briefer extensions, aborted reigns, precarious continuities.

This vulnerability of political extension affects the security of the thinker's conceptual extension. The potential collapse of a political order involves the viability of the cognitive order, since the cognitive discourse first presented itself as counsel for successful action. As the implicit distance widens between model and realistic goal, as the demeaning decline of culture stands revealed, then the double *operazioni* of imitation appear less and less plausible. The extension of the conceptual clearing assumes a fund of relevant nonmythical examples to be drawn upon to meet each problem of praxis. But this fund in *The Prince* proves to be shallow. The situation of Machiavelli as innovative thinker can be compared most readily to the situation of that prince who is a newcomer in a *principatus novus.* Of such a prince's task it can be said that "nothing is more difficult to arrange, more doubtful of success, and more dangerous to carry through" (51). To achieve something like decorous closure under these circumstances may require the surrender of hope for a single extended clearing; it may require one to settle for random patches of relative order, clusters of insight connected arbitrarily. The closing chapters of *The Prince* will be decisive in determining whether in fact it does adumbrate a calculus capable of scientific coherence.

III

This determination proves to be negative: analysis leading to precept is progressively abandoned in the last third of the book. Scientific pretensions are quietly withdrawn as the semblance of conclusive law fades from the text. In this progressive capitulation, a few stages can be roughly distinguished. Quite early one can trace a disturbing gap between example and precept: in the failures of the exemplary figures Cesare Borgia and Oliverotto da Fermo, in the blurred distinction between Borgia and Agothocles, in the success of Scipio whose leniency should in principle have proven fatal, in the success of French armies employing those mercenaries which are allegedly the root cause of Italian military disgrace. As the analysis proceeds one can follow the increasing effort of the precept to disengage itself from the entangling texts of recorded history and remembered history. *This* text begins with gestures ostensibly grounding precepts in past experience and then goes on essentially to unground them, to demonstrate as it were in spite of itself the difficult struggle of the precept to stem directly from experience.

This struggle is rendered still more arduous by the progressive recalcitrance of the precept to remain simple, pure, clearcut. The famous chapter 17 ("Cruelty and compassion; and whether it is better to be loved than feared, or the reverse") has been noticed chiefly for its ethical brutality, but for our purposes it can serve to exemplify the intensifying discursive qualification. Brutal this chapter may be, but the harshness emerges from an undergrowth of distinctions, reversals, exceptions, and modifications. The text is finding it increasingly necessary to complicate generalizations, turning back on its own discourse to raise objections or modify rules. One can work through chapter 17 noting the complications in purely lexical terms, in the frequency of expressions like "nevertheless," "but," "however," "on the other hand" ("nondimanco," "pertanto," "ma," "pure," "dall'una parte," "dall' altra"). Not every usage involves a qualification of the argument, but taken together they underscore the difficulty of reaching guidelines in the shifting morass of human affairs. The conceptual clearing becomes more visibly overgrown.

In the chapters that follow, the ability to elicit unqualified rules from history will grow feebler. The long chapter 19 ("The need to avoid contempt and hatred") presents a new stage in the deterioration of analysis, a stage which substitutes contradiction for qualification and which in effect offers an alternative to precept. Two cases of contradiction can suffice. First instance: Machiavelli's lifelong support of the standing militia in preference to mercenary armies, support which is expressed elsewhere in *The Prince* (chapter 12), is subverted in chapter 19 by his analysis of the Roman army's destructive role in the empire and his congratulation of modern rulers on their freedom from this threat. Second instance: the confusing discussion of conspiracies argues that "there have been many conspiracies but few of them have achieved their end" (103) ("si vede molte essere state le coniure e poche avere avuto buon fine" [47–48]). A survey of the factors that cause their failures and which should deter a potential conspirator leads to the surprising assertion that "it is unthinkable that anyone should be so rash as to conspire" (104) ("è impossibile che alcuno sia sì temerario che coniuri" [48]), an assertion that denies the facts and denies what immediately precedes it. The contradiction remains if both generalizations are restricted to those regimes which have won popular support. This is the case of the one example offered: the Canneschi family conspired against and assassinated Annibale Bentivogli, prince of Bologna. But the Bolognese so loved the dynasty that they killed the Canneschi, then found a bastard scion of the Bentivogli and allowed him to rule until the rightful heir had time to come of age. Thus I conclude, writes Machiavelli, "that when a prince has the good will of the people he should not worry about conspiracies" (105) ("uno principe debbe tenere delle coniure poco conto, quando el popolo gli sia benivolo" [48]). This will not comfort Annibale, who perhaps should have worried about conspiracies somewhat more than he did. In his case men *were* rash enough to conspire and they succeeded in doing him in.

The alternative which in effect replaces the crumbling analytic precept in chapter 19 has maintained a vigorous presence through most of the treatise but is only now explicitly permitted to dominate the argument. This is the undefined, perhaps undefinable gift of *virtù*, whose mysterious significance in this book can only be grasped by triangulating contexts, and whose contexts themselves are richly, perversely various. What we learn from this chapter is that politics cannot be mastered as a science but intuited as an art beyond the reach of rules. Politics becomes an arena for flair, instinct, genius, which no treatise can circumscribe and whose description can never be closed because it cannot, properly speaking, be begun. Why did the emperor Severus, a "new prince," keep his throne, when all the other emperors of his era who, like him, had recourse to undue cruelty were killed?

> In Severo fu tanta virtù che, mantenendosi e soldati amici, ancora che i populi fussino da lui gravati, possé sempre regnare felicemente; perché quelle sua virtù lo facevano nel conspetto de' soldati e de' populi si mirabile che questi rimanevano *quodam modo* attoniti e stupidi, e quelli reverenti e satisfatti. (50)

> Severus was a man of such *virtù* that, keeping the soldiers friendly, even though the people were oppressed by him, he reigned successfully to the end; this was because his *virtù* so impressed the soldiers and the people that the latter were continuously left astonished and stupefied and the former stayed respectful and content.(109)

The narrative that follows fails to distinguish persuasively Severus' conduct from the others'; the basis of his success was simply his *virtù*, which the text cannot really concretize. The *virtù* remains an absolute, impervious to description or even to understanding.

> A Caracalla, Commodo e Massimino [fu] cosa perniziosa imitare Severo, per non avere auta tanta virtù che bastassi a seguitare le vestigie sua. (53)

> It was fatal for Caracalla, Commodus, and Maximinus to imitate Severus, since they lacked the *virtù* to follow in his footsteps. (114)

We seem on the brink of a tautology wherein *virtù* obtains success and success results from *virtù*. The close of this long chapter can add little to this semantic circle.

      The following chapter 20 foregrounds a factor which will complete the subversion of a prescriptive political science— the factor of the unique set of circumstances, the unpredictable, asystematic *kairos*. Should the prince disarm his subjects, deliberately antagonize them, foster divisions among them, build fortresses?

> Di tutte queste cose non si possi dare determinata sentenzia se non si viene a' particulari di quelli stati dove si avessi a pigliare alcuna simile deliberazione. (54)

> It is impossible to give a final verdict on any of these policies, unless one examines the particular circumstances of the states in which such decisions have had to be taken. (114)

Despite this impossibility Machiavelli states his intention to discuss each question in general terms, but each discussion tends to appeal finally to "i particulari," "i tempi." The appeal implicitly calls into question the analysis and the counsel of the preceding chapters, since these have been presented as transcending concrete occasions and as generally valid. Here rather in the dominance of circumstances lies the vindication of that instinctive *virtù* which will seize upon the essentials of each concrete occasion and manipulate them with daring and imagination. Just as the writer ends his treatment of the fortresses by commending those who build them and those who do not, so his choice of able advisers is a choice beyond rules: "Good advice, whomever it comes from, depends on the shrewdness of the prince who seeks it, and not the shrewdness of the prince on good advice" (127). ("Li buoni consigli, da qualunque venghino, conviene naschino dalla prudenzia del principe, e non la prudenzia del principe da' buoni consigli" [61].) The closing sentence of chapter 24, the last ostensibly analytic chapter, seems to offer the only version of closure the book is now capable of.

> Quelle difese solamente sono buone, sono certe, sono durabili, che dependano da te proprio e dalla virtù tua. (63)

> The only sound, sure, and enduring methods of defense are those based on your own actions and *virtù*. (129)

The activity of the prince is now fundamentally improvisatory. All courses of action are risky in the nature of things ("l'ordine delle cose"). The prince as we last view him is profoundly lonely, extemporizing stratagems and precautions to extend his hazardous rule, unable to count on his people, his allies, his advisers, or ancient models of achievement. He must adapt himself ceaselessly, restlessly, to the caprice of changing circumstance, as the penultimate chapter 25 affirms, but to do this is to be extravagantly, inhumanly volatile.

> Se uno che si governa con respetti e pazienzia, e tempi e le cose girono in modo che il governo suo sia buono, e' viene felicitando; ma se li tempi e le cose si mutano, e' rovina, perché non muta modo di procedere. Né si truova uomo si prudente che si sappi accomodare a questo. (64)

> If a man behaves with patience and circumspection and the time and circumstances are such that this method is called for, he will prosper; but if time and circumstances change he will be ruined because he does not change his policy. Nor do we find any man shrewd enough to know how to adapt his policy in this way. (132)

The lonely ruler, shifting his balance and his policy, remaking his own character as he remakes his style, listening for each whisper of change in the times, will nonetheless falter in the end from a tragic insufficiency of pliancy.

      This failure of the prince betokens the failure of the analyst whose admission of circumstance has caused his conceptual space definitively to implode. Stage by stage, he has withdrawn from dogmatism to qualification to contradiction to a surrender before pure contingency. The text, unable to perpetuate its order, unable to validate imitation, acts out its own version of the prince's failure. The analyst has been unequal to the volatility of his own subject and if, in his penultimate chapter, he leaves open, or tries to, the struggle between Fortune and *virtù*, his own rational power seems defeated by Fortune. Counsel based on experience is impracticable; success lies in the harmonizing of conduct with occasion; and this book, by maintaining ostensibly its function as manual, has evidently denied itself any meaningful statement. The final conclusion, given this collapse of system, would appear to be necessarily confessional or duplicitous. The only real question, apparently, is how much failure to admit.

IV.

The final, twenty-sixth chapter of *The Prince* ("Exhortation to liberate Italy from the barbarians") may have been written well after the others, as though the writer were dissatisfied with his original close. It radically alters the rhetorical mode from deliberation to apocalypse. A desperate urgency, hertofore barely discernible, produces calls for a redeemer like Moses, Cyrus, and Theseus, and the very prostrate condition of Italy, personified pathetically, becomes an argument for her future salvation. Stylistic restraint gives way to oratorical melodrama, and the scorn for myth gives way to the invocation of a savior.

In this last chapter the repressed visionary in the author returns to life, the visionary of the *capitoli* and the *Asino d'oro*. The strained hope of the vision results in ironies beyond his control: irony in the evocation of "unheard of wonders" ("estraordinarii, sanza esemplo"), in the predicted defeat of the Swiss and Spanish infantry by newly trained Italians, in the identification of the Medici with the hypothetical redeemer, in the concluding quotation from Petrarch, 150 years old, predicting a speedy victory of native *virtù* over the barbarians. The desperate urgency of this chapter apparently derives from the ruinous military situation, but one wonders whether the deeper cause is not the deterioration of the writer's enterprise. If in fact he had established with calm logic the prescriptive science his book had seemed to promise, there would be no need for miracles and messiahs. This conclusion could not properly be called either confessional or duplicitous, but it does not seem free from a degree of self-deception.

To say this however is not seriously to deal with the problematic question of the book's closure, nor to determine ultimately what we are left with. One way to respond to these questions would be to point to the text's increasing dependence on a single signifier, *virtù*, which possesses at once too much and too little siginificance. The meanings of this word as derived from context "go round in an endless series of incompatibilities," according to one critic,[3] and from this circular plethora of meaning, stable meaning might plausibly be seen to leak away. Thus it might be argued that Machiavelli's book is progressively usurped by a signifier which is essentially vacant, pretending to denote a referent which cannot be shown to exist. Historical analysis and political analysis would stand revealed as dependent on a term which is radically blurred, so that the text as a whole could be said to reach an impasse or to move around endlessly in that vortex of incompatibilities. This account would postulate then a helpless closure of decentered or hollow statement, feebly circling around its weakness.

An alternative account would recognize in the messianic close an admission that the book had begun by misrepresenting its own character and that it truly belongs to that flow of cultural production it had initially wanted to repudiate. The close restores the book to cultural discourse, "literary" discourse, as against that ulterior, detached, purely analytic discourse it had seemed to claim for itself. The "Exhortation" reveals a mode of imitation which breaks down the segregation of rhetorician and activist, which accepts models from poetry as well as from praxis. The ruler/reader is no longer situated side by side with the writer, engaged in a common *operazione*, but rather opposite the writer, the object of his exhortation. In this view of *The Prince*, the presumption of scientific, systematic closure would be regarded as a distraction which the book gradually, then dramatically, dispels. The text could thus be understood as acting out the discovery of its authentic goal, which is the goal of "literature" and all culture, namely the fabrication of a vulnerable construct. The prince Machiavelli fabricates, the conniver with a hundred faces, belongs to the realm of the mythical which the text has never exorcised, and the prince's *virtù* retains that potent and volatile opacity which is the property of imaginative fictions.

The construct of *The Prince* is of course ungrounded like all cultural contructs. It achieves the shaky validity of an extemporized invention which is exposed, precarious, *bricolé*, conative. If the signifier *virtù* is vulnerable through its simultaneous superfluity/emptiness of meaning, then like other problematic signifiers it calls for the intervention of the reader to drain and fill it, to penetrate its opacity and grasp the emergent integrity of its

"incompatibilities." If in the politico-geographic realm the fragmentation of Italy invites a redeemer, in the textual realm the
fragmented meanings invite more plausibly the intrusion of the
reader's synthesizing and flexible understanding. The invulnerable
construct, if such a monster could be conceived, the construct
lacking this text's polysemous density, would be condemned to
sterility. *Virtù* as a signifier is incontestably imprecise, but it makes
demonstrably a somber, obsessive aggression upon the mind
which could not be propelled either by pure precision or pure
vacancy. *Something* is there in the text, something not wholly
unstable, that sort of thing we look to culture to provide. As a
scientific concept, *virtù* blurs; as an otherwise unnamable, explosive, newly isolated property of experience, it can be received as
seminal. Machiavelli's book does open up a clearing of space, not
so much for analysis as for the historical imagination, a space of
suggestive uncertainty surrounding a word, and this space becomes a constitutive element of the text, perhaps the most valuable
element.

From this view of the book, *The Prince* reaches its close
when having discovered its own mystery and mythicality, it comes
at last to admit and proclaim them. This mystical dimension does
not cancel out the play of analytic intelligence which has governed
earlier chapters. It does not discredit the effort to generalize political action and to read performatively all history as a text. But it
does seal the analogy between writer and ruler more firmly, since
the writer like his most prestigious models is a prophet, a *profeto*.
His book can end decorously when he accepts the role of prophet,
and if his crudest concluding prophecy invites irony, we can find
in the body of his work a prophetic vision of bitter dignity, a
composite image of brilliant, beleaguered fury which cannot effectively be deconstructed. He dismisses in a famous aphorism the
role of unarmed prophet: "All armed prophets have conquered,
and unarmed prophets have come to grief" (52). ("Tutti e profeti
armati vinsono, e gli disarmati ruinorno"[18].) This dismissal does
not really affect his own role. As a prophet, Machiavelli is not
totally disarmed: he is armed with that fury of *virtù*. Closure then
is not a matter of completing a design; it fulfills no ideal propor-

tions; it does not allow an intellectual order to expand to its outermost limits. Closure in this case constitutes rather a recognition that the text belongs in the sphere of other texts, the sphere of human society—improvisatory, groundless, metamorphic, fictive—the sphere of tragic conation where it finally places and joins its hero.

5

The Hair of the Dog
That Bit You:
Rabelais' Thirst

"Je ne sçay que diable cecy veult dire," remarks Panurge shortly after he enters Rabelais' narrative; "ce vin est fort bon et bien delicieux, mais plus j'en boy, plus j'ai de soif. Je croy que l'ombre de Monseigneur Pantagruel engendre les alterez, comme la lune les catharres." ("I don't know what the devil this means. This wine is very good and most delicious, but the more I drink of it the thirstier I am. I believe that the shadow of my lord Pantagruel makes men thirsty, as the moon breeds catarrhs.")[1] The reader may be or ought to be inclined to share Panurge's puzzlement. The motif of thirst in this book, so ubiquitous and so ostensibly transparent, still invites reflection, and not least its property of increasing with satisfaction. One may well ask with Panurge what that means, and one may ask whether Panurge's own analogy between thirst and a form of illness ("catharres") is appropriate or misplaced.

Thirst is not in itself a condition limited to the characters we are invited to admire. "Dipsodes" means "Altérés"; Janotus and his companions are heavy drinkers; Jobelin Bridé drinks "théologalement" in the early editions (1:64 n. 3), as does his pupil, the young Gargantua:

A boyre n'avoit poinct fin ny canon, car il disoit que les metes et bournes de boyre estoient quand, la personne beuvant, le liege de ses pantoufles enfloit en hault d'un demy pied. (1:82)

For drinking he had neither end nor rule. For he said that the ends and limits of drinking were when the cork-sole of the drinker's shoe swelled up half a foot as he drank. (83)

The same pupil will drink far less under Ponocrates. The hypocritical *caphars* are obsessed with thirst and hunger, "guarniz de
alteration inextinguible et manducation insatiable" (1:403)
("possesed of an inexhaustible thirst and insatiable powers of
mastication" [286].) This insatiability is not on its face readily
distinguishable from the influence Panurge attributes to Pantagruel. Among the Papimanes, the "beuvettes" are "numereuses"
(2:189). The impulse to drink is not consistently represented as
appealing.

The word *altéré*, Panurge's word and Rabelais' most
common word for "thirsty," tended to have negative implications
during the sixteenth century. Although Rabelais uses the verb
alterer routinely in the sense "to excite thirst," this would not
appear to have been one of its readiest meanings during his own
era. Huguet omits it altogether from his entry devoted to the verb
and suggests a related meaning only cautiously and tentatively in
his long entry devoted to the noun *altere*, despite the abundant
evidence in the Rabelaisian text. *Alterer* in the sixteenth century
meant primarily to change something but also to trouble somebody, to upset and to anger. The cognate noun *altere* meant "mal-
heur," "état pénible." The participle *altéré* could mean "avid,"
even "greedy," as a tiger is avid for blood. The reflexive verb
s'alterer meant "to be disturbed" and is so used by Rabelais ("sans
plus vous fascher ne alterer," 2:18). But it also had the meaning
"to change" intransitively, with a negative nuance; medieval writers had already used it with an implication of deterioration, an
implication which remains in Amyot and Montaigne.[2] When the
narrator of the *Quart Livre* prologue archly compliments the
reader—"Vous avez remede trouvé infinable contre toutes alter-
ations." (2:11)—this last word refers to an unhealthy deterioration of the balance of humors. It is conceivable that the neutrality
of the modern French *altéré* owes something to Rabelais' own
usage, but this neutrality does not correspond to the assumptions
his readers would have brought to his book. He may well have
wanted to modify or complicate these assumptions, but he could
not abolish them.

The associations with thirst already present in the pre-

Rabelaisian name "Pantagruel" were scarcely positive. The minor demon who poured salt down the throat of sleepers to make them thirsty was considered to be mischievous; he was not, clearly, bestowing a favor upon his victims. Demerson connects the etymology of this demon's name with his capacity to render people *pantois* or *pantelants*.[3] This element of intense thirst shifts from mischief to catastrophe at the opening of Pantagruel's history in Rabelais, in the terrible description of the drought. After the equivocal fertility of the first chapter and the equivocal reference to Noah as a deceived or confused *(trompé)* drinker, it is the drought in chapter 2 of the *Pantagruel* which initiates the narrative proper. "Qui feut premier, soif ou beuverye?" (Which came first, drinking or thirst?" [48–49]) asks one of the *bien yvres* in the *Gargantua*. He receives two answers.

> "Soif, car qui eust beu sans soif durant le temps de innocence?"
> "Beuverye, car *privatio presupponit habitum*. Je suis clerc." (1:23)

> "Thirst. For who could have drunk without a thirst in the time of innocence?
> "Drinking, for *privatio praesupponit habitum*. I'm a Latinist." (49)

In Rabelais' bibulous version of the chicken and the egg, the balance of infinite regress may tilt slightly toward the second, clerical response, but in his own narrative there is no doubt that *soif* is primary and that it is first represented as cruelly, prodigiously murderous of man and his fellow creatures. The nightmare images of the drought—the parched birds falling from the sky, the fish flip-flopping on dry land, the suicides throwing themselves into wells—provide an initial vision of the horror of thirst which ensuing chapters will never entirely cancel.

The element of salt, already present in the fifteenth-century folk material, recurs now in a guise which is not easy to understand. Salt in the second chapter is initially associated with the parching effect produced by Phaeton, whose wayward course through the sky caused the earth to sweat and thus to produce

the seas, salty like all other sweat. ("Taste your own and see for
yourself," recommends the narrator in effect, thus drawing the
reader into the narrative.) The supplicatory processions organized
by the pious during the drought produce watery exhalations from
the ground, but these too prove to be salty. It is immediately after
these episodes that the birth of Pantagruel is recounted, a birth
preceded by the emergence from his mother's womb of sixty-eight
mules laden with salt, then nine dromedaries laden with ham,
followed by further supplies of thirst-producing edibles. The infant
Pantagruel makes his appearance at the tail of this procession. The
account is both repellent and suggestive. Salt would appear to be
the staple least needed amid the universal disaster, but the end of
the chapter veers toward a hint of good augury. Some of the
midwives present take heart.

> "Voicy bonne provision. Aussy bien ne bevyons nous
> que lachement, non en lancement; cecy n'est que bon signe, ce
> sont aguillons de vin."[4]

> "Here is fine fare. We were only drinking slackly, not
> like Saxons. This is bound to be a good sign. These are spurs to
> wine." (176)

The allegedly propitious *aguillons* are followed by the propitiously
hirsute appearance of the newborn child ("Il est né à tout le poil,
il fera choses merveilleuses" [1:231]). ("He is born with all his
hair. He will perform wonders" [177].) The midwives' auguries
may be merely old wives' superstitions, but we hear nothing more
of the drought; in effect, it has ended with Pantagruel's birth. How
to interpret, if interpretation be needed, this grotesque and pro-
digious delivery with its monstrous parade? Salt, the source of
thirst, emerges from the organ of generation, preceding a creature
who will himself be a source and an incarnation of thirst. The
privation which was death is transformed inexplicably into a privation which is life, which is happily or painfully bound up with
life. Salt lies on both sides of the renewal.

Thirst had already become in the sixteenth century a
metaphor for a more generalized desire resulting from privation.
Perhaps the metaphor is inherent in the physical experience. It is

impossible at any rate to disentangle the element of thirst from the broader theme of lack, and no attempt to segregate them will be made in what follows here. The connection can be traced in Rabelais' text between the readers who are drinkers in the *Gargantua* prologue (1:5), the readers who are *alterez* in the *Tiers Livre* prologue (1:402), and the readers who in the *Ancien Prologue* of the *Quart Livre* are "malades . . . goutteux . . . infortunés" (2:576). (The dedication to cardinal Odet de Chastillon refers to them as "affligez et malades absens" [2:3].) Thirst, whatever else it implies, contains the implication of need, and the whole book reinforces that implication, perhaps more than has been recognized. Need in turn leads to mutual dependence.

"Il n'est si riche," remarks Pantagruel, "qui quelques foys ne doibve. Il n'est si paovre, de qui quelques foys on ne puisse emprunter" (1:425). ("No man is so rich that he does not sometimes owe money. No man is so poor that sometimes one may not borrow from him" [302].) Pantagruel is in effect conceding a point which Panurge has just made in his praise of debts: "Les hommes sont nez pour l'ayde et secours des hommes" (1:419) "Men are born to aid and succour one another." [298]). Thus the myth of the sack recalled by the priestess Bacbuc, a myth deliberately distorted from a fable by Aesop, must be admitted to correspond to the thought of Rabelais even by those who deny its authenticity.

"Vous dites en vostre monde que *sac* est vocable in toute langue, et à bon droit, et justement de toutes nations receu. Car, comme est l'Apologue d'Esope, tous humains naissent un sac au col, souffreteux par nature et mandians l'un de l'autre. Roy souz le Ciel tant puissant n'est qui passer se puisse d'autruy; pauvre n'est tant arrogant qui passer se puisse du riche. . . .Encores moins se passe l'on de boire qu'on ne fait de sac." (2:454)

"You say in your world that *sack* is a noun common to all tongues, and that it is rightly and justly understood by all nations. For, as Aesop's fable has it, all human beings are born with a sack round their necks, being by nature needy and begging from one another. There is no king under the firmament so powerful that he can do without other men's help. There is no poor man so proud that he can do without the rich. . . . And if one cannot do without a sack, even less can one do without drinking. (704–5)

The myth might appear at first reading as a digression in an explication of the oracle's panomphean "Trinch," but the relation of drinking to the innate indigence of man is direct and crucial. We cannot really read Rabelais without sensing that economic or existential or metaphysical indigence as the ground behind the narrative.

     The stress on the carnivalesque elements in this work initiated by Bakhtin has not in fact been carried so far as to lay bare the inference it entails. Carnival, as everyone knows, violates a norm essential to its extraordinary status. Carnival is inverted "reality" or antireality. Carnival requires its opposite in order to be carnival. Thus the presence of abundance, freedom, uninterrupted laughter, at the extraordinary moment out of time silently implies need, constraint, sorrow, within time. The prefatory verses to the *Gargantua* volume allude to this opposition in defending the author's choice of laughter: "Voyant le dueil qui vous mine et consomme / Mieulx est de ris que larmes escripre" (1:3). ("When I see grief consume and rot / You, mirth's my theme and tears are not" [36].) The *dueil,* chagrin, sorrow, which the writer already knows afflicts his readers, seems to call into question the Aristotelean formula in the last verse: "Rire est le propre de l'homme" ("Laughter is man's proper lot" [36]). Laughter is extravagant and fantastic; it is secondary; it responds to an anterior, basic condition, which is *dueil.* (Bacbuc will assert that in drinking rather than laughter lies the essence of man [2:454].) As an enormous if inconsistent reversal, the entire book might be compared to the microreversal that Epistemon encounters in the other world.

     En ceste façon, ceulx qui avoient esté gros seigneurs en ce monde icy, guaingnoyent leur pauvre meschante et paillarde vie là bas. Au contraire, les philosophes et ceulx qui avoient esté indigens en ce monde, de par de là estoient gros seigneurs en leur tour. (1:371)

     Thus did those who had been great lords in this world here gain their poor, miserable, scurvy livelihood down there. On

the other hand, the philosophers and those who had been penurious in this world, had their turn at being great lords down below.
(268)

This world on earth seems to consist in a minority of "gros seigneurs" and a majority of "indigens" whose roles have been happily exchanged in the afterlife. But the reader only learns about
the prevalence of indigence by hearing of the reversal. The book
adopts the perspective of the peasant or proletarian who fantasizes
plenitude without wanting or needing to articulate all that is too
grim for fantasy. But this inarticulable dimension is really incarnate in the book's central antihero, a figure who remains throughout what he is seen to be at his first appearance, a creature of
"penurie et indigence" (1:263), a creature impervious to wealth.
In Panurge's story as in so much of the book, privation is the
semivisible ground against which the narrative is enacted. It possesses that status of archaic awareness and automatic presuppo-
sition which cultural historians assign to the "mentality" of a class
and an era. It belongs to an outlook of millennial antiquity, im-
memorial, prerational, almost preverbal. The thirst of almost all
the characters can be read as an oblique expression of this
"mentalité."

   The narrational and existential priority of drought, *soif,*
need, to drinking, *beuverye,* can be seen to correspond to other
fundamental priorities: *dueil* is primary, laughter secondary; nature is primary, culture secondary; silence is primary, language
secondary; curiosity is primary, learning secondary; sexual desire
(like Panurge's) is primary, satisfaction secondary; poverty (like
Couillatris') is primary, wealth secondary. The second member in
each case can be envisioned as a filling up of a void, just as the
text of the book fills the void within the empty reader. "Sus à ce
vin, compaings! Enfans, beuvez à pleins goudetz" (1:401). ("Up
lads, and to the wine! Gulp it down, my boys, in brimming cups"
[286].) The process of filling up in any given pair of antinomies
may prove to be problematic; it may lead to frustration, denial,
leakage; it may lead to the death encountered by Couillatris'
imitators; it may more often lead as Panurge noticed to an inten-
sification of the primary need. But we understand the text in a

way most comfortable to its own basic tropes, I submit, if we recognize each priority and if we privilege the relationship evoked in the fifty-seventh and sixty-first chapters of the *Quart Livre*, those chapters which establish Messer Gaster's claim to be the first Master of Arts of this world.

The opening shift from the infertile, rocky, ugly, and formless base of Gaster's island to its paradisiac summit of virtue anticipates the antinomy which governs the episode that follows: the primary emptiness of the hollow Gaster endlessly filled by a process which necessitates the civilized arts. Virtue, excellence, *areté*, are produced by an activity which is perpetual, cruel, and creative. Gaster himself is a "paovre, vile, chetifve creature"; his worshipers are hideously wrongheaded; but the act of replenishing his void is constructive. It would be reductive to confine the suggestive implications of this section to the narrow limits of its sources in Aritophanes and Persius,[5] or to the literal meaning of *gaster*. Rabelais leads us beyond the reductive interpretation by inventing a new mother of the Muses, no longer Mnemosyne but "la bonne dame Penie, aultrement dite Souffrete" (2:209) ("Dame Penia, otherwise called Poverty" [571]). He transforms the predatory jungle into a ballet.

> Les elephans, les lyons, les rhinocerotes, les ours, les chevaulx, les chiens il faict danser, baller, voltiger, combatre, nager, soy cacher, aporter ce qu'il veult, prendre ce qu'il veult. Et tout pour la trippe! (2:211)

> Elephants, lions, rhinoceroses, bears, horses, and dogs, he makes to dance, jump, caper, fight, swim, hide, bring him anything he wants, or carry what he wishes. And all for the sake of the belly! (572)

By the close of the section he has modulated away from the physiological altogether in favor of the quest by "gens saiges et studieux" for heavenly music, "celeste, divine, angelique" (2:230). The master of this art cannot be crudely corporeal. It is possible to take the repeated formula "Et tout pour la trippe!" as a kind of epigram for the work as a whole, but "la trippe" would then have to receive the semantic expansion it deserves. It is more finally than a physiological belly; it can stand metaphorically for all the versions of emptiness the text contains. And the process whereby emptiness engenders *areté* can stand as an ideal model which any given act of replenishment will more or less closely approximate.

Replenishment appears as the quintessential human act, and the act in particular of the Muses' devotee, the musician and the writer. Replenishment, as we already know from the *Tiers Livre* prologue, is the act allegedly performed by the writer for the reader through the medium of this text. The revised parenthood of the Muses authorizes us to extend the condition of lack to the written word, to understand texts themselves as requiring replenishment. The need which first appears as economic and physiological proves to be equally literary, linguistic, hermeneutic, semiotic. The danger of indigence, which this text is supposed to combat, becomes a danger the text itself may have to deal with. The play with lists and catalogues, the litanies of epithets, the gigantism of style, can be construed as constituent gestures in a struggle with hollowness. Behind the litany lies a threatened drought of verbal *joyeuseté. Beuverye* in all its forms responds to a primal *soif.*

An interpretive paradigm which reverses this relation, which attributes priority to a mythical cornucopian plenitude and represents lack as a disguised contamination, will necessarily conclude with the perception of textual exhaustion or entropy. But the lack is nowhere disguised; it is universal thirst; it emerges in the community of indigence; it threatens the foundation of Thélemè through the ambiguous "Enigme en prophetie"; it produces the black hole of meaning into which Humevesne follows Baisecul; it haunts Panurge in various forms through his successive incarnations; it shadows quite explicitly the character of human communication and interpretation; it finds its archetype in Messer Gaster; it provides a peremptory undertone to the oracle's command "Trinch!" The thirst which is lack in this book anticipates the argument of Sartre that scarcity, *la rareté,* is the fundamental framework in which man acts.[6] Rather than beginning with a mythical plenitude which always betrays its insufficiency, the text

requires us to begin with dearth and to ask how it might be
mitigated. Is there a thirst which will not, like Panurge's, be intensified in the quenching?

　　　Before trying to respond, we should note that Rabelais
inherited the problem of a thirst difficult to quench from Florentine
Neoplatonism. The neoplatonic version of the metaphor doubtless
forms a strand in Rabelais' symbolism, although the two are not
coterminous. Among Ficino's numerous usages, one can cite as
particularly relevant a passage in a letter to Lorenzo de' Medici
(already published in the quattrocento.)

> We are all Tantali. In fact we all thirst for the good and the true,
> yet all drink dreams. While, with wide open jaws, we let the lethal
> waters of Lethe flood down our throats, meantime we scarcely
> sense the shadowy faint trace of nectar and ambrosia, lapping our
> upper-most lip. Thence, a panting thirst continuously burns up the
> wretched Tantali.
>
> 　　　If by nature the mind desires certain things, we should
> acquire them. And certainly, in acquiring them, the soul would at
> some time be fulfilled by them, either wholly or in greatest part.
> But the more we acquire mortal things from all sides, by so much
> the more is the appetite of the soul inflamed.

Ficino's letter will go on to envision a hypothetical human condition wherein man is freed of his dreams and thus of his role as
Tantalus. Or rather it envisions some degree of liberation: "Insofar
as we shall be cleansed, so shall we be serene."[7] The "insofar"
(Latin "quam . . . tam") really leaves the question open and allows
the sweeping description of all men as Tantali to stand. Rabelais
problematizes the metaphor by refusing to articulate Ficino's dual-
ism. He does not make a clear distinction between Lethe and
nectar. But Ficino's powerful image of Tantalian man, confused
by the duality of his thirsts, contributes a prestigious analogue to
Rabelais' less transparent reformulation.

　　　Ficino's drinker is beset by an unappeasable thirst he
is conceivably able to redirect. The redirection is less clearly available in Rabelais, but the one visible alternative, the choice not to
drink, is harshly represented. Whether or not thirst can be
quenched, it is proper to try; it is improper and self-destructive

simply to refuse. This is the first step toward an answer to the riddle of thirst; it is made clear by the most disturbing, the most dense, the most elusive image of penury in Rabelais, Quaresmeprenant, all the more disturbing because in this case penury can be said to be willed. The description of the monster is made to appear almost interminably long, with its grueling parataxis and its flirtation with opacity, yet it remains curiously reticent. One must take care not to interpret it too quickly or too reductively. Quaresmeprenant in its ominous silence and sickly immobility is doubtless many things at once. It is first of all a recurrent period of time. But the divisions of the church calender can be regarded as reflecting divisions both within society and within the individual, more or less permanent tensions or conflicts plotted as alternations within the round of the year. Thus Quaresmeprenant would seem to incarnate that enduring will to privation which has appeared so often in human history and has been institutionalized by Christianity. There is a will not to drink and even a will not to be thirsty.

In Rabelais the impulse to self-denial has become pathological, hideous, self-destructive, nourished by fantasies. "Rien ne mangeoit jeusnant, jeusnoit rien ne mangeant. Grignotait par soubson, beuvoit par imagination" (2:134–35). ("When he fasted, he ate nothing, and when he ate nothing he fasted. He nibbled at a mere morsel, and drank only in his imagination." [519].) Dwelling on the "isle de Tapinois," the creature has become furtive, twisted, slobbering, sluggish. Thus it is both timeless and time-specific; it corresponds to a rooted human impulse but also to an early modern perversion of that impulse, an umbrella-disease which attacks both Calvin and *papelars*. The bizarre similes which approach surrealism, the inert parallelisms of the syntax, seem to adumbrate a poverty inextricable from the language that evokes it. This is the supreme figuration in the work of the contagion of asceticism. However harsh the innate privation of existence, its acceptance leads to a ghastly imitation of death. Even if thirst produces *alteration*, that infirmity is not poisonous; it is proper to choose the restless catarrh of desire, whether or not one can be satisfied.

This is a choice which is, it seems, particularly incumbent upon the writer. Fasting, remarks Pantagruel in another connection, produces sickly writing.

> "Souvenir assez vous peut comment Gargantua mon pere . . . nous a souvent dict les escriptz de ces hermites jeusneurs autant estre fades, jejunes et de maulvaise salive, comme estoient leurs corps lors qu'ilz composoient." (1:455)

> "You may easily remember how my father Gargantua . . . has often told us that the writings of the fasting hermits are as flat, meagre, and sour-spittled as were their bodies when they composed them." (322)

The "sympathie . . . indissoluble" (1:456) between mind and body is seldom affirmed so plainly, mingling as it also does here reading and consuming, language and nourishment. Physician blends with writer, as at the Isle de Tapinois. The writer needs to be replenished in order to replenish his reader; the alternative is the foul saliva of Quaresmeprenant, whose symbolic fasting is not only of the body.

Although the *Tiers Livre* prologue promises the reader's replenishment, presents its text *as* replenishing wine, the text of that volume raises questions about the facility of restorative communication. The prologue recognizes the possibility of failure, the possibility that *thesaur* may prove to be *charbons* (1:401). It dismisses this possibility in the case of the Pantagruelist reader who will know how to profit from textual *joyeuseté*. The body of the volume, however, confronts the reader with a permanent shadow over communication—the problem of interpretation. It confronts him or her in two distincts ways: first by thematizing the problem of communication in Panurge's consultations with authorities, and second by offering its own text as a problem in explication culminating with the perversely obscure symbol of the Pantagruelion.[8] The instrument of communication, the signifier, is itself impoverished, uncertain, open to misinterpretation. The *Tiers Livre* reveals all signifiers to suffer from that partial opacity which Pantagruel attributes to the soul newly awakened from dreaming of realities.

"Vray est qu'elle ne les raporte en telle syncerité comme les avoit veues, obstant l'imperfection et fragilité des sens corporelz: comme la Lune recevant du Soleil sa lumière, ne nous la communicque telle, tant lucide, tant pure, tant vive et ardente comme l'avoit receue." (1:453)

"It is true that it does not report them as straight-forwardly as it saw them, being prevented by the imperfection and frailty of the bodily senses; even as the moon, receiving her light from the sun, does not communicate it to us as clearly, purely, vividly, and ardently as she received it." (321)

Earthly man is condemned to that reflected light which distorts and blurs, that *moonlight* of knowledge which the *Tiers Livre* dramatizes with compassion but with unsparing repetition. Human signifiers are not purely natural like the chimes of Varenes, whose sound can be construed at will either to mean "Marie toy" or "Marie poinct." Yet our signifiers are not altogether proof against this type of projection. The messages that reach us from authorities may tend ostensibly to overlap, but they are fatally subject to interpretation, which is to say to conflict and perversion. These messages may be deciphered with a relatively high degree of plausibility, as is the case with Pantagruel's explications, or a relatively low degree, as is the case with Panurge's. But the fact remains that man understands and communicates through codes admitting of probabilities but not of certainties. The truth is written on leaves like those scattered by the sibyl of Panzoust, leaves we must try to find and arrange if we can: "Allez les chercher, si voulez; trouvez les, si povez" (1:473). ("Go and look for them if you like; find them if you can" [335].) We have to find a meaning for the sibyl's "bon bout," for the *membra* of Virgil, for the *chouette* of Panurge's dream, the bagpipe of Triboullet, the sneezing of Nazdecabre. These are expressions and symbols that carry dim associations, at best ascertainable in part with effort, with knowledge, with ideal objectivity. The signifier, apparently firm and clear, can only produce a shadowy signified. The *manoir de Verité*, home of unimpaired Words, Ideas, Models, excludes this world, which only receives its catarrhal drippings, fragments like the incoherent and explosive *parolles gelées* (2:204–5). All symbols leak significance, and among the others those symbols that make up this book. Here is another form, and not the least, of human privation.

Thus there is a semiotic lack, a semiotic frustration analogous to the sexual frustration which afflicts Panurge and prompts his quest. It would be a mistake to minimize the implications of the semiotic indeterminacy. The necessity of interpretation, the burden and risk of interpretation, deny to man the full satisfaction of his legitimate intellectual curiosity, that thirst so intense that its earthly frustration becomes, in the *Almanach de 1535*, the strongest argument for immortality. The language of the *Almanach*, not coincidentally, employs an alimentary metaphor.

> L'entendement n'est jamais rassasié d'entendre, comme l'oeil n'est jamais sans convoitise de voire, ny l'aureille de ouyre, *Eccl.* I, et nature n'a rien fait sans cause, ny donné appetit ou desir de chose qu'on ne peut quelquefois obtenir, autrement seroit iceluy appetit ou frustatoire ou depravé. (2:521)

> The understanding is never surfeited with understanding, as the eye is never without a craving to see, nor the ear to hear, Ecclesiastes I, and nature does nothing without a cause, nor does it bestow an appetite for something which cannot sometimes be obtained; otherwise this appetite would be frustrated or perverted.

The biblical verse alluded to reads: "The eye is not satisfied with seeing, nor the ear filled with hearing" (Eccles. 1:8). It would be a cruel injustice to leave man with this appetite unassuaged, man as he leads his life of demi-ignorance on earth. Thus the necessity of life after death. Here, despite the reverent tone, *soif* is harsh and present, *beuverye* is delectable but future.

It would of course reduce improperly the semantic range of Rabelais' *soif* to privilege unduly this epistemological insufficiency. The affirmation of the priestess that man is indigent by nature is appropriately read at many levels, or read rather in terms of a specturm along which any privileged meaning of *souffreteux* must not be allowed to exclude adjacent meanings or even all possible meanings. The text allows no firm line to be drawn between the mentality of the peasant and the Christian Humanist.

The drought of II, 2 will properly recall the literal drought parching France at the time of the volume's compositon; it will suggest obliquely the literal neediness of beggar, vagrant, and husband man; but within the context of the work as a whole, it will adumbrate all forms of privation—economic, moral, sexual, social, intellectual, spiritual, semiotic—which surface in turn as successive or mingled versions of a single impoverished condition. If finally it is the epistemological or semiotic thirst which tends to concern the reader most pressingly, this priority derives precisely from his role as reader, engaged in a process of communication intensifying his own self-conscious thirst for meaning. The reader, wanting to act the role of Pantagruelist drinker, wanting to receive the promised wine of gaiety, has to strive to understand this promise through the associated images of Tantalus, Pandora, and a mountain of salt (1:402).[9] More broadly he has to strive to fill up the vacancies of signification that punctuate the text. To fill up the text is to satisfy one's thirst to understand it.

One reason for attributing authenticity to the final episode of the *Cinquième Livre* is its sophisticated treatment of the polysemous motif of thirst and its approximation to a resolution which will abide our questions. If in fact the gifted author of this episode was not Rabelais, this supposition need not oblige us to neglect its profundity and its pertinence to the original four volumes. The oracle's word "Trinch!" in the context of the entire book invites a double reading—as hortatory encouragement and as inescapable command. One may consent, or deceive oneself into consenting, to the exhortation. Or one may recognize that there is no choice, that one's peremptory need compels one to obey the command. What says the inscription in the temple of the oracle? "Ducunt volentem fata, nolentem trahunt" (2:428). We can choose to accept or suffer compulsion. Panurge at any rate experiences a release when he chooses to accept marriage. To marry is to assume consciously the burdens and risks of a complete humanity. It is unnatural and painful to refuse, as Panurge himself has stated: "Poine par nature est au refusant interminée" (1:424). ("Penalties are inflicted by Nature on those who refuse to pay" [301].) Panurge at the end is liberated by choosing his proper human destiny; he has ignored as long as he could the pressure of the need, the *indigence*, which follows him from his first appearance in the work. But the decision to marry will not exempt him from future pain; it will simply make available to him the response of Pantagruelist courage.

The priestess elaborates on the oracle's decree by describing man as inherently *alphestes*, questing (2:462), and perhaps this interpretation also lends itself to two perspectives. To quest for truth may be said to be man's glory. To pursue truth perpetually, with the eye unsatisfied and the ear unfilled, may be said to be his curse. "En vin est verité cachée" (2:454) ("The truth lies hidden in wine" [705]), she has told her guests earlier. Is that concealment an invitation to hope or to despair? To portray man as *alphestes* is to equate experience with desire. Wine may be a source of power, wisdom, divinity, but there is never enough, apparently, to free man from his search and his thirst. The god which is truth and wealth lies underground, concealed—"l'Abscond, le Mussé, le Caché" (2:461). Experience becomes archaeology or speleology, the search for the god of wealth who will put an end to need, the subterranean Plutus, whom man will never wholly disinter.

It is unclear whether the Pantagrueline travelers have completed their odyssey by the close of the *Cinquième Livre*. Their enterprise has led them to the discovery that their lives are nothing but enterprise. The symbols of drinking, marrying, voyaging, borrowing, searching, appear to converge. They may all be reducible to the need to fill the void we are born with, the penury that wears so many aspects that the command "Trinch!" remains vastly, tragically polysemous. Does the text offer any escape from this reduction of the symbolic verbs to their lowest denominator?

It could be said to offer two. One escape from lack would lie paradoxically in generosity. "Ça bas, en ces regions circoncentrales," affirms Bacbuc, "nous establissons le bien souverain, non en prendre et recevoir, ains en eslargir et donner" (2:460). ("Down here, in these circumcentral regions, we place the supreme good, not in taking or receiving, but in giving and bestowing" [709].) This has been a perceived value since the first

volume, from the *contion* of Gargantua and the inscription at Thélème: "Or donné par don / Ordonne pardon / A cil qui le donne"
(1:197). ("Gold freely given, / A man's freely shriven / In exchange
for awards" [155].) To give or to share mitigates by a peculiar
logic the sharpness of need. But is this giving conceivable in the
shadowy realm of human knowledge? How does one share understanding which is immutably partial?

One moves to the second conceivable escape from
reductivity. "Soyez vous mesmes interpretes de vostre entreprise"
(2:454) ("You must be your own interpreters in this matter"
[705]), Bacbuc recommends in a famous formula. The effect of
this instruction is to transform the enterprise into an interpretation, and if two chapters later all experience becomes an enterprise
of questing, questing then becomes in turn a hermeneutic activity.
If we regard interpretation as it is represented in the *Tiers Livre*,
enterprise would thus be reduced still further to the moonlight
dimness of opinion. But the close of the *Cinquième Livre* offers an
alternative version of interpretation, veiled by transparent symbolism, in that forty-second chapter entitled "Comment l'eau de
la fontaine rendoit goust de vin, selon l'imagination des beuvans"
("How the Water of the Fountain tasted of different Wines, according to the imagination of the Drinkers" [700]). Here what
was perplexing and tormenting earlier, interpretation, becomes
creative and restorative. "Beuvans de ceste liqueur mirifique,"
says the priestess, "sentirez goust de tel vin comme l'aurez imag-
iné. Or, imaginez et beuvez."

> Ce que nous fismes. Puis s'escria Panurge, disant:
> "Par Dieu, c'est ici vin de Beaune, meilleur onques
> jamais je beus, ou je me donne à nonante et seize diables . . ."
> "Foy de lanternier," s'escria frere Jean, "c'est vin de
> Greve, gallant et voltigeant. O pour Dieu, amye, enseignez moi la
> maniere tel le faictes."
> "A moy," dist Pantagruel, "il ne semble que sont vins
> de Mirevaux . . ."
> "Beuvez," dist Bacbuc, "une, deux ou trois fois, De
> rechef, changeans d'imagination, telle trouverez au goust, saveur
> ou liqueur, comme l'aurez imaginé." (2:447–48)

"... as you drink of this miraculous liquor you will detect the taste
of whatever wine you may imagine."

This we did, and Panurge cried out: "By God, this is
the wine of Beaune, and the best that I ever tasted, and may a
hundred and six devils run away with me if it isn't! ..."

"I swear as a Lanterner!" exclaimed Friar John, "that
it's Graves wine, gay and sparkling. Pray teach me, lady, the way
you make it like this."

"To me," said Pantagruel, "it seems like wine of Mir-
evaux ..."

"Drink," said Bacbuc, "once, twice, and three times.
And now again, changing your thoughts, and each time you'll find
the taste and savour of the liquor just as you imagined it." (701)

This gift of transformation by the subjective ego is described by
the priestess as God-given. It resembles that transformation of
manna by the collective imagination of the children of Israel,
during their deliverance from Egypt "en extreme famine." To
experience this transformation is to know that nothing is impossible to God (2:447, 448). The drinker alters the objective element
to accord with his own taste, but this subjectification of reality is
not the perverse product of *philautia;* it does not deform, as Panurge's interpretations of his authorities arguably deform; rather it
delights and brings together. It is a token of human dignity and
divine grace. It ennobles the liquor consumed as it ennobles the
recipient.

If we understand interpretation (broadly construed) in
the terms of this chapter, then the interpretation of enterprise, of
questing and of drinking, need not be regarded as suspect. It opens
into a theory of culture as an exchange of shared myths. Interpretation remains vulnerable; it remains a construct; but it adds to
the filling of a void that extraneous element of imagination, which
can be allowed to retain its sixteenth-century definition. The wine
supplied the reader by the *architriclin* of the *Tiers Livre* prologue can
begin to acquire a meaning, despite the leakage of its negative
associated myths, because the reader generously places a welcom-
ing construction upon it. Thus in spite of textual cross-purposes,
the banquet that closes the *Quart Livre* succeeds in creating a

community by the communal assumption of a sacrament. To begin thus to replenish is not to achieve a perpetually abundant cornucopia, but it is to *haulsser le temps,* raise the time and the gesture out of compulsive response, to avoid that cycle whereby drinking merely, mechanically, begets more thirst. It allows the writer and reader to climb a step toward that plateau of civilized virtue where the deaf, pitiless monster creates a culture about him.

What is it finally which the priestess wants men and women to give each other? They cannot exchange pure knowledge, since the overwhelming mass of it, by her own report, lies hidden, as she says, "underground." Presumably in our endless communal archaeology, we can exchange what she herself offers—glosses, myths (like the myth of the sack), tropes (like the very metaphors of drinking, questing, digging, the metaphors of underground wealth and an underground god). We can exchange what the *architriclin* of the *Tiers Livre* offers—a dimly symbolic narrative, an obscurely allegorical herb. We can exchange the sort of rapturous, dubious vision contained in the praise of debts or the glosses patiently proffered by Pantagruel when faced with palpable obscurity. We can exchange money but only when, as at the founding of Thélème, the money itself has moral, social, and religious implications. We cannot give or receive absolutes—absolute certainty or clarity, absolute happiness, absolute divinity, absolute "wealth." We can only give what humanity and human culture empower us to give—versions, tropes, fictions, partial insights, visions like the Utopia of indebtedness which are always open to suspicion. We can only give with the *mediocrité* of this world, and our hope for generosity must be attended with a corresponding *mediocrité.* The ear ultimately will never be truly filled nor the eye satisfied nor the belly replenished. The glosses we exchange—and all narratives, constructs, myths, jokes, allegories, metaphors, are essentially glosses on the mysterious— these remain perpetually vulnerable to skepticism, incomprehension, dissatisfaction, obscurity. We can never finally know whether Bridoye's metaphor of ripeness is the product of wisdom or self-interest. We can only know that human exchanges are subject to pathology, as among the Chicquanous or the Papimanes or on the ship carrying Dindenault. The Muses born to Dame Souffrete are not invariably and perpetually healthy. They are, like the humans they inspire, *alterées,* volatile, vulnerable, unprotected from the threat of deterioration.

The enormous text which takes alteration as its theme and working principle is no more protected than other fictions and constructs, other interpretations which through imagination turn the water of the outer world into the regional wine of experience. If that text is required to provide an absolute plenitude of joy or of truth, of meaning or of closure, it will always prove inadequate; it will always appear to be leaking. We can only locate its fragmented substance if we bring to it a readerly *mediocrité,* aware that it will never fully quench our thirst, that it may well make us thirstier. What it gives us is not simply and merely a function of what we give it, but there must be nonetheless a kind of transaction, our gloss upon the text for its gloss upon "the world." It will only continue to give us successive versions of what it has already given us, the hair of the dog that bit us. "Reprendra il du poil de ce chien qui le mordit?" asks Frere Jean about Panurge (2:456) ("Will he take some more of the hair of the dog that bit him?" [706].) This at least is what the reader of this book will do, impoverished as he or she is and afflicted with *dueil.* We return to the book, *continue* the book, as our exchange temporarily fills both it and ourselves a little. The breviary flask is at best half full or half empty. The book offers us restoration through a restorative hero, who however is preceded on the page by mule after mule bearing salt, the salt that hurts, that flavors, that quickens, and that kills, that *alters* as it provokes us to alter our own insufficient world.

6

Rescue from the Abyss:
Scève's Dizain 378

This reading of a dizain from the *Délie* of Maurice Scève rests on the conception of a literary text as *vulnerable,* and perhaps the most useful preface to my reading would be an explanation of the ways this term seems to me to be pertinent to textual analysis. As a kind of epigraph or subtext I want to cite Valéry's poem "Aurore," which like Scève's dizain describes a return to consciousness. This liminary or auroral preface to the volume *Charmes* evokes the awakening of the poetic intelligence and its simultaneous recognition of a host of analogies and ideas at its disposal. They have been close to the poet, they tell him, throughout the night of his slumber.

> Nous étions non éloignées,
> Mais secrètes araignées
> Dans les ténèbres de toi! . . . .
> Regarde ce que nous fîmes:
> Nous avons sur tes abîmes
> Tendu nos fils primitifs.

(We were not far off, but were secret spiders in your shadows. . . . See what we have done: we have stretched our crude threads over your abysses.)

The sleeping mind of the poet has been an abyss across which the spider-metaphor has woven its fragile network ("une trame ténue") of threads. The poet then enters a "sensual forest" of Being where every vine and tree offers images ripe for plucking, though surrounded by thorns.

> Je ne crains pas les épines!
> L'éveil est bon, même dur!

Ces idéales rapines
Ne veulent pas qu'on soit sûr:
Il n'est pour ravir un monde
De blessure si profonde
Qui ne soit au ravasseur
Une féconde blessure,
Et son propre sang l'assure
D'être le vrai possesseur.

(I don't fear the thorns! Waking is good, even if harsh! These ideal plunderings do not permit one to be certain. To carry off a world, no wound is so deep that it is not for the pillager a fecund wound, and his own blood assures him that he is the true possessor.)

The paradoxical "féconde blessure," the wound whose blood is a sign of fertility and power, can serve to emblematize the character of poetry this analysis will assume. Valéry is thinking primarily of the creative consciousness, but his thought will not be seriously falsified if his image is transferred to the structure of the poem itself. The text wins its privileged status as a poem, as *literary* text, partly because it accepts a beneficent incision.

The vulnerability of poetry stems from four basic conditions of language: its historicity, its dialogic function, its referential function, and its dependence on figuration. We can approach the first of these conditions by considering how unprotected, at a macrocosmic level, is a given culture and all that it produces. This is to say not only that cultures are subject to change and decay, nor even that they are incipiently threatened by contact with other cultures, although this latter threat is not without its importance. But more fundamentally, the very role of a culture—as provider of rationales and myths, liturgies and symbols, in response to the individual's quest for identity and purpose—rests on fictions that can always be exposed as ungrounded by a demystifying mind. Culture as a product of history partakes of historical contingency and can create only constructs, *ad hoc* fabrications, including those codes, images, forms, and metaphors that will govern its works of art. Contact with another culture is dangerous precisely because acculturation betrays the arbitrary particularity of each myth and code. Culture exists partly to shield the individual from the random chaos of history by imposing mythical patterns upon it, but culture is not itself shielded from fortuitous violence, neither from the violence of the field of battle nor the violence of skepticism.

Books are often praised for outlasting violence, but to pretend that their survival exacts no price is to sentimentalize their "immortality." In fact they reach us as vestigial fragments of a once-living civilization we are unable to reconstruct in its dynamic fullness. We are condemned to labor to restore a power to the symbols and a density to the codes of an inherited text that will never fully overcome its estrangement. Thus the text is vulnerable simply through the historicity of its signifiers. The reader who hopes to bypass this historicity and to appropriate the remote text immediately as "modern" will only flounder in the bog of hermeneutic narcissism. Historicity is a fact that makes the text vulnerable to a slippage of understanding, just as its origin and the fabricated, arbitrary character of its code or codes have exposed it to the challenge of alternative codes. One can define this exposure most simply by noting that any literary text, possessing as it does a specific historical origin and specific moral style, is always potentially subject to parody.

An analogous vulnerability stems from the involvement of any text in a perennial series of exchanges, allusions, and responses, an involvement that constitutes that dialogic character which in our century has been studied most searchingly by Mikhail Bakhtin. Bakhtin has shown how speech in the novel and other novelistic modes is never "pure" but is always to some degree invaded by voices other than the speaker's, even if the "speaker" is the narrator. The resultant interplay of voices within a given discourse always carries with it alternative or antithetical discourses. Bakhtin associates this interplay with what he calls the novelistic, but this category in fact expands to embrace a large part of the canon. Indeed Bakhtin may not have allowed it to expand far enough; arguably, every literary work contains a dialogic element. Every poem contained in a collection maintains a dialogic relation with the other poems surrounding it,[1] and also with the antecedent poems of its tradition. This admission of dialogue is an admission of vulnerability, since the poetic discourse is open to the challenge of divergent or opposing utterances, reminding the reader of alternatives, pointing to potential weaknesses, underscoring the partiality of the ostensibly unflawed and complete statement. Although the poetic text may appear to withdraw from the dialogues that make up our daily life, although it may appear to isolate itself from the ongoing extra-textual dialogues of history, it only exchanges one dialogue for another. In this exchange, if it deserves our attention, it will neither swerve from its exposure to the alien nor be capable of deconstructing its subtexts; it will remain toward them in a state of dialectical tension. Intertextuality imposes vulnerability.

In a different sense the signifying function of language also imposes risks upon the poetic text. Poems call into being entities for which no names exist and for which no single term can adequately be coined, since that term would require a definition still to be supplied. Poems thus intensify a problem that seems to be inherent in language: the signifier tends to possess sharper clarity and firmer presence than the signified. The invisible arrow from signifier to signified is itself a cultural construct, fabricated within history and subject to historical distortion. Poems are commonly located near the border of the ineffable, and in that location lies a willed heightening of the problem of signifying; there lies the danger that the border may be overstepped and the act of meaning may fail. The poem participates, and invites the reader to participate, in the quintessentially human quest to fix meanings behind representations, and it characteristically chooses meanings closest to the unrepresentable. Some poems allude to this proximity by invoking the ineffability topos, as though to call attention to their flirtation with failure. Poems act out the noble, persistent struggle to win through to the unnamable, to that which resists reference, and in this struggle they reveal a conative character that excludes absolute fulfillment.

To carry on this struggle, poetry attempts to control and elaborate a fourth condition of language, its involvement in figuration. Poetry employs metaphor and other figures in order to denominate more finely, but in this employment there lies a further risk, since a figure is a kind of wound; commonly it introduces what is a literal non-sense. The poem misuses deliberately the names that exist in order to evoke the unnamable, but in doing this it courts the perilous obliquity of figuration. The metaphor is perhaps the riskiest of all figures, since it violates literal sense most visibly, and since its interpretation requires sensitivity to the particular force of its expressed or unexpressed copula. The metaphor may raise the level of discourse to a "higher" plane, but it also introduces nodes of uncertainty, centers of explosive resonance whose precise overtones may have to remain indeterminate. In the potent metaphor that closes Scève's dizain 378 there lies a large (fatal?) degree of hermeneutic indeterminacy. The poetic structure must contain as best it can the violent outbreaks of its tropes.

To speak of the vulnerability inherent in a poem's cultural origin, in its historicity, in its dialogic and intertextual character, in its effort to mean and to name, in its involvement with figuration, is not to exhaust all the sources of potential damage. Each poem runs its own risks. But what distinguishes those poems that deserve our interest is their survival in spite of, or perhaps because of, their risks. Exposure to subversion does not necessarily doom a poem to collapse, chaos, or aporia. We tend to underestimate of late its tolerance of dissonance. A wounding may confer, in Valéry's language, a waking alertness, a power, a fecundity. Thus the analytic phase that registers a text's exposure has to be followed by a phase that asks whether, and how, the text survives. The reader should be sensitive to the rewards which textual courage can win, the strategies of containment, the harmony within dissonance. The idea of a vulnerable text does not exclude it from the tragic hazards, divisions, fragmentations, of human experience; the idea assumes rather what might be called the text's *humanity*. But it also recognizes the possibility of a paradox that is not self-destructive, a tension which is not aporetic, an oxymoron that produces fresh meaning, such as "une féconde blessure." It would be possible to deconstruct that antithesis and the poem that rests upon it, but not without the danger of reduction. It might be more rewarding to ask how the oxymoron could hold together, how it could justify itself and justify poetry.

The successful poem can be regarded as a linguistic

structure in which limits and specificities reveal their profundity, the explosive reveals its brilliance, and oppositions reveal their tensile strength. The poem's vulnerability is not the authorial, Philoctetean neurosis Edmund Wilson analyzed; it is not psychologistic. It might be compared to the relative weakness of the Aristotelian enthymeme in relation to the syllogism. The enthymeme, the principal tool of rhetoric, deals with probabilities and contingencies where the syllogism deals with certainties.[2] Each literary text, also resting on probabilities and contingencies, always failing to achieve the unflawed precision of logic, produces at best a construct, reaches at best a microcosmic, relative stability of which the macrocosm is the relatively stable culture standing as its vulnerable matrix.

The *Délie* of Maurice Scève (Lyon, 1544) is a sequence of 449 poems, each composed of ten decasyllabic lines. Most are love poems showing the influence of Petrarch and his Italian imitators. A prefatory poem of eight lines entitled "A sa Délie" is followed by a motto which also follows the concluding poem: "Souffrir non souffrir." Beginning with dizain 6, every ninth poem is preceded by an *impresa* or device, conventionally if misleadingly referred to as an emblem. The "emblem" consists of a woodcut picture accompanied by a motto; the motto is then echoed in the final line of the following dizain. Thus emblem XLII represents a bat, with the motto "Quand tout repose point ie ne cesse" (When all is at rest I do not stop). This motto is echoed by the close of the following dizain 375.

> Et sur la nuict tacite, & sommeillante,
> Quand tout repose, encor moins elle cesse.

(And during the silent and sleeping night, when all is at rest, still less does it [the poet's soul] stop [admiring and praying to the remembered image of the lady Délie].)[3]

Although it is rare for the eight poems following the emblem-poem to refer back to the emblem, the dizain to be analyzed, 378, does contain a common element—a troubled night. Although this retrospective reference is not an essential aspect of 378, it deserves to be noted because it involves that poem directly with a *dated* semiotic construction.

I quote 378 in its original version of 1544.

La blanche Aurore a peine finyssoit
D'orner son chef d'or luisant, & de roses,
Quand mon Esprit, qui du tout perissoit
4   Au fons confus de tant diuerses choses,
Reuint a moy soubz les Custodes closes
Pour plus me rendre enuers Mort inuincible,
Mais toy, qui as (toy seule) le possible
8   De donner heur a ma fatalité,
Tu me seras la Myrrhe incorruptible
Contre les vers de ma mortalité.

(The white Dawn had scarcely finished adorning her head with gleaming gold and roses when my Mind, which was perishing altogether in the turbid depths of many multifarious things, returned to me under the closed curtains to render me more invincible against Death.

But you who have [you alone] the capacity to bring favor to my destiny, you will be to me the incorruptible myrrh against the worms of my mortality.)

Analysis can begin by clarifying a difficulty at the literal level. Line 6 is somewhat obscure and has led to some scholarly controversy. I follow Dorothy Coleman in reading the return to waking consciousness in line 5 as a return to relative security from death. The sleeping mind has been perishing totally ("du tout perissoit") while unconscious. Wakefulness renders the poet less subject to this psychic foundering, somewhat safer ("plus . . . invincible") in the face of death, but only to a degree. It is the woman alone, "Délie," as the final four lines affirm, who offers a form of absolute protection.[4] Thus Scève's poem is itself about vulnerability; it distinguishes three degrees of exposure to mortality.

This poem is also, like Valéry's, about an awakening, a dawn of consciousness, and in fact certain images associated with sleep in "Aurore" are found in Scève. Valéry writes of the inner darkness (*ténèbres*) and gulfs (*abîmes*) over which his "Ideas" have spun their webs, spiderlike, during his sleep. The *Délie* is haunted by the fear of an experience of psychic dissolution, the dissipation in confusion of lines 3–4 above, an experience for which the most common metaphor is "abysme." Another metaphor is "tenebres." Often the two appear together, as in another dizain of sleep and awakening, 79, where consciousness is at first swallowed up in

> [le] profond des tenebreux Abysmes,
> Ou mon penser par ses fascheux ennuyz
> Me fait souvent percer les longues nuictz.

(the depth of the shadowy abysses, where my mind through its grievous torments often causes me to pass long nights.)

Here as in the "fons confus" of 378, the experience of the abyss seems to consist of a disintegration into multiplicity, a psychic unravelment. In Scève there is no counterpart to Valéry's "trame ténue," the fragile web over the abyss that anticipates the fragile texture of the poem. In the *Délie* the *abysme* is naked and fearful. The chasm can swallow the poet even when, paradoxically, he receives from the woman a spiritual illumination.

> plus m'allume, & plus, dont m'esmerueille,
> Elle m'abysme en profondes tenebres. (7)

(The more she illumines me, the more [I marvel at it] she engulfs me in deep shadows.)

Dizain 164 recounts a kind of equivocal awakening from a bitter vortex of consciousness, a "Gouffre amer," which in this case is not bodily sleep but a slough of listless self-abandonment.

> Lors toy, Espoir, qui en ce poinct te fondes
> Sur le confus de mes vaines merueilles,
> Soudain au nom d'elle tu me resueilles
> De cest abysme, auquel ie perissoys.

(Then you, Hope, who at this moment base yourself on the confusion of my futile imaginings, suddenly, hearing her name, you wake me from that abyss where I was perishing.)

The substantivized adjective *confus* and the verb *perissoit* link this experience with the disintegration of our original poem 378. The ominous repetition of this motif in the *Délie* and its extension beyond mere physiological sleep permit us to identify the experience of the *abysme* as the dominant traumatism of the work. The abyss of nonbeing is the ontological opposite of that reality incarnated by the female presence called "Délie." The final line of the entire sequence—"Non offensé d'aulcun mortel Letharge" (unravaged by any mortal lethargy)—seems to affirm at last the speaker's freedom from the abyss of somnolent dissolution. All of these passages can be read as a gloss on lines 3–4 of 378. The epithets *confus* (confused, disorderly, uncertain, obscure) and *diverses* (various, far-off, inconstant, strange, painful) evoke a recurrent danger threatening the speaker with cognitive fragmentation. In view of this danger, the image of the bat, emblematic of the soul's nocturnal anguished restlessness, assumes a more sinister coloring. A certain kind of sleep may resemble a certain kind of sleeplessness.

This danger to the speaker can be construed as a danger to the poem as well, since the poem's coherence would normally depend on his own cognitive coherence. Because the return from the death of confusion is presented as only a relative return, we may ask whether his regained consciousness is firm enough or reliable enough to build a poem on. If psychic incoherence remains a recurrent experience in the *Délie*, then perhaps its poetry reflects a failed struggle for personal integration. Under this interpretation, the speaker's vulnerability would become the work's and in particular this dizain's. It is significant that the heraldic term *mise en abyme* has been appropriated by modern criticism to mean any structure containing a smaller representation of itself that in turn contains an infinite series of progressively smaller representations. The deconstructive school of criticism has associated this series with the semantic vortex that is alleged to engulf all texts. Perhaps Scève was self-conscious enough to thematize his own text's vortex in his own obsessive *abysme*. To raise this possibility is not to affirm it but to suggest the degree of potential disturbance inherent in line 4 of 378.

The implication of fragmentation is intensified by the quasi-allegorical figure of "mon Esprit," represented as distin-

guishable from the speaker's selfhood and even relatively independent. The region of confusion where the Esprit is languishing
seems to lie outside the essential self, since the Esprit is said to
return in line 5. The phrasing suggests that it (he?) has made a
conscious decision to return that is not the poet's decision. Does
the voice we hear speak for a self into which the Esprit is integrated? We cannot immediately be sure. In one sense, the confused depths lie within the self; in another, they lie outside. We
have to strain to intuit the implied epistemology, as we strain to
grasp the semi-allegorized world that also includes a vaguely personified "Mort" and, in a somewhat different rhetorical register,
the mythographic "Aurore." The same world also includes a Petrarchan "toy" apart from these personifications, and a "moy"
who exists both in their world and in hers. A historical explanation
for this commingling of codes would note Scève's transitional
position between an older poetic rhetoric dependent on allegoresis
and an emergent rhetoric mingling mythography with Petrarchan
topoi. Analysis thus leads us to confront the historicity of this
poem's eclectic language. The poetry of the *Délie* commonly formulates sophisticated insights through the dramatic interplay of
shadowy faculties: le Coeur, l'Ame, Espoir, le Sens, le Desir, Vou-
loir, and, inevitably, Amour. Sometimes, as in 378, the psychom-
achias lie in a gray area between weak allegory and sustained
metaphor. The vulnerability of the poetry is made more acute by
a rhetorical irresolution connected with the inner irresolution of
the speaking self.

　　　　Our impression of this self is further qualified by the
remarkable detail of the "Custodes closes" in line 5. These can be
taken as bed-curtains, as in the translation above; this is also
McFarlane's gloss. This reading is inevitable but it may also be
incomplete. A second reading might be "eyelids." A third would
locate the "Custodes" within the speaker to imply a kind of mental
curtaining or closing off. There may be a suggestion of protection
anticipating the "plus . . . invincible" of the following line (Latin
custos: guardian, watchman). But there surely emerges as well a
sense of occlusion from the external world, and specifically from
the gorgeous brilliance of Dawn. The evocation of Dawn at the

opening gathers together all that the curtained self must lose. The temporal coincidence presented as the ostensible link between outer and inner world (". . . a peine finyssoit . . . quand . . .") conceals a more important discontinuity. The poet is removed, voluntarily or involuntarily, behind his "Custodes," limited to shades of black and gray, their sobriety set off by the threefold repetition of the syllable *or* (gold) in lines 1–2.

> La blanche Aur*or*e a peine finyssoit
> D'*or*ner son chef d'*or* luisant, & de roses.

The cosmic coquetry of Aurore, in her gleaming and youthful vitality, draws both on natural adornments ("roses") and precious artifacts ("or luisant") to heighten her seductiveness. Of this immense polychromatic effulgence the poet is deprived, as the poem itself turns away, underscoring the contrast of its own drama, drawing so to speak its *custodes* about itself. Its solution to the threat of mortality will necessarily exclude that universal, periodic, inhuman dynamism, but will reach at the end an intuition of eternity that implicitly belittles the brevity of the precise moment when the first glow of auroral white first turns to pink and gold. The criticism works in both directions: the cosmic vitality is excluded from the drama of mortality that follows, but it remains in the poem to set limits to the drama. It is neither rejected nor vindicated; it exists in tension with its antitheses, the mortal man and the immortalizing woman.

At the affective and imagistic pole from auroral brilliance, the Esprit returns to the dormant self, curtained off from all that light. The prepositional phrase "soubz les Custodes closes" can be taken to modify both the pronoun "moy" and the verb "Revint"; taken with the verb it hints at an added effort by the Esprit to pass through a barrier. This return constitutes a kind of reunion, a homecoming which averts, at least on this occasion, a drowning in confusion. It implies a recapture of clear-sighted self-possession by the poet, and thus a provisional salvation from dissolution. In the struggle with Death which occupies life, a struggle that ebbs and flows irregularly, this homecoming represents a modest victory; it strengthens the living man's defenses, though not without an ambiguity stemming from the application of the adverb "plus" to an adjective, "invincible," that does not commonly admit distinctions of degree. Line 6 leaves the reader hesitating uncertainly between a comparative and an absolute invulnerability.

The verb "Revint" also represents a modest victory in another, more obscure struggle which might be described as a striving with Petrarch. The verb is actually anti-Petrarchan. The basic pattern of movement in all Petrarchan poetry is a continuous, incomplete repetition of suffering, or a repetitive cycle of suffering and illusory hope. Frequently this cycle spins so fast that it produces oxymorons (such as Scève's "agreables terreurs," an oxymoron in dizain 1 that accompanies his initial wounding by love and authenticates, so to speak, its Petrarchan character). This incomplete experience of suffering may sometimes be evoked in the imperfect tense ("J'errois flottant parmy ce Gouffre amer"), but its most common vehicle is the iterative present: Petrarch's "Vegghio, penso, ardo, piango" (I wake, think, burn, weep), Scève's "Mon mal se paist de mon propre dommage" (My suffering feeds upon its own injury), Sidney's "My youth doth waste, my knowledge brings forth toys." This iterative present, with its associations of entrapment, frustration, and (frequently) narcissism, is fundamental to Petrarchan poetry and to the *Délie*.[5] Lines 3–4 of dizain 378, read out of context, would seem to perpetuate a Petrarchan indefinite repetition, depending as they do on a verb in the imperfect tense *(perissoit)* which lacks precise limits. But in the *Délie* this repetition is intermittently interrupted by single, detachable events that are embedded in it but that provide a kind of surcease from it. This is the case with the "Revint" of line 5; it offers a salutary specificity. It even offers a glimpsed alternative to the endless cycle of the claustrophobic Petrarchan consciousness—a willed choice of independent, lucid consciousness. The *Délie* assumes a certain vulnerability by admitting these agonistic patterns of experience, but it averts collapse by hierarchizing the patterns. In the first six lines of 378, the specific event overcomes repetition, both in the cosmos and within the poet. Here Scève might be said to tip the balance against Petrarch and thus make it possible for his sequence as a whole to reach some kind of closure, as the *Canzoniere* totally fails to do.

But from the perspective of the last four lines, the relative victory of reunion and specificity in lines 5–6 proves, uncharacteristically, to have been inadequate. The closing lines go on to present still another pattern of experience which supersedes the temporary repossession of the self. This new pattern is introduced by the hinge conjunction "Mais" in line 7. It shifts the poetic focus away from the private, curtained interior of the poet's consciousness to an interpersonal relation between him and Délie, here named simply "toy." Délie enters the poem dramatically with the reiterated pronouns of line 7 and the pronoun of line 9, all of which receive accentual stress; the two strong syllables of the parenthetical "toy seule" are adroitly placed to receive particular stress, creating a dramatic spondee that the following mute *e* helps to isolate and lengthen further. This shift of focus, which also exchanges allegoresis for metaphor, does not, however, split the poem altogether, since the contest with death remains to provide thematic continuity.

The abrupt entry of Délie is also related to the textual striving with Petrarch. Petrarch's Augustinian self-rejection led him, as supposed lover, to an almost total self-involvement. A counterpart of Petrarchan repetition is a certain haziness or even unreality of the woman, who figures in the lover's narcissistic sensibility chiefly as fantasy, memory, angel, or dream. Thus the struggle in the *Délie* against the oxymoronic circularity of Petrarch is also a struggle to make contact with an actual woman. Here in 378 she is suddenly revealed, as the work's subtitle describes her, as an "obiect de plus haulte vertu," a source of the highest power. She is not a fantasy; she has an actual talismanic potency. It is she who will bring *heur* (favor, good fortune) to his *fatalité*, his lot or destiny, a word normally lacking in sixteenth-century usage the modern meaning of doom, but in this context unmistakably including death. She will not utterly transform this human lot; she will confer an aura of felicity upon a course of life whose outlines may remain unchanged. After his death her existence will act as a kind of myrrh, a preservative balm, against the worms devouring his body. This affirmation does not state, as I read it, that there will be no worms, just as line 8 does not cancel fatality. We are left simultaneously with the myrrh *and* the worms in the state of opposition denoted by the preposition *contre*. The copula, which appears here in a very rare (for Scève) and strongly affirmative future tense *(seras)*, leaves room for mystery and indeed creates it. But with their mystery these final two lines do offer a stable (though always vulnerable) image of redemption, all the more credible because it includes decay. They offer a continuity that is not Petrarchan.

The pattern of experience of the last four lines might best be described as a simultaneity of opposites. The Italian Neo-platonic tradition in which Scève was steeped contained theories of a coincidence of antitheses (Pico della Mirandola: "Contradic-toria coincidunt in natura uniali"). Scève stops short of a coinci-dence to affirm a mutuality of opposed forces, deepening and arresting the Petrarchan oxymoronic cycle to produce, as here, an equilibrated metaphoric paradox. The "seras" of line 9 is really a magical copula, affirming a talismanic and transformative power, a copula which displays its own power by asserting the counter-logical identity of Délie with myrrh. The metaphor resting on this very strong copula creates a space for reflection, for exploration and inquisition. It constructs a myth, a fabricated, mysterious assertion of a human power equal no longer to an allegorized external "Mort" but to a personal, bodily, intimate "mortalité." Any single answer to the question, of *how* Délie protects the poet against death—by her exemplary character, by her role as poetic muse—any attempt to salve the textual incision of this metaphoric non-sense, would only reduce the space that the metaphor opens for meditation.

The final line is vulnerable of course to a second inter-pretation, which would read "vers" as lines of poetry. Few readers will fail to weigh this interpretive option, but the decision to adopt it is not easily made. Our contemporary obsession with textual auto-referentiality should not lead us to project thoughtlessly an anachronistic meaning on a work that resists it. Scève as love poet does *not* thematize consistently and explicitly the act of poetic composition as do Petrarch, Ronsard, Sidney, and Shakespeare. In 378 nothing before the last line would lead the reader to expect this kind of auto-referentiality. It is possible, though not easy, to devise a conceivable interpretation taking "vers" as lines of verse. These last lines might mean that the lover's poetry is destined to oblivion without the saving honor and power of the woman they celebrate. Without her, the poetry could be imagined as languishing, like the Esprit, in a gulf of turbid incoherence. This interpretation *may* be appropriate to lines 9–10, but it has to be forced a little. The metaphor that closes this little poem may be a node of exceptional semantic resonance, but it is also a node of uncertainty. It offers a possible secondary meaning which is difficult either to reject or adopt, and in this ambiguity it demonstrates one type of vulnerability inherent in figurative language.

What is not ambiguous in the last four lines is the tone of awed reverence attained by a voice whose spiritual serenity is conveyed with luminous expressivity. Tone in any poem is governed by what I have called moral style, that area of meaning where verbal style becomes synecdochic of a recognizable, existential posture, a style of experiencing. The moral style of the *Délie* emanates from the density and economy of its language, from the intensity of the alternating pain and joy, from a certain abstract dryness occasionally shot through with images of sensuous immediacy, from its intricate, sometimes crabbed syntax, from a play with pointed antithesis that can lapse into sterility, but also from a spiritual seriousness that survives despair and engulfment. The stretches of verbal and affective dryness augment the intensity of those privileged moments that reward the patience of both speaker and reader. Dizain 378 concludes with one of these moments, replacing the somewhat jagged hypotaxis and cool manner of the first sentence with the extraordinarily harmonious, warm, tranquil, and voluptuous fluency of the second. The closing lines represent at once a marvelous achievement of rhythm, trope, and tone.

Tone is the slightest of poetic elements; it does not lend itself to structural and diagrammatic analysis; it is easily neglected and easily mistaken. But it plays nonetheless a critical structural role: it hierarchizes conflicting forces through its delicate and subtle pressures. Here in Scève's dizain it validates the final metaphor as a spiritual attainment, privileging it above the initial cosmic brilliance and the repossession of integrated selfhood. The role of Délie in this poem as in the sequence is always vulnerable to a hermeneutic of suspicion; we know her after all only through figures; she might arguably be regarded as merely a Petrarchan fantasy. For her to become what she is affirmed to be, a source of real power, the poetry has to manifest its own *vertu*, its own transformative magic. If we are to believe in the poet's recovery from incoherence, his language must assume a credible coherence. The poem does in fact achieve these things, does deal with its vulnerabilities and dissonances, by means of the calm solemnity that informs its resolution. It does not of course *dispel* the dissonances it has admitted. As a time-specific construct of codes and fictions, it is always exposed to demystifying skepticism. Its effort to formulate an ineffable and mysterious relationship may always be charged with obscurantism. Its *vers* may prove to be *mortels*. But it has avoided that equality of polarized components leading to the aporetic *abyme*. It has succeeded in this because its modulations of tone and intensity have made distinctions, have assigned hierarchical values. It has also dealt with the historicity of its inherited traditions by privileging a metaphor over mythography and allegoresis, recognizing and organizing its own cultural past.

A printer's device on the 1544 title page portrays a great rock battered by sea and wind with the motto "Adversis duro," which seems not unfitting to the volume that follows. The phrase would normally be translated "I endure against adversities." But in the case of Scève's book the more appropriate rendering might be "I endure because of adversities"; I endure, that is, because of oppositions, antitheses, subversions, paradoxes. Scève's book begins and ends with the simplest and briefest expression of paradoxical simultaneity, "Souffrir non souffrir," which means essentially "To suffer through contact with transformative power is not to suffer." That is the kernel of unreason at the heart of the *Délie*. Perhaps in a larger sense it is the unreason of poetry, fecundated by its wounds. Great poetry assumes the parochialisms, the contradictions, the tensions, of the semiotic world from which it issues; it takes them upon itself and from them it acquires its tensile strength. Even its violations of its inherited codes pay a kind of homage. If it were to repress the contingencies of its historical moment, the modalities of its particular signifiers, the illogic of its particular tropes, it would interest us less.

Each poem is a wager of the mind struggling for mastery over its babble, its obsessions and anxieties, its conflicting metaphors, its divergent rhetorics, the expressive limitations of its cultural vocabulary, its distance from its subtexts and its readers, its resistances to closure. The wager is won when the text proves its own tolerance of subversions and its strength of containment, its capacity to confront without reducing. The wager is lost when the text fails to contain, when it fails to organize and distinguish, or when it contains too strictly, leaving no room for the play of meditation. Dizain 378 involves a wager that its construct can rest on a power and a presence known only through an ambiguous analogy. If the analogy collapses, the poem sinks to a confused depth with so many other jumbled things. If the analogy holds, in its oracular and hieratic dignity, the poem remains exposed but coherent, a fragile web, humanly, precariously, sufficiently coherent, enduring within and through its adversities.

7

Dangerous Parleys—Montaigne's *Essais* 1:5 and 6

"Tout ce qu'on peut dire de la plupart
de ces chapitres-là, c'est qu'il n'y a
rien à en dire."

Pierre Villey

The opening page of the *Essais* introduces the reader to terror—
the massacre of a city's inhabitants by the Black Prince, who
has taken it by force and who is finally deterred only by the
exemplary heroism of three defenders. This first essay continues
with anecdotes instancing other examples of cruelty and compassion, most of them involving a military siege: Conrad III at Guelph,
Dionysius at Rhegium, Pompey at the city of the Mamertines,
Sylla at Perusia, Alexander at Gaza, Alexander at Thebes. The
concluding paragraph records the slaughter of 6,000 Thebans and
the enslavement of the remaining 30,000. This terror at the opening of the book is anything but rare. The elements of horror and
cruelty in the earlier essays of Montaigne have been insufficiently
noted and insufficiently explained. Their presence is all the more
remarkable in view of their comparative infrequence in the mature
essays. It is equally remarkable that the ubiquitous military anecdotes in the very earliest essays (most of them preceding I:1 in the
chronology of composition) tend to involve the siege of a city or
fortress. The siege is the locale of peculiar menace, the contest
which exacerbates cruelty and, when successful, conventionally
authorizes the harshest carnage.

Specific anecdotes add substance to these impressions.
For the defender, even the limited choice of military options can
be perilous. Essay I:15 ("On est puny pour s'opiniastrer à une
place sans raison") (One is punished for defending a place obsti-

nately without reason) cites a number of recorded massacres victimizing those foolhardy enough to resist too long. Yet the succeeding essay ("De la punition de la couardise") (Of the punishment of cowardice) cites examples of those commanders who exposed themselves to the charge of cowardice by yielding too easily and who were justly punished by degradation. The defender, it appears, must walk a fine line, if indeed one exists. The next essay but one ("De la peur") (Of fear) opens with examples of self-destructive madness which overwhelms terrified men under siege. Essay I:34 offers a series of miracles: walls of invested cities which fall by divine will without attack, or the most recent case, truly wonderful, of a wall blown up which settled down neatly into place again. Essay I:47 cites the case of the Roman commander Vitellius whose siege of a city was repelled because his troops taunted the defenders too caustically. Essay II:3 ("Coustume de l'isle de Cea") (A custom of the island of Cea) in its long catalogue of recorded suicides, individual and communal, returns again and again to the city reduced to despair by an encircling army. Essay I:24 narrates an incident clearly analogous to these others which Montaigne witnessed as a child: the governor of a city walks out from a secure building to address a frenzied mob and is killed. Miracles aside, all of these stories evoke an intensity of violence whose narrow spectrum runs from peril to nightmare. As a set, they outdo in brutality the other military anecdotes which accompany them.

I have not yet mentioned one more early essay, or rather two twin essays, whose organizing situation is the siege. These are I:5 ("Si le chef d'une place assiégée doit sortir pour parlementer") (Whether the governor of a besieged place should go out to parley) and I:6 ("L'heure des parlemens dangereuse") (Parley time is dangerous). These are apparently among the earliest of all (1571–72), and in the 1580 edition they are among the very simplest in structure: a bare series of brief stories scarcely mortised by minimal commentary. Although they mute to a degree the explicit brutality of their companion essays, they offer a useful focus for the study of the motif or obsession which unifies them. They also introduce a distinctive element missing elsewhere,

a third tactical option—the possibility of a parley, a verbal negotiation, between the opposing forces. This element complicates
the primitive oppositions of the other anecdotes and confers a
special interest on these crude and laconic texts.

For all their ostensible simplicity, however, they do
not lack their puzzles and reversals. First reversal: I:5 opens not
with the decision of the defending commander posed by the title
but with the corresponding decision of the investing commander
(should he win an advantage by faking a truce to negotiate?).

(a) Lucius Marcius legat des Romains en la guerre contre Perseus
roy de Macedoine voulant gaigner le temps qu'il lui falloit encore
a metre en point son armée, sema des entregets d'accord, desquels
le roy endormi accorda trefve pour quelques jours, fournissant par
ce moyen son ennemy d'opportunité & loisir pour s'armer: d'ou le
roy encourut sa dernier[e] ruine. Si est ce que le Senat Romain, a
qui le seul advantage de la vertu sembloit moyen juste pour acquerir
la victoire trouva ceste pratique laide et des-honneste, n'ayant
encores ouy sonner a ses oreilles ceste belle sentence, *dolus an virtus
quis in hoste requirat?* [*Aeneid* II.390] Quand a nous moings superstitieux, qui tenons celuy avoir l'honneur de la guerre, qui en a le
profit, & qui apres Lysander, disons que ou la peau du lyon ne peut
suffire, qu'il y faut coudre ung lopin de celle du renard, les plus
ordinaires occasions de surprinse se tirent de ceste pratique: & n'est
heure, disons nous, ou un chef doive avoir plus l'oeil au guet, que
celle des parlemens & traites d'accord. Et pour ceste cause c'est une
reigle en la bouche de tous les hommes de guerre de nostre temps,
qu'il ne faut jamais que le gouverneur en une place assiegée sorte
luy mesmes pour parlementer.[1]

Lucius Marcius, legate of the Romans in the war against Perseus,
king of Macedonia, wishing to gain the time he still needed to get
his army fully ready, made some propositions pointing to an agree-
ment, which lulled the king into granting a truce for a few days
and thereby furnished his enemy with opportunity and leisure to
arm. As a result, the king incurred his final ruin. Yet the Roman
Senate, judging that valor alone was the just means for winning a
victory, deemed this strategem ugly and dishonest, not yet having
heard this fine saying ringing in their ears: "Courage or ruse—
against an enemy, who cares?" As for us, who, less superstitious,

hold that the man who has the profit of war has the honor of it, and who say, after Lysander, that where the lion's skin will not suffice we must sew on a bit of the fox's, the most usual chances for surprise are derived from this practice of trickery. And there is no time, we say, when a leader must be more on the watch than that of parleys and peace treaties. And for that reason there is a rule in the mouth of all military men of our time, that the governor of a besieged place must never go out to parley. (16–17)

There are really two questions at issue: the *ethical* choice of a Lucius Marcius, chastised by the senate for his unscrupulous strategem, and the *tactical* choice of the captain who must weigh the advantages of the proffered armistice. In the incident cited, both commanders appear to have selected the wrong alternative; Lucius commits an error of morality and Perseus of prudence. Both errors seem to stem from the ambiguity of a truce wich fails to conclude hostilities for good and creates a gray area of ethics and judgment suspending all conventional rules. The polarity attacker/defender then yields to a second polarity, ancient/modern, since the contemporaneous world is represented as heedless of all promises, ironically "moings superstitieux," less scrupulous regarding good faith than the Roman senate. Yet in another reversal, the integrity of antiquity is blurred by the Virgilian quotation (Courage or ruse—against an enemy, who cares?), which subdivides the ancient member of the polarity by distinguishing republican honesty from imperial deceit. Aeneas' aphorism might be the motto of faithless modernity. He seems to share a gray area of history with the Spartan general Lysander.

Up to this point, the evidence presented would dictate a negative answer to the question of the essay's title; under the given circumstances, negotiation is suicidal. This will also be the conclusion of the sequel essay; the hour of parleying *is* dangerous. But here in I:5, in another reversal, this implication receives a qualification.

Du temps de nos peres cela fut reproché aus seigneurs de Montmord & de l'Assigni deffandans Mouson contre le Conte de Nansaut, mais aussi à ce conte celuy la seroit excusable, qui sortiroit en telle facon, que la surté & l'advantaige demeurat de son costé, comme

fit on la ville de Regge, le Conte Guy de Rangon (s'il en faut croire
Monsieur du Bellay: car Guichardin dit que ce fut luy mesmes) lors
que le seigneur de l'Escut s'en approcha, pour parlementer: car il
abandonna de si peu son fort, que un trouble s'estant esmeu pan-
dant ce parlement, non seulement monsieur de l'Escut & sa
trouppe, qui estoit approchée avec lui se trouva la plus foible, de
façon que Alexandre Trivulce y fut tué, mais lui mesmes fust con-
trainct, pour le plus seur, de suivre le Conte, & se getter sur sa foy
a l'abri des coups, dans la ville.[2]

In our fathers' day the seigneurs de Montmord and de Lassigny,
defending Mouzon against the count of Nassau, were blamed for
this. But also, by this reckoning, a man would be excusable who
went out in such a way that the security and advantage remained
on his side; as Count Guido Rangone did at the city of Reggio (if
we are to believe Du Bellay, for Guicciardini says it was he himself)
when the seigneur de l'Escut approached to parley. For he stayed
so close to his fort that when trouble broke out during this parley,
Monsieur de l'Escut not only found himself and his accompanying
troop the weaker, so that Alessandro Trivulzio was killed there,
but was constrained, for greater security, to follow the count and
trust himself to his good faith, taking shelter from the shots inside
the town. (17)

Properly managed, a sortie to parley *can* be profitable. The tortuous
syntactic convolution of this long sentence and the factual uncertainty (does the credit go to Rangone or Guicciardini?) introduce
new types of blurring, but through the distractions one can isolate
the crucial tactical factor on the victor's side: he left behind his
bastion *only a little*. This crucial calculation not only leads to the
death of a prestigious enemy leader but forces a humiliating reverse upon the besieging leader, who ends within the walls dependent upon the defender's goodwill. We assume, without learning from Montaigne, that the supplicant is accorded grace. The
text leads us to question only the word of the outsider, not the
insider. The defender tends to appear as a moral virgin; only the
attacker is a potential rapist or seducer.

　　　　The incident at Reggio throws into doubt the negative
answer to the title-question which the Macedonian incident had
appeared to imply. It remains for a final incident to obscure the

question definitely by providing the one remaining outcome which is theoretically possible.

Si est ce que encores en y a il, qui se sont tres bien trouvés de sortir sur la parolle de l'assaillant: tesmoing Henry de Vaux, Chevalier Champenois, lequel estant assiegé dans le chasteau de Commercy par les Anglois, & Berthelemy de Bonnes, qui commandoit au siege ayant par dehors faict sapper la plus part du chasteau, si qu'il ne restoit que le feu pour acabler les assiegés soubs les ruines, somma ledict Henry de sortir a parlementer pour son profict, comme il fit luy quatriesme, & son evidante ruyne luy ayant esté monstrée a l'oeil il s'en sentit singulierement obligé a l'ennemy, a la discretion duquel apres qu'il se fut rendu & sa trouppe, le feu estant mis a la mine les estansons de bois venant a faillir le chasteau fut emporté de fons en comble.[3]

Yet it is true that there are some who have done very well by coming out on the attacker's word. Witness Henri de Vaux, a knight of Champagne, who was besieged in the castle of Commercy by the English. Barthélemy de Bonnes, who commanded the siege, after having the greater part of the castle sapped from outside, so that nothing remained but setting fire in order to overwhelm the besieged beneath the ruins, asked the aforesaid Henri to come out and parley for his own good; this Henri did, preceded by three other men. And, convinced by what he was shown that he would have been ruined without fail, he felt remarkably obliged to his enemy, to whose discretion he surrendered himself and his forces. After this, the fire was set to the mine, the wooden props gave way, and the castle was demolished from top to bottom. (17)

This final reversal ends the original published version of the essay, which I have now quoted in its entirety. It leaves the hostile parties pacifically together outside the castle as the previous story left them inside the city, and here, one gathers, the "discretion" of the attacker is to be trusted as it could not be earlier. The essay might be said to leave the question whether to go out to parley permanently up in the air, so to speak, since the text is void of authorial intervention beyond the sarcasm of the two phrases: "belle sentence" (fine saying), applied to Virgil, "moings superstitieux" (less superstitious), applied to modern tacticians. Yet even this conclusive inconclusiveness will be reversed as we turn to the opening of the sequel essay. "Toute-fois" (However), it begins, and after a longer catalogue of disastrous sorties by gullible defenders, it in turn ends with a timid authorial leap onto the shoulders of a Stoic philosopher. The writer's position on the *tactical* question, the options of the besieged, can only be inferred from the ambiguous evidence of the twin but divergent essays. On the *ethical* question he edges into the second essay through the opposition of two other voices. We just catch sight of Montaigne as thinker in the final antithesis of Ariosto and Chrysippus.

> Fu il vincer sempremai laudabil cosa
> Vincasi o per fortuna o per ingegno [*Orlando furioso*, 14, I]
> disent-ils mais le philosophe Chrisippus n'eust pas esté de c'est advis: car il disoit que ceux, qui courrent a lenvy doivent bien employer toutes leurs forces a la vistesse, mais il ne leur est pourtant aucunement loisible de mettre la main sur leur adversaire pour l'arrester, ny de lui tendre la jambe, pour le faire cheoir.[4]

> To conquer always was a glorious thing,
> Whether achieved by fortune or by skill, (Ariosto)
> so they say. But the philosopher Chrysippus would not have been of that opinion. For he used to say that those who run a race should indeed employ their whole strength for speed but that, nevertheless, it was not in the least permissible for them to lay a hand on their adversary to stop him, or to stick out a leg to make him fall. (19)

This seems to align the essayist with the philosopher, but the alignment is tacit, merely implicit. And even this tiny, almost imperceptible gesture of approval is made after the terrible problem of the siege has been elided into a metaphorical footrace. Later published versions would render the approval slightly more visible ("Le philosophe Chrisippus n'eust pas esté de cet advis, *et moy aussi peu*" [29][5] (The philosopher Chrysippus would not have been of that opinion, *and I just as little)*; they would also introduce further incidents, complications, quotations, citations of authority, together with a fuller though somewhat straddling comment on the ethical issue in I:6, and in I:5 a new auto-referential ending affirming the writer's quickness to accept the word of others. This credulity, which cuts against those prudential concerns present earlier, represents one more reversal in the form of an afterthought.

Considered an an integral text, this fifth essay might be said to possess unity only in the persistence of its portentous theme and in the consistency of its failure to resolve its own questions. Together with its companion, it stands as a chaos of diverging or conflicting events, quotations, opinions, perspectives, shifts of the issue at hand. All we can ascertain with certainty as we stand back from the two conflicted texts as from Book One as a whole is that the dilemma of the man surrounded and the question whether speech is of use to him are indeed of pressing concern to the writer.

What remains obscure is the basis of this concern, and given the reticence of these little sketches, especially taciturn in their original form, the interpreter is obliged to turn to the appropriate larger context, which can only be the entire work in which they take their modest place. But this step, though necessary, is problematic, since the *Essais* repeatedly throw out versions of inside/outside antitheses.[6] Many of the antitheses can be read back into the siege motif so as to render it in varying degrees metaphoric. One could then consider the work as a series of explications or unpackings of a dramatic situation transformed into a trope. This becomes problematic only because the potential "explications" are so numerous and entangled that the original obsession will emerge as overdetermined to the point of meaninglessness. If in other words we scrutinize the *Essais* for all the ways in which the siege motif might be understood to "symbolize," we may be left with a blur as inconclusive as the uninterpreted point of departure. To avoid this impasse, the most promising procedure would be to follow those directions which the texts themselves offer most insistently, to privilege those hints whose networks of reinforcement prove most dense, without denying the potential relevance of other networks and other metaphoric displacements.

The most obvious extrapolation is biographical. Montaigne is a landowner whose property is walled during a period of civil conflict and routine pillage. He marvels in fact that it has remained intact, "(b) encore vierge de sang et de sac, soubs un si long orage, tant de changemens et agitations voisines" (966) ("still virgin of blood and pillage, under so long a storm, with so many changes and disturbances in the neighborhood" [737]). The sexual metaphor is not to be disregarded; for the proprietor, the invasion of his house would be experienced as the breaking of a hymen. Domestic anxiety, remarks Montaigne, is the peculiar product of civil war alone. "(b) Les guerres civiles ont cela de pire que les autres guerres, de nous mettre chacun en eschaugette en sa propre maison. . . . C'est grande extremité d'estre pressé jusques dans son mesnage et repos domestique" (971). ("Civil wars are worse in this respect than other wars, that they make us all sentinels in our own houses. . . . It is a great extremity to be beset even in our household and domestic repose" [741–42].) A passage toward the end of "De la phisionomie" (Of physiognomy) narrates the attempt by a neighbor to capture Montaigne's house by a ruse, a ruse which fails through the intended victim's trusting manner.

　　This threat of violence is not however altogether distinct from the threat of daily affairs to the man of letters. The significant interior may not be the property as such but the tower library. "(c) C'est là mon siege. J'essaie . . . à soustraire ce seul coin à la communauté. . . . Miserable à mon gré, qui n'a chez soy où estre à soy" (828). ("There is my throne. I try . . . to withdraw this one corner from all society. . . . Sorry the man, to my mind, who has not in his own home a place to be all by himself" [629].) It is impossible to distinguish firmly the military press which threatens the landowner from the press of affairs which threatens the meditative solitary. But the physical withdrawal to a quiet place is impossible to distinguish in turn from the mental withdrawal to an inner quietude. The *coin*, the corner where one can reign alone, already contains in germ a metaphor of psychological space which other contexts will make explicit. "(b) Si je ne suis chez moy, j'en suis tousjours bien pres" (811). ("If I am not at home, I am always very near it" [615].) This metaphoric dimension of the "chez moy" in the *Essais* emerges so commonly and spontaneously that the reader almost overlooks its figurative force.

In a passage justifying his failure to fortify his house against marauders, Montaigne writes that "any defense bears the aspect of war" and invites attack, then remarks of his house: "(c) C'est la retraite à me reposer des guerres. J'essaye de soubstraire ce coing à la tempeste publique, comme je fay un autre coing en mon ame" (617). ("It is my retreat to rest myself from the wars. I try to withdraw this corner from the public tempest, as I do another corner in my soul" [467].) This internal corner clearly corresponds to the "arriereboutique" (back shop) of the essay on solitude (I:39): "(a) . . . en laquelle nous establissons nostre vraye liberté et principale retraicte et solitude" (241) ("in which to establish our real liberty and our principal retreat and solitude" [177]. The evocation of this internal withdrawal does not lack military imagery. "(a) Nous avons une ame contournable en soy mesme; elle se peut faire compagnie; ella a dequoy assaillir et dequoy defendre, dequoy recevoir et dequoy donner" (241). ("We have a soul that can be turned upon itself; it can keep itself company; it has the means to attack and the means to defend, the means to receive and the means to give" [177].) But the most powerful image at the close of the essay suggests a defensive cunning and contracted force still more absolute: "(a) Il faut faire comme les animaux qui effacent la trace, à la porte de leur taniere" (247). ("We must do like the animals that rub out their tracks at the entrance to their lairs" [182].) It was this profound impulse to lie still in a spiritual center, beleaguered, alert, solicited but cautious, which brought Montaigne home from the Bordeaux *parlement*, and it is this impulse, more than any other, which seems to underlie the obsession with the siege.[7]

The experience of the *parlement* may not be irrelevant to the twin essays that concern us, since the title of I:6 ("L'heure des parlemens dangereuse") contains the word, and the title of I:5, a cognate form ("parlementer"). A useful gloss on these essays can be found in the opening pages of "De l'experience" [On experience] (III.13), where legal abuses bring into focus the capacity of language for obliquity, ambiguity, treachery, and self-subversion. "(b) Cette justice qui nous regit . . . est un vray temoignage de l'humaine imbecillité, tant il y a de contradiction et

d'erreur" (1070). ("This justice that governs us . . . is a true tes-
timony of human imbecility, so full it is of contradiction and error"
[819].) Jurisprudence is "(b) generatrice d'altercation et division"
(1066) ("generating altercation and division" [816]). Law does
not offer "(b) aucune maniere de se declarer qui ne tombe en
doubte et contradiction" (1066) ("a way of speaking [one's] mind
that does not fall into doubt and contradiction" [816]). The wish
for an absolute intercourse beyond ambiguity and contradiction
is already present in I:5, which begins by positing a Roman purity
betrayed both by event (Lucius Marcius' stratagem) and by quotation ("Dolus an virtus . . ."). The military *parlement*, like the
judicial, places the heaviest pressure on direct language since, as
we have seen, there is no time when a commander must be more
wary.

The quotation from Virgil that closes I:6 (added in
1588) can be read as an expression of Montaigne's fantasized
escape from the verbal and the equivocal.

> (b) Atque idem fugientem haud est dignatus Orodem
> Sternere, nec jacta caecum dare cuspide vulnus:
> Obvius, adversosque occurrit, seque viro vir
> Contulit, haud furto melior, sed fortibus armis.
> (Aeneid X, 732–35 [291])

> Nor did he deign to knock down from the rear
> Fleeing Orodes with an unseen spear:
> He passes, veers, and man to man, in fight,
> He proves the better, not by stealth but might. (19)

To attack from behind would savor of linguistic obliquity, would
be analogous to the tricky indirections of negotiations; the ideal
struggle is silent, face to face, on a plain outside a city, as here in
the *Aeneid*. It matters little if even this fantasy, having descended
to language, is faintly undermined by our remembrance that it
depicts the brutal tyrant Mezentius. The only alternative would
be mutual confidence, *fiance*, which the opening of I:6 has ruled
out in modern times. "(a) Ne se doit attendre fiance des uns aux
autres, que le dernier seau d'obligation n'y soit passé: encore y a

il lors assés affaire" (28). ("Parties should not trust one another until the last binding seal has been set. Even then there is plenty of room for wariness" [18].) The final seal of commitment (real or metaphorical?) points back again to a judicial parallel; the effect of the analogy is to imply a nostalgia for a finality which is supra-diplomatic, suprajudicial, supralinguistic. Even after the ostensibly final seal, one must be on one's guard. In effect there is no conclusion to a conflict; that might only be produced by the frontal, mute assault of a Mezentius, slugging it out hand to hand—a kind of salvation. The Mezentius quotation is immediately preceded by an anecdote wherein Alexander refuses a lieutenant's advice to "(b) se servir de l'avantage que l'obscurité de la nuit luy donnoit pour assaillir Darius" (20) ("to take advantage of the darkness of night to attack Darius" [19]). It is tempting to extend this obscurity metaphorically to evoke that dimness of indirect, verbal engagement which the writer wants to evade.

Thus these apprentice essays seem to condone indirectly their author's choice to withdraw from a parliament into his tower bastion. Here one might suppose that there would be fewer *heures des parlemens dangereuses*. Yet if we look to the early essays as products of pure interiority, we will of course be disappointed. The first versions of I:5 and 6 appear to be almost entirely the contrary, a collection of actions by other men reported in other writers' books, bearing as we have noted only the barest traces of authorial commentary. What is besieging the mind on these pages are the words, experiences, and opinions of cultural memory, to the degree that the writer's own voice seems scarcely audible. Montaigne has opened his text as Montmord and Assigni opened their gates, and seems to have suffered something of their fate, a fate he fails to specify though we gather it to have been unpleasant. Even in this essay's later versions, where the authorial voice can intermittently be made out, it merely makes one in a somewhat cacophonous chorus. The self is hedged about by all those who solicit entrance to the allegedly self-defining text; the self is exposed to the wounds, the subversions, the variances of opinion, the linguistic and moral codes pressing about it.

In the final versions of I:5 and 6 the writer's own

outlook, to the degree that it is felt at all, is jostled by that of the
Roman senate, the Achaians, the ancient Florentines, contemporaneous Frenchmen, of Virgil (or Aeneas), Cleomenes, Xenophon, Ariosto, Alexander. There is no "arriereboutique," no un-
traceable lair, although the yearning for one might well be a
reasonable consequence of the crowded page. Montaigne, one
might say, has taken a step which is called in "L'heure des parlemens dangereuse" a "pas de clerc."

> A Yvoile seigneur Jullian Rommero *aiant fait ce pas de clerc* de sortir
> pour parlementer avec monsieur le Constable, trouva au retour sa
> place saisie. (29)

> At Yvoy, Signor Giuliano Romero, having made the novice's blun-
> der of going out to parley with the Constable, on his return found
> his place seized.(19)

Modern French has lost this idiom, which associates the clerkly
with the naive, but we understand it here with more clarity than
its author may have intended. A cleric may, in certain situations,
be reasonably associated with the unworldly; the question hovers
whether this handicap extends to all who have taken it upon
themselves to write.

Thus if we consider the essays themselves, we have no
difficulty in making out a textual equivalent to the military drama.
Wherever else in Montaigne's experience the threat of invasion
lies, it can be found unmistakably upon the pages he is beginning
to produce. In a later essay he would confront clairvoyantly the
aggressive dimension, the *murderous* dimension of this solicitation
from outside.

> (b) Or j'ay une condition singeresse et imitatrice:
> quand je me melois de faire des vers . . . ils accusoient evidemment
> le poete que je venois dernierement de lire; et, de mes premiers
> essays, aucuns puent un peu à l'estranger. . . . Qui que je regarde
> avec attention m'imprime facilement quelque chose du sien. Ce
> que je considere, je l'usurpe: une sotte contenance, une deplaisante
> grimace, une forme de parler ridicule. . . .
> (c) Imitation meurtriere comme celle des singes hor

ribles en grandeur et en force que le Roy Alexandre rencontra en certaine contrée des Indes. (875)

> Now I have an aping and imitative nature. When I used to dabble in composing verse . . . it clearly revealed the poet I had last been reading. And of my first essays, some smell a bit foreign. . . . Anyone I regard with attention easily imprints on me something of himself. What I consider, I usurp: a foolish countenance, an unpleasant grimace, a ridiculous way of speaking. . . .
>
> A murderous imitation, like that of the horribly big and strong apes that King Alexander encountered in a certain region of the Indies. (667)

The anecdote that follows tells how these apes were led to hobble or strangle themselves by men who exploited their imitative bent. The murderous capacity of compulsive imitation can apparently be directed either at one's models or at oneself. Montaigne finds it both in his nature ("condition") and his book, malodorous and destructive. The early essays which stink of others are those precisely haunted by the terror of the siege. Perhaps the younger Montaigne fears the fate of those captains in I: 16 who surrendered their bastions too quickly and suffered for it. Perhaps he fears (or envies?) the fate of Henry de Vaux; he might, through the act of writing, pass outside himself altogether, yield to his besiegers, turn around and see his self explode forever.

To write at any rate is to face the risk of invasion, capture, destruction, murder. Perhaps the struggle between inside and outside is the struggle imposed by the composition of the *Essais*. We can follow this struggle *metaphorically* through the various implications of Montaigne's intersecting images and anecdotes, or we can follow it *intrinsically*, through the unevenly developing power of assimilation, the absorption of anecdote, allusion, and quotation by a unique, recognizable voice, a distinctive moral style. One allows oneself to be conquered, one surrenders one's tower, one's city, if one reads and writes credulously, obsequiously, without independent judgment. One has to learn how to speak without leaving the gate behind.

In view of the felt risk, one may wonder how the first essays ever came into being. Two or three answers can be made.

One can point first of all to the freedom of reception as a mark of underlying assurance. The apparently humble and gullible hospitality may mask a secret pride, a reserve which is not hospitable, a confidence on the writer's part that he can be strengthened by his chosen and willed vulnerability. From this minuscule egoism, almost invisible in the first version of I:5, would grow the bulk of the *Essais*. The caution, the wariness, the ambivalent receptiveness, of these early sketches would remain in their more dense and more poised successors; we can watch the interplay in simpler form at the outset, where we are given a radical metaphor with which to trace the intertextual drama.

But aside from the nascent confidence, Montaigne seems sometimes to perceive the act of writing not as exposure but protection, not as centrifugal but centripetal. This at least is the basis of the apology in the brief but fascinating "De l'oisiveté" (Of idleness) (I:8), where writing involves the exorcism of wild and disorderly fantasies, just as the cultivation of a field removes weeds and just as the fertilization of a woman by an alien seed ("une autre semence") produces normal offspring rather than shapeless lumps. Here it is the mind abandoned to reverie, undisciplined by writing, which runs off like an escaped horse ("faisant le cheval eschappé"). Writing centers and fortifies the mind, even if it admits a little of the alien. In this formulation the writer maneuvers like Guy de Rangon, emerging just a little to make his capture and then retire. We remember that in I:15 those who defend their cities *too* stubbornly are exposed to terrible vengeance.

In still other formulations of the apprenticeship phase, we find repeated images of tremendous pressures unhealthily bottled up. Too much sexual desire can make a man impotent.

(a) De là s'engendre par fois la défaillance fortuite, qui surprent les amoureux si hors de saison, et cette glace qui les saisit par la force d'une ardeur extreme, au giron mesme de la jouyssance. (13)

From that is sometimes engendered the accidental failing that surprises lovers so unseasonably, and that frigidity that seizes them by the force of extreme ardor in the very lap of enjoyment. (7)

The news of bad fortune can paralyze response, until relief comes in an outpouring of tears and speech (I:2). Too much eagerness to write well hampers composition, just as water in a full bottle is hampered by its own pressure from issuing through the neck (I:10). Images like these bespeak a terrific expansive energy acutely in need of release. But there is also a recognition that the release must be guided by an authentic external resistance.

> (a) L'ame esbranlé et esmeuë se perde en soymesme, si on ne luy donne prinse: et faut tousjours luy fournir d'object où elle s'abutte et agisse. (22)

> The soul, once stirred and set in motion, is lost in itself unless we give it something to grasp; and we must always give it an object to aim at and act on. (14)

The essay from which this is quoted (I:4—"Comme l'ame descharge ses passions sur des objects faux, quand les vrais lui defaillent") (How the soul discharges its passions on false objects when the true are wanting) fails to specify what the *object vrai* would be; one might presume it to be the thought and writing of another man. Here the *prinse*, the clutch of otherness, is not dangerous but necessary, a tonic encounter which saves the soul from its unbridled solitude.

The conflict of the siege then is both life-threatening and life-preserving. We cannot miss in any case the debate just below the surface of the apprentice essays over the prudence, the ethics, and the hygiene of their composition. The question whether or not to parley contains the question whether or not to write. To use language is to be invaded and to invade. To parley is to assume the vulnerability of a writer, to enter the gray area of language, of interchange, of the *prinse* of oppositions. Montaigne was by no means insensitive to this contingent, dialogic, oppositional character of discourse.

> (c) Nous raisonnons hazardeusement et inconsidereement, dict Timaeus en Platon, par ce que, comme nous, nos discours ont grande participation au hazard. (286)

> "We reason rashly and inconsiderately," says Timaeus in Plato, "because, like ourselves, our reason has in it a large element of chance." (209)

We hear in this remark the appeal and the safety of silence, which is opposed to speech and perhaps more authentic.

> (a) Le nom, ce n'est pas une partie de la chose ny de la substance, c'est une piece estrangere joincte à la chose, et *hors d'elle.* (618, my italics)

> The name is not a part of the thing or of the substance, it is an extraneous piece attached to the thing, and *outside of it.* (468)

This exteriority of the name is the exteriority, and thus the inferiority, of all words, artificially and arbitrarily connected to the thing, the true, valid, inner, voiceless substance, the silent *res.* Between this authenticity and hazardous expression lie the crucial thresholds of the lips and the page. Any utterance or act of writing is a *sortie,* a leaving behind the bastion of the private self. A *parlement* is an *essai,* a hazardous initiative, a lowering of defenses. Speech will betray the beleaguerment of those forces which only silence can hold at bay. Speech is already an acceptance of infiltration and contamination, because language to have meaning has always already been used, because Montaigne's language in particular is composed of external examples, opinions, tropes, sentences. One defines one's position in relation to others (Chrisippus, the Roman senate) and against others (Xenophon, Cleomenes, Ariosto). The alternative is that refusal of contact which is seen intermittently as sterile, as producing shapeless lumps, and as sustaining: "(a) Ce n'est pas pour la montre que nostre ame doit jouer son rolle, c'est chez nous, au dedans, où nuls yeux ne donnent que les nostres" (623). ("It is not for show that our soul must play its part, it is at home, within us, where no eyes penetrate but our own" [472].) In writing this tribute to the *chez nous,* Montaigne is of course exposing it to others; he is violating that pure interiority which he entrusts to paper (and thus violates) so often. The muteness of pure interiority, of the beast in its den, is often praised but in the very praising subverted. Elsewhere he resigns himself to the dialogue within all discourse.

> (c) Je propose les fantasies humaines et miennes, simplement comme humaines fantasies, et separement considerées, non comme arrestées et reglées par l'ordonnance celeste, incapables de doubte

et d'altercation: matiere d'opinion, non matiere de foy; ce que je
discours selon moy, non ce que je croy selon Dieu. (323)

I set forth notions that are human and my own, simply as human
notions considered in themselves, not as determined and decreed
by heavenly ordinance and permitting neither doubt nor dispute;
matter of opinion, not matter of faith; what I reason out according
to me, not what I believe according to God. (234)

Here an implication emerges which anticipates Bakhtin, that human discourse necessarily contains "altercation."

We have noted the oddity of an essay whose titular
concern is with the prudence of a defender but whose opening
paragraph, among others, deals with the ethics of the besieger.
These two pairs of options, ostensibly so different in military terms,
begin to approach each other in discursive terms. Once one has
made a verbal foray from one's bastion, one is already on the road
to becoming an invader, if not a seducer. Montaigne is alert to the
risk.

(b) Il y a tant de mauvais pas que, pour le plus seur, il faut un peu
legierement et superficiellement couler ce monde. (c) Il le faut
glisser, non pas s'y enfoncer. (b) La Volupté mesme est douloureuse
en sa profondeur. (1005)

There are so many bad spots that, for greatest safety, we must slide
over this world a bit lightly and on the surface. We must glide over
it, not break through into it. Even sensual pleasure is painful in its
depth. (768)

(b) J'essaie à tenir mon ame et mes pensées en repos. . . . Et si
elles se desbauchent à quelque impression rude et penetrante, c'est
à la verité sans mon conseil. (1020)

I try to keep my soul and my thoughts in repose. . . . And if they
sometimes veer under some rough and penetrating attack, it is in
truth without my consent. (781)

Both passages betray a certain ambiguity which blurs the image
of penetration. Is the writer's sensibility male or female? Perhaps
it partakes of both. The element of aggression is present in any
case, and it is subject to considerations of both prudence and

ethics. There is the risk of penetrating too far; there is also the risk of attacking too much "(b) Nous empeschons . . . la prise et la serre de l'ame à luy donner tant de choses à saisir" (1009). ("We impede the mind's grasp and grip by giving it so many things to seize" [771].) The last of the essays seems to attribute a certain "animosité" (animosity) and "aspreté" (bitterness) to all writing (1066). And the "Institution des enfans" will discuss the risk of assaulting the classics too directly. "(c) Je ne luitte point en gros ces vieux champions là, et corps à corps: c'est par reprinses, menues et legieres attaintes" (147–48). ("I do not wrestle with those old champions wholesale and body against body; I do so by snatches, by little light attacks" [108].) Even for the post-Humanist that Montaigne became, engagement with antiquity involved a circumspect struggle. Thus beneath the concern for the threatened center, one distinguishes an interest in the policy of attack. To go out to parley is already to begin to take the offensive.

Revisions of the first paragraph of I:5 will suggest subtly that speech and action lie upon a single spectrum. The Roman senate, disapproving the strategem of Lucius Marcius,

(a) "accuserent cette pratique de leur *stile* (c) antien. . . . C'estoient les *formes* vrayment Romaines. . . . (a) Il appert bien par le *langage* de ces bonnes gens qu'il n'avoient encore receu cette belle sentence: 'dolus an virtus quis in hoste requirat?' " (25)

"condemned this practice as hostile to their old style. . . . These were truly Roman forms. . . . It clearly appears from the language of these good men that they had not yet accepted this fine saying: 'Courage or ruse—against an enemy, who cares?' " (16)[8]

Here the word *stile* adumbrates a moral code. Today we may feel the word as a metaphor, since a rhetorical term seems to have replaced a normative one. But for Montaigne there may have been no sense of transferal; for him ethics and language interpenetrate each other, as they do for most Renaissance writers. Each utterance and each act of writing possesses a moral character, so that soldier, legislator, and writer can be judged by a single criterion. Each is governed by a moral style. In the gradual emergence of a moral style lies the interest of the earlier essays, and also their achievement. In the apprentice essays, one feels the resistance the composed self has to overcome in order to declare itself. One cannot really speak of subtexts, since the appropriations lie on the surface; one can only speak of a subself which gradually reveals itself through its power to absorb, which is to say rewrite, Seneca, Plutarch, Lucretius, Diogenes Laertius. We come progressively to respect this composed self precisely because it has accepted its vulnerability, its engagement in discourse, and has struggled with the resistance of alterities.

The siege may fade from the mature essays because Montaigne acquires confidence in his own moral style and its capacity for assimilation without risk. The self-destructive reception without assimilation is what Montaigne calls *pedantisme.*

> (a) Nous prenons en garde les opinions et le sçavoir d'autruy, et puis c'est tout. Il les faut nostres. . . . (b) Nous nous laissons si fort aller sur les bras d'autruy, que nous aneantissons nos forces. (137)

> We take the opinions and the knowledge of others into our keeping, and that is all. We must make them our own. . . . We let ourselves lean so heavily on the arms of others that we annihilate our own powers. (101)

As Montaigne matures, the danger of this annihilation, this pillage or rape, tends to diminish without altogether disappearing. A posthumous addition to "L'heure des parlemens dangereuse" signals a new willingness to enter the equivocal play of diplomacy.

> (c) Il n'est pas dict, que, en temps et lieu, il ne soit permis de nous prevaloir de la sottise de nos ennemis, comme nous faisons de leur lascheté. Et certes la guerre a naturellement beaucoup de privileges raisonnables au prejudice de la raison. (28–29)

> It is not said that, at a given time and place, it is not permissible for us to take advantage of the stupidity of our enemies, as we do of their cowardice. And indeed war has by nature many privileges that are reasonable even at the expense of reason. (18)

With the passing of years, parleying became less dangerous and less reprehensible, the siege motif less relevant, because the self could allow itself to be permeable. A passage in the essay I:50

("De Democritus et Heraclitus") constitutes a kind of manifesto of the soul's transformative energy.

> (c) Les choses à part elles ont peut estre leurs poids et mesures et conditions; mais au dedans, en nous, elle [l'ame] les leur taille comme elle l'entend. . . . La santé, la conscience, l'authorité, la science, la richesse, la beauté et leurs contraires se despouillent à l'entrée, et recoivent de l'ame nouvelle vesture et de la teinture qu'il lui plaist: brune, verte, claire, obscure, aigre, douce, profonde, superficielle, et ce qu'il plaist à chacune d'elles: car elles n'ont pas verifié en commun leurs stiles, regles et formes: chacune est Royne en son estat. (302)

> Things in themselves may have their own weights and measures and qualities; but once inside, within us, she [the soul] allots them their qualities as she sees fit. . . . Health, conscience, authority, knowledge, riches, beauty, and their opposites—all are stripped on entry and receive from the soul new clothing, and the coloring that she chooses—brown, green, bright, dark, bitter, sweet, deep, superficial—and which each individual soul chooses; for they have not agreed together on their styles, rules and forms; each one is queen in her realm. (220)

Each soul has its *stile, regle,* and *forme,* which not only render matter profound or superficial, but also brown or green; the style tinctures matter with its own indissoluble shading. This is the victory of the soul and preeminently of the writer, since it liberates him from beleaguering hostilities. It is not too much to say that the ultimate subject of the *Essais* is this transformative *stile* of their author's soul. "(a) Qu'on ne s'attende pas aux matieres, mais à la façon que j'y donne" (408). ("Let attention be paid not to the matter, but to the shape I give it" [296].) This indeed is what essentially he seeks in other writers. "(c) Tous les jours m'amuse à lire en des autheurs, sans soin de leur science, y cherchant leur façon, non leur subject" (928). ("Every day I amuse myself reading authors without any care for their learning, looking for their style, not their subject" [708].) If one neglects this progressive discovery of the *façon* as his own final accomplishment as well as others', one is likely to misunderstand Montaigne's book. If one reduces this *stile* to a purely linguistic or rhetorical comportment, then one misses anachronistically its energy and breadth. As Montaigne writes, his trust grows in the integrity of his own *façon* and its power to negotiate with his classics.

There remains, to be sure, a certain wariness.

(b) Quand j'escris, je me passe bien de la compaignie et souvenance des livres, de peur qu'ils n'interrompent ma forme. Aussi que, à la verité, les bons autheurs m'abattent par trop et rompent le courage. (874)

When I write, I prefer to do without the company and remembrance of books, for fear they may interfere with my style. Also because, in truth, the good authors humble me and dishearten me too much. (666)

The impulse to withdraw remains a temptation, but each page belies this alleged surrender of the literary memory; the *souvenance* is not so easily or perhaps so willingly abandoned. The strongest defense against marauders, we learn from the careful householder of "De la vanité" (Of vanity), is not to lock one's gates. The third book bears witness to a less private conception of solitude.

(c) Qui ne vit aucunement à autruy, ne vit guere à soy. (1007)

He who lives not at all unto others, hardly lives unto himself. (769)

(c) Ma forme essentielle est propre à la communication et à la production: je suis tout au dehors et en evidence, nay à la société et à l'amitié. (823)

My essential pattern is suited to communication and revelation. I am all in the open and in full view, born for company and friendship. (625)

It is true that a yearning emerges in "De l'experience" (Of experience) for a purely uninterpreted experience, for pure and absolute knowledge without commentary and without a secondary voice. But this desire, which remains active, can be balanced against the willing acceptance of linguistic duality in the same essay: each word belongs equally and rightfully to its speaker and its auditor. "(b) La parole est moitié à celuy qui parle, moitié à celui qui l'escoute" (1088). ("Speech belongs half to the speaker, half to the listener" [834].)

Terence Cave discerns a vacuum at the center of the *Essais*, which constitute a failed attempt to compensate for the loss of La Boétie.

> As they proliferate around the space left by the absence of La Boétie—like decorative motifs around a missing painting—they can only designate with greater and greater intricacy their own condition of exile and *écoulement*, so that finally the focal absence reveals itself to be that of Montaigne himself.[9]

Each reader of Montaigne will find the metaphor that suits best his own impressions. But Cave's focal absence at the center fails to account for that tincturing of the external as, in Montaigne's own metaphor, it enters and crosses the threshold of the soul. This stylization or coloring of things by a central sensibility is the dominant activity of the *Essais;* it defines that human *façon* which brings us to them as it brought Montaigne to his preferred masters. If in place of the Renaissance vocabulary one substitutes the terms of post-Saussurian linguistics, one skirts anachronism. Cave writes:

> Discourse can never be a transparent vehicle for a given content. Asserting its own presence, it contaminates, obscures, and renders invisible its reference; the resolution of meaning is deferred to some future articulation which will never occur.[10]

This contamination and postponement constitute the text's "diseased nature." But if Renaissance rhetoric approves the technique of *contaminatio,* if discourse pretends neither to transparence nor to reference but to a tincturing *stile,* then there is no pathology of obscurity or deferral; the creation of a transformative moral style is everywhere achieved. Cave cites effectively the myth of the Danaids, whose leaking buckets forestall plenitude, but Montaigne's predilections lead more frequently to images of solid centers and surroundings which encroach upon each other as the center expands or contracts, negotiates or withdraws, stiffens or softens. Each alternative might be regarded as "a movement toward death,"[11] but only if it is understood always to stop short. Death would lie in the collapse of centric resistance, in the suicidal *imitation meurtriere,* or it would lie antithetically in the absolute resistance of silence, the permanent closing of the gate, the refusal of speech. We know that there is a living self when there is a locus of dialogic "altercation." Speech contaminates Montaigne as it contaminates everyone, but for the cunning negotiator, speech saves as well as threatens; it preserves the fortress-self from the two mortal tactical extremes.

The neighbor who invades Montaigne's estate by a ruse of murderous intent is disarmed finally by his host's trustfulness, an apparent simplicity which is spontaneous but not naive. "(b) Je suis peu deffiant et soubçonneux de ma nature," he remarks (1060) ("I am by nature little given to distrust and suspicion" [812]), and it is this clear-eyed credulity that preserves his life. The essay with which we began (I:5) ends on the same note, in an addition of 1588.

> (b) Je me fie ayseement à la foy d'autruy. Mais malaiseement le fairoy je lors que je donnerois à juger l'avoir plustost faict par desespoir et faute de coeur que par franchise et fiance de sa loyauté. (27)

> I put my trust easily in another man's word. But I should do so reluctantly whenever I would give the impression of acting from despair and want of courage rather than freely and through trust in his honesty. (17)

Trust seems both spontaneous and tactical; it may coexist with fear, but not so as to reveal fear. This partial and qualified trust is Montaigne's response to the problem of these twin essays, "l'heure des parlemens dangereuse." His book reveals his cautious, gradual extension of faith to the voices who encircle him on its pages, as he gained faith that his own quirky, placid voice could be heard through theirs and above theirs and *in* theirs. The *Essais* might be said to adumbrate a textual theology like one their author hated: Lutheranism. A man accepts both the estrangement of the word and its promise of engagement: in a gray area without rules, he is saved by his *fiance*. But here this perennial interchange is embraced with a secular temperance: "(b) Celuy qui se porte plus moderéement envers le gain et la perte, il est tousjours chez soy" (1009). ("He who bears himself more moderately toward winning and losing is always at home" [771].)[12]

8

Love's Labour's Lost:
The Grace of Society

The qualities of *Love's Labour's Lost* determine its limitations. The arabesques of wit, the elaborations of courtly artifice, the coolness of tone—these sources of its charm contribute to that brittleness and thinness and faded superficiality for which some critics of several generations have reproached it. For its admirers, a heavy stress upon these limitations is likely to appear irrelevant. But even admirers must acknowledge that, placed against its author's work, *Love's Labour's Lost* is distinguished by a certain slenderness of feeling, a delicate insubstantiality. It is most certainly not a trivial play, but its subtlety remains a little disembodied.

One source of that impression may be the play's lack, unique in Shakespeare, of any firm social underpinning. Not only is there missing any incarnation of responsible authority, any strong and wise center of political power, but there is equally missing any representative of a stable and dependable citizenry. There is nobody here who, however quirky or foolish or provincial, can be counted on, when he is multiplied enough times, to keep society functioning. Or if there is such a figure in the person of Constable Dull, we are struck with how very marginal a role his creator has permitted him. The patently comic figures— Armado, Holofernes, Costard, Nathaniel, Moth—are all too thin or specialized or socially peripheral to suggest any sort of living society. They may be contrasted with the mechanicals of *A Midsummer Night's Dream*, who, for all their splendid ineptness, do persuade us that a kind of Athenian proletariat exists. The earlier play may owe its peculiar airiness in part to a lack of that social solidity.

Yet despite its lack of a ballasted society, the play is

really about "society," in a slightly different sense of the word. Its true subject is caught in an offhand remark by one of its funny men: "Societie (saith the text) is the happiness of life" (IV.ii.177–78).[1] The play does not challenge Nathaniel's text, however insubstantial its dramatic sociology. It is much concerned with society, and the happiness of life in society. If it does not present a living society in action, it presents and comments on configurations of conduct which sustain living societies in and out of plays. It is concerned with *styles,* modes of language and gesture and action which befit, in varying degrees, the intercourse of civilized people. And being a comedy, it is concerned with the failures of inadequate styles, since this is the perennial source of elegant comedy from Homer to Proust. Only at the end, and much more surprisingly, does it turn out to reflect the failure of all style.

To distinguish most sensibly the play's hierarchy of moral styles, one may adopt the vantage point of the princess of France and her three attendant ladies. These four women, being women, cannot provide a strong political center, but they do constitute a certain spirited and witty center of social judgment. In their vivacious and spontaneous taste, limited in range and depth but not in accuracy, each is a poised, Meredithian arbitress of style. This power of discrimination is established by the first speech each lady makes onstage. In the cases of the three attendants, the speech consists in a sketch of the gentleman who is to become the given lady's suitor, and each speech, in its alert and finely qualified appreciation, does credit to the speaker as well as to its subject. Thus Maria:

> I know him Madame, . . .
> A man of soveraigne parts he is esteem'd:
> Well fitted in Arts, glorious in Armes:
> Nothing becomes him ill that he would well.
> The onely soyle of his faire vertues glosse,
> If vertues glosse will staine with any soile,
> Is a sharp wit match'd with too blunt a Will:
> Whose edge hath power to cut whose will still wills,
> It should none spare that come within his power.
>
> (II.i.44, 48–55)

As regards the princess, it is her modesty, her impervious disregard of flattery, the sense of proportion regulating her pride of birth, which betoken most frequently her moral poise. The princess' first speech opens with a mild rebuke of the spongy Lord Boyet for his gratuitous compliments:

> Good L. *Boyet,* my beauty though but mean,
> Needs not the painted flourish of your praise: . . .
> I am lesse proud to heare you tell my worth,
> Then you much wiling to be counted wise,
> In spending your wit in the praise of mine.
>
> (II.i.16–17, 20–22)

She refuses coolly to be hoodwinked by the flattery her station conventionally attracts, with an acuteness which sets off the fool- ish egotism of the king. His first speech, the opening speech of the play, is full of tiresome talk of fame and honor, posturing predic- tions of immortality and glory. The princess' view of "glory" is plain enough after her quick disposal of Boyet, as it is in a later scene when she laughingly dismisses with a tip an unwitting blunder by the forester. Indeed she follows that incident with reflections which are painfully apposite to the king's foolish en- terprise, even if they are ostensibly and deprecatingly directed at herself:

> And out of question, so it is sometimes:
> Glory growes guiltie of detested crimes,
> When for Fames sake, for praise and outward part,
> We bend to that, the working of the hart.
>
> (IV.i.34–37)

This last phrase about bending to externals the work- ing of the heart touches very nearly the heart of the play. For *Love's Labour's Lost* explores the relation of feeling and forms, feeling and the funny distortions of feeling which our social ex- perience beguiles us to fashion. The four gentlemen, quite clearly, begin by denying the workings of their hearts and libidos for the outward part of fame, just as Armado squirms from his distressing passion for a girl who is outwardly—i.e., socially—his inferior. The distinction of the ladies is that their feelings and their style, their outward parts, are attuned; they know what they feel and they are in control of its expression. Although they are as quick to admire as the four gentlemen, they are slower to think they are falling in love. They are also, to their credit, far clearer about the physiological dimension of their interest. The freedom of their byplay about sex may have lost with time some of its comic sprightliness, but next to the dogged Petrarchan vaporizings of their suitors that freedom still emerges as the healthier and more refreshing mode of speech. The four ladies are, in the best sense, self-possessed, although the play does not try to pretend that the *scope* of their feelings or their experience is any wider than most girls'. An older person with no wider a scope would risk the hollowness of the ambiguous, slightly sterile Boyet. The ladies are so engaging because their spirited and untested freshness is tempered by instinctive good sense.

The roles of the gentlemen—Navarre and his three courtiers—are slightly more complicated. For they must justify to some degree the interest the ladies conceive in them. Longaville may not be quite the "man of sovereign parts" Maria says he is, but he must remain within hailing distance of that distinguished man she thought she saw and liked. We must always be able to assume that the gentlemen are salvageable as social animals and potential husbands, and need only the kind of education provided by laughter and the penances to which, at the close, they are assigned. But granting them a basic attractiveness, we have to confess that they resemble a little—in their deplorable affectations, their wayward rhetoric, their callow blindness to themselves— the caricatured figures of the subplot. There is a difference of degree, not of kind, between the doggerel of, say, Holofernes (IV.ii.66–76) and the mediocrity of Dumain's verses:

> A huge translation of hypocrisie,
> Vildly compiled, profound simplicitie
> (V.ii.55–56)

Like Holofernes, Armado, and Nathaniel, the gentlemen "have been at a great feast of languages and stolen the scraps"; all steal indifferently from a common alms-basket of words. They are failures as poseurs because their poses are never original, and as Holofernes himself is able to recognize, "imitari is nothing." The successive defeats of the gentlemen in their sets of wits with the ladies betray an ineptitude of social intelligence and style.

Shakespeare will tolerate cheerfully enough the fashionable inanities of sentimental rhetoric, but he sees the risk of mistaking rhetoric for real sentiment. It is the risk which anguished Pirandello, but it works in this more comical world to expose the gentlemen to their mistresses' ridicule. For the ladies, who are not all wise, know enough to distinguish language in touch with feeling from the language which does duty for feeling, or, more accurately, which papers over adolescent confusions of feeling. The ladies' rhetoric, cooler, more bracing, more alert than the lords', enlivened by the freedom of its casual license, finds a natural recreation in a kind of amiable flyting, a "civil war of wits." The ladies vanquish their suitors unfailingly in this civil badinage because they are, so to speak, in practice. The suitors are not, having attempted to exclude from their still and contemplative academy what they call "the world's debate." Or rather, they have allowed the debate to impinge only at second hand, as a recreative fancy and linguistic toy. They may hear, says the king, from Armado:

> In high-borne words the worth of many a Knight:
> From tawnie *Spaine* lost in the worlds debate.
>
> (I.i.184–85)

Perhaps it is their unwillingness to be so lost—save in fantasy, through the mediation of high-colored language—which loses them the verbal battles under the banner of Saint Cupid. The play will end with a calendary debate, reminding us that nature itself, and the human lives it governs, are subject to the amoebean conflicts of the seasons.

The war of wits is "civil" in more meanings than one, since the term *civility* gathers up all of the play's central values. The term as Elizabethans used it embraced all those configurations of political and social and moral conduct which can render society the happiness of life. The gentlemen, in their cocksure unworldliness, have only bungling conceptions of civility, and for all their fumbling efforts toward urbanity, their parochial manners unflaggingly show through. The ideal is defined partly by its breaches: the ascetic breach represented by the academy's austere statutes; or the inhuman breach of the decree which would deprive an interloping woman of her tongue: "a dangerous law against gentilitie" (I.i.139); or the inhospitable breach which denies the princess welcome to the court of Navarre; or the rhetorical breaches of the gentlemen's poetastical love complaints; or the fantastical breach of the Muscovite embassy:

> Their shallow showes, and Prologue vildely pen'd:
> And their rough carriage so ridiculous;
>   (V.ii.342–43)

or the final blunder which asks the bereaved princess to listen still to her lover's suit. This variety of gaffes is filled out by the cruder affectations of the minor comic characters. Virtually all the men in the play violate, each in his peculiar way, the values of "civility," which meant at once civilization, social polish, government, courtesy, decorum, manners, and simple human kindness.

Of these various participant values, the play lays particular stress on the virtue of decorum, which becomes here a sense of the conduct appropriate to a given situation. Berowne's main charge against Navarre's academy appeals implicitly to that virtue:

> FERDINAND: *Berowne* is like an envious sneaping Frost,
> That bites the first borne infants of the Spring.
>   BEROWNE: Wel, say I am, why should proud Summer boast,
> Before the Birds have any cause to sing?
> Why should I ioy in any abortive birth?
> At Christmas I no more desire a Rose,
> Then wish a Snow in Mayes new fangled showes:
> But like of each thing that in season growes.
> So you to studie now it is too late,
> That were to clymbe ore the house to unlocke the gate.
>   (I.i.110–19)

Enterprise blossoms when, in Berowne's phrase, it is "fit in his place and time" (I.i.107); comedy wells up from the disjuncture of act and occasion. The lords' intuition of this great Renaissance virtue is blunted equally in their roles as students and as suitors, so that an especial irony tinges the king's summons to courtship:

> Away, away, no time shall be omitted,
> That will be time, and may by us be fitted.
> (IV.iii.400–401)

That cry will receive an unwitting answer in Rosaline's fantasy:

> O that I knew he were but in by th'weeke,
> How I would make him fawne, and begge, and seeke,
> And wait the season, and observe the times.
> (V.ii.65–67)

and finds another faint echo later in the princess' rejection of Navarre's last plea:

> KING: Now at the latest minute of the houre,
> Grant us your loves.
> QUEEN: A time me thinkes too short,
> To make a world-without-end bargaine in.
> (V.ii.861–64)

This fault of abusing season and "time" is implicitly caught up in Berowne's incoherent apology for the misconduct of himself and his companions, whose errors he ruefully confesses to have sinned against decorum.

> Your beautie Ladies
> Hath much deformed us, fashioning our humors
> Even to the opposed end of our intents.
> And what in us hath seem'd ridiculous:
> As Love is full of unbefitting straines,
> All wanton as a childe, skipping and vaine . . .
> Which partie-coated presence of loose love
> Put on by us, if in your heavenly eies,
> Have misbecom'd our oathes and gravities.
> Those heavenlie eies that looke into these faults,
> Suggested us to make. (V.ii.829–34, 839–43)

The key words are "deformed," "unbefitting," and "misbecom'd," suggesting offenses against that value of propriety which had not yet, in the sixteenth century, become the fossilized austerity we have learned to deplore.

The relationship of Berowne to the ideals of civility is rather more complex than his fellows', since he understands so much more than they without ever saving himself from their muddles. He has traits in common with Shaw's John Tanner: both are brilliant, ineffectual talkers who never quite learn how useless are even their best lines. Berowne for all his brilliance is easily put in his place by the securer wit of Rosaline. But despite his frustrations he remains the most original, interesting, and complicated character in the play. He is insincere from the outset; he knows of course that he will sign the articles of the academic oath, even as he calls attention to himself by pretending to refuse. He plays with life, and his life is a play within the play. It is the last word he speaks, in the famous regretful line that gives us—had we been so obtuse as to miss it—the key to his character: "That's too long for a play" (V.ii.955). Ironist, sophist, scoffer, he has one small, delusory faith: he believes in language, and it fails him. He is almost saved by his capacity to laugh at himself, but not quite; his worst muddle is his last, when he tries to chasten his rhetoric before the fact of death, and cannot shake his inveterate cleverness:

> We to our selves prove false,
> By being once false, for ever to be true
> To those that make us both, faire Ladies you.
> (V.ii.845–47)

To themselves they do indeed prove false, and to the motto "Honest plain words, best pierce the ears of griefe" (V.ii.826).

Berowne's teasing dilettantism is not up to death— nor (more surprisingly?) is it up to sex. His sexuality, like his fellow suitors', is visual, not to say voyeuristic. Their obsession with the eye transcends the Petrarchan cliché; it betokens their callow and adolescent virginity. It is symptomatic that the most sleazy joke the gentlemen permit themselves has to do with looking;[2] when the ladies' talk is bawdy, they refer to the more relevant organs. Their ribaldry is the cleaner. None of these women would say of her lover what Berowne is so foolish to admit:

O but her eye: by this light, but for her eye, I would not love her; yes, for her two eyes. (IV.iii.10–12)

And again later:

From womens eyes this doctrine I derive.
They sparcle still the right promethean fire,
They are the Bookes, the Arts, the Achademes,
That shew, containe, and nourish all the world.
Else none at all in ought proves excellent.
(IV.iii.369–73)

This fascination is echoed in the rhetoric of the other suitors, and enters the plot with the misleading exchange of favors:

The ladies did change Favours; and then we
Following the signes, woo'd but the signe of she.
(V.ii.521–22)

The sign of she! That is always the object of immature desire. To know and love the complex living creature takes more time and a wiser heart.

The comedy of the gentlemen's sentimental inadequacies is reflected obliquely in the comedy of their inferiors. This reflection receives dramatic expression in Costard's mistaken interchange of Berowne's poem with Armado's letter. The confusion suggests a common element which we recognize as the vice of affectation, a vice which is only a few degrees more marked in the style of Armado and spills over into humor. One might almost say that we are invited to share Costard's error. But from another perspective the gentlemen as gallants emerge from the contrast with even less credit than the ostensible clowns. Costard at least represents the closest thing to good sense in the flights of folly of the opening scene; through his malapropising nonsense a few primitive truths are sounded which shatter all the foregoing silliness about asceticism:

Now sir for the manner; It is the manner of a man to speake to a woman. (I.i.221–22)

Such is the simplicitie of man to harken after the flesh. (I.i.229–30)

Armado of course is more closely parallel to the gentlemen because, unlike Costard, he fancies himself to be in love. Armado is the most suggestive of the comic figures and one of the richest of any in Shakespeare's early comedies, although his potentialities are not consistently developed. There is a resonance to his humor which is lacking, say, in the humor of his fellow pomposity, Holofernes. This is because Shakespeare invests Armado's grandiloquence with a touch of melancholy. We are allowed to catch a bat's squeak of pathos behind the tawny splendor, and a lonely desire for Jaquenetta behind the clumsy condescension to her. The pathos is really affecting when he must decline Costard's challenge and confess his shirtlessness, infamonized among potentates. Nothing so touching overshadows the presentation of the gentlemen. Armado's courtship is more desperate, more clouded, and more believable.

A conventional reading of the play places the main turning point at the end of the fourth act, with the fourfold exposure of the quondam academics and their abjuration of study in the name of Saint Cupid. But to read in this way is to be taken in by the gentlemen's own self-delusions. For their apparent conversion is at bottom a pseudo-conversion, the exchange of one pretentious fiction for another, and we are meant to view ironically their naive release of enthusiasm, as we view Caliban's "Freedom, high-day!" The Muscovite embassy represents the culmination of the gentlemen's clumsy posing, their inept sophistication, and their empty formalism. Never yet in the play have manner and mien been quite so far from feeling, and we learn merely that courtship as performance can be just as silly as the performance of monastic seclusion. The real turning point begins with Berowne's second abjuration and its potentially deeper renunciation of rhetorical affectation.

> Taffata phrases, silken tearmes precise,
> Three-pil'd Hyperboles, spruce affection;
> Figures pedanticall, these summer flies

> Have blowne me full of maggot ostentation.
> I do forsweare them. (V.ii.452–56)

Berowne underestimates the difficulty of the sacrifice, as Rosaline finds a way to suggest, but we are allowed to hope that the seed of understanding has been planted. Indeed the remaining action of this rich last scene—almost a one-act play in itself—can be regarded as a progressive and painful exorcism of the gentlemen's pretenses and pretensions. The first step involves a humiliating sincerity.

> KING: Teach us sweete Madame, for our rude trans-
> gression, some faire excuse.
> QUEEN: The fairest is confession.
> Were you not heere but even now, disguis'd?
> KING: Madam, I was. (V.ii.478–82)

That step leads to the further humbling discovery of the exchanged favors and mistaken identities, and that in turn to the puzzling but clearly important episode of the Worthies' pageant.[3]

The intrusion of this interlude, so cruelly and even pathetically routed at the climax of the action, has troubled more than one reader,[4] and indeed it is not easily justified by our common standards of daily morality. Yet I think that Shakespeare has given us a key to its interpretation, a key which no critic to my knowledge has noticed. The essential point is the reluctance of the gentlemen to watch the pageant, chastened as they already are at this point by their sense of their own absurdity. Yet in fact they do watch. The exchange is notable that immediately precedes this ambiguous entertainment:

> KING: *Berowne,* they will shame us:
> Let them not approach.
> BEROWNE: We are shame-proofe my Lord: and 'tis some
> policie, to have one shew worse then the Kings and his
> companie.
> KING: I say they shall not come.
> QUEEN: Nay my good Lord, let me ore-rule you now;
> That sport best pleases, that does least know how.
> Where Zeale strives to content, and the contents

Dies in the Zeale of that which it presents:
Their forme confounded, makes most forme in mirth,
When great things labouring perish in their birth.
BEROWNE: A right description of our sport my Lord.
(V.ii.567–79)

The clumsy pageant will imitate uncomfortably the fumbling Muscovite masquing. The analogy is painfully close, as both the king and Berowne are alert enough to perceive. The princess' wise insistence on the performance—"That sport best pleases, that does least know how"—creates a small moral dilemma for the lords which they come to resolve by mocking their own unwitting mockers. They recognize, not without a certain rueful courage, that the pageant represents a quintessential parody of their own offenses against propriety; so they choose to follow Boyet in turning upon that parody as though to exorcise their own folly. The telling line is Dumaine's:

Though my mockes come home by me, I will now be merrie.
(V.ii.704–5)

Unforgivable in itself, the routing of the pageant is dramatically right as ritual action, as a symbolic rejection of a mask beginning to be outworn. Indeed only the savage shame one feels toward an unworthy part of one's self could motivate the gentlemen's quite uncharacteristic cruelty.

Considered in this way, the ridicule of the pageant needs no palliation, and yet two palliative observations can be made. The first is that the ridicule is not heaped equally on all five performers. Moth as Hercules remains silent while presented by Holofernes-Maccabaeus and is allowed to leave the stage after the six-line presentation without any interruption. Costard is interrupted twice and corrected once at the outset, but is then heard out quietly, thanked by the princess, and complimented by Berowne. Nathaniel fares somewhat worse, but the most scathing ridicule is reserved for the two most outrageous (if charming) pomposities, Holofernes and Armado. This careful apportioning of embarrassment is not accidental, nor is the circumstance that the two most harried victims achieve individually their finest, and simplest, moments under fire. Holofernes' reproach is his last line and his one stroke of quiet dignity: "This is not generous, not gentle, not humble" (V.ii.696). Armado, the richer character, is vouchsafed by his creator a felicity close to eloquence:

> The sweet War-man is dead and rotten,
> Sweet chuckes, beat not the bones of the buried:
> When he breathed he was a man (V.ii.731–33)

and by the end something like a transformation seems to be operating even upon his stiff and shallow playing-card magnificence. ("For mine owne part, I breath free breath: I have seene the day of wrong, through the little hole of discretion, and I will right my selfe like a soldier"—V.ii.795–97.) He too will serve a penance like his betters.[5] Thus the lash of comic criticism chastens with bitter success all the surquedry of this dramatic world. Thus all men are taught, with Nathaniel, not to o'erpart themselves.

The final and most telling chastisement appears with the entrance of Marcade, who brings the fact of death. Even a few minutes earlier, this fact would have shattered the play; now it can be borne. Heretofore death has been itself rhetorical, as in the very first lines:

> Let *Fame,* that all hunt after in their lives,
> Live registred upon our brazen Tombes,
> And then grace us in the disgrace of death. (I.i.6–8)

Then an abstract unreality, death now is a particular event. No one of the characters has the emotional depth fully to command a rhetoric commensurate with the event, but in the speeches following Marcade's entry three degrees of rhetorical inadequacy can be distinguished. The princess falls short only in the reserve with which she receives her bereavement, a reserve which betrays no feeling and risks the appearance of coldness. Otherwise she is sensible, brief, even, briskly courteous, alert to the relative inconsequence of all the badinage that has preceded. In contrast, the poverty of the king's rhetoric is painfully manifest:

> The extreme parts of time, extremelie formes
> All causes to the purpose of his speed: (V.ii.813–14)

a rhetorical failure because it cannot conceal the underlying poverty of sympathy or even of decent respect. In essence, the king is making a request which is shockingly improper—that his courtship not be neglected because of her loss—and perhaps it is his consciousness of this indecorum that produces such monstrous linguistic convolutions and elicits her wryly polite answer: "I understand you not, my greefes are double" (V.ii.825). Berowne's essay at a valediction, as we have seen, opens with a gesture toward the proper simplicity but winds up with an equally inappropriate contortion. Berowne at least recognizes the rhetorical problem; the lesson of *his* failure seems to be that habits of feeling and language are not quickly overcome. Earlier he had confessed:

> beare with me, I am sicke.
> Ile leave it by degrees. (V.ii.464–65)

The degrees do indeed come slowly.

In the light of the lords' inadequacies before the fact of death, the penances set them by the ladies constitute a kind of final prodding toward maturation. Berowne's will test the relevance of his dilettantish jesting to human suffering[6] and thereby purge perhaps the frivolity of his ironies. In these closing moments of the last scene, one has the impression of the comedy turning back upon itself, withdrawing from those modes of speech and laughter which have in fact constituted its distinctiveness. Pater is surely right when he suggests that the play contains "a delicate raillery by Shakespeare himself at his own chosen manner"[7]—at least of the manner chosen for this work. The raillery has been there throughout, diffused and subtle, but now at the end it has become something more serious and has determined the conclusion. Could this final verdict have been introduced in the later version, "newly corrected and augmented," as the title page of the 1598 quarto informs us? The judgment on Berowne comes to seem like a judgment on the slenderness of a certain moral style that has been outgrown.

There could be no greater mistake than to conclude from this judgment that Shakespeare disliked rhetorics and forms, patterns of words and of experience. He was not, needless to say, in favor of the crude expression of raw passion. He knew that society, the happiness of life, depends on configurations and rituals. He represented the Muscovite masquing to be silly not because it was artificial but because, in his sense of the word, it was not artificial enough; it was "shallow" and "rough" and "vilely penned." This being so, one may ask whether Shakespeare did not provide within the play an instance of authentic artifice, and the answer is that he did provide it, in the form of the two concluding songs.

If we regard the presentation of these songs literally, as a part of the pageant they are designed to conclude, then their artistic finish is out of place. But if we regard them as rhetorical touchstones by which to estimate the foregoing funny abuses of language, they form an ideal ending. In their careful balance, elaborate refrain, and lyric poise, the songs are artificial in the good old sense, but in their freshness and freedom from stale tradition, they blithely escape the stilted modern sense. They violate the cliché preference of spring to winter and adumbrate a finer decorum; they "like of each thing that in season grows." They like of each thing, but not conventionally or sentimentally; the "unpleasing" word of the cuckoo sounds in the spring, while the wintry cry of the owl is "merry." Joseph Westlund points out suggestively that the more attractively "realistic" world of Hiems lies further from the effete world of the play itself, and closer to the experience the gentlemen must come to face.[8] The winter song achieves a mingling of the lyrical and the humbly truthful which none of the courtly poetasters in Navarre could manage.

"The Words of Mercurie, / Are harsh after the songs of Apollo" concludes Armado (V.ii.1012–13). A recent editor paraphrases:

i.e., let us end with the songs, because clever words of the god Mercury would come harshly after the songs of Apollo, the god of poetry.[9]

Such may well be Armado's meaning, but his words can bear an ulterior construction. He might be taken to mean that the songs we have just heard, with their bracing directness, are to the rest of the play and its pseudo-golden poetry as Mercury is to Apollo. From the narrow world of neo-Petrarchan sentiment, the experience of the songs may well seem "harsh," since they treat of cuckolds and red noses and frozen milk. With that adjective in our ears, Armado ends the comedy: "You that way; we this way" (V.ii.1014). Who is "you"? The actors on the other side of the stage? Or we in the audience, who must leave the theater and exchange one set of conventions and disguises for another, less tractable to laughter?

Society may be, ideally, the happiness of life, but the end of the play has not placed us in it. Perhaps Nathaniel's text is fallacious. But by one very faint, almost surreptitious means, Shakespeare seems to me to remind us repeatedly of the possible felicity into which society can flower. This means is the unusual frequence and special prominence accorded the word "grace"— the word, we remember, with which the opening sentence plays (quoted above, p. 152). As the play continues, the many extensions and intricate variations of "grace" in all its meanings are explored with deliberate subtlety. In no other play by Shakespeare is the address "Your Grace" to a sovereign so alive with suggestiveness. The princess is represented explicitly and emphatically as endowed with "grace," from the first mention of her:

> For well you know here comes in Embassie
> The *French* Kings daughter, with your selfe to speake:
> A Maide of grace and compleate maiestie
>
> (I.i.145–47)

and again at her first appearance, in Boyet's injunction:

> Be now as prodigall of all deare grace,
> As Nature was in making Graces deare,
> When she did starve the generall world beside,
> And prodigally gave them all to you. (II.i.12–15)

The princess' grace has something to do presumably with the comely carriage of her physical bearing, but also with a certain courtesy and sweetness of manner which transcend the body. As the multiple meanings of the word quietly exfoliated, educated Elizabethan playgoers may have remembered the quality of *grazia* in Castiglione's *Cortegiano*, that indefinable air which represents the courtier's supreme distinction, and which is repeatedly and emphatically opposed to affectation.[10] Such an echo could only heighten the ironies of the honorific "Your Grace" addressed to the king, and indeed on one occasion his fitness for it is indirectly questioned:

> Good heart, What grace hast thou thus to reprove
> These wormes for loving, that art most in love?
> (IV.iii.158–59)

The word in these contexts signifies a virtue a person can possess, but other contexts remind us that it is something that can be given to another. It is what lovers want, as Longaville's poem shows:

> Thy grace being gain'd, cures all disgrace in me
> (IV.iii.68)

and what the ladies determine to refuse:

> And not a man of them shall have the grace
> Despight of sute, to see a Ladies face. (V.ii.134–35)

> No, to the death we will not move a foot,
> Nor to their pen'd speech render we no grace.
> (V.ii.152–53)

Grace is what a wit desires from his audience, perhaps meretriciously:

> For he hath wit to make an ill shape good,
> And shape to win grace though she had no wit.
> (II.i.63–64)

> Why that's the way to choke a gibing spirit,
> Whose influence is begot of that loose grace,
> Which shallow laughing hearers give to fooles
> (V.ii.934–36)

but it is also the very ability to amuse:

> He is Wits Pedler, and retailes his Wares,
> At Wakes, and Wassels, Meetings, Markets, Faires.
> And we that sell by grosse, the Lord doth know,

    Have not the grace to grace it with such show.
                    (V.ii.356–59)

These last passages suggest the paradoxical openness of this ability to perversion or manipulation, and other usages imply the same double-edged danger:

    Follie in Wisedome hatch'd:
    Hath wisedoms warrant, and the helpe of Schoole,
    And Wits own grace to grace a learned Foole? (V.ii.74–76)

But all these failures, real or potential, of the virtue never quite suppress the hope which the word embodies: the hope for felicitous human conversation. And although the hope is firmly rooted in the affairs of this world, at least one usage holds the word open briefly to its theological sense:

    For every man with his affects is borne,
    Not by might mastred, but by speciall grace. (I.i.163–64)

That is Berowne on the resilience of human passion, to be echoed later by his flip cynicism: "God give him grace to grone" (IV.iii.20). Is it fanciful to think that the word is introduced deliberately, to enrich its resonance still further, in the invitation of Holofernes to Nathaniel?

    I do dine to day at the fathers of a certaine Pupill of mine, where if (being repast) it shall please you to gratifie the table with a Grace, I will . . . undertake your *bien vonuto*. . .I beseech your Societie.
    NATHANIEL: And thanke you to: for societie (saith the text) is the happinesse of life. (IV.ii.169–73, 175–78)

Here, just below the amusing surface, two or three meanings of the word seem to coalesce.

        The grace of entertainment, the grace of love, the grace of wit, the grace of civility—*Love's Labour's Lost* is about the pursuit of all these fragile goals. Its opening adumbrates the need of some ulterior, metaphysical principle to "grace us in the disgrace of death," though the principle of fame proposed there is quickly forgotten. The reader may ask what means the play holds out to us to confront that disgrace, since in fact we are forced at the end to consider it, and the disgrace also of "the speechless sick" and "the pained impotent." Perhaps the upshot is a wry surrender and such a devaluation of grace as Kokeritz teaches us to find in the irreverent play of *The Comedy of Errors* on the word's Elizabethan homonym: "Marry, sir, she's the kitchen-wench, and all grease."[11] But *Love's Labour's Lost* is not, in the last analysis, devaluative, and in a sense its object is to live with the best sort of grace—with enlightened intercourse between the sexes, with gaiety and true wit, with poise, taste, decorum, and charity. The ending does not discredit this object, even if it acknowledges the helplessness of wit before suffering, and even if it extends the realm of grace to unexpected social strata. For the play does not leave us with the princess; it leaves us with a pun on greasy Joan who keels the pot.

We can be grateful to the playwright for not attempting to put onstage the truly enlightened society. He leaves that achievement where it belongs, in the indefinite future, not altogether remote, but much too long for a play. In 1598 he was beginning to outgrow comedy as he knew it, and to question the truth of a comic resolution. Shortly he would reach his own Twelfth Night, an end to merriment. At the end of this comedy, we hardly know where we are, as Berowne goes off to the hospital and the king to a naked hermitage, and Armado to his plow, and the princess to her loss, all off to the world's debate, and we are left with our former mirth a little suspect, and are signaled to leave, almost enigmatically: "You that way; we this way."

9

Anti-Hermeneutics: The Case
of Shakespeare's Sonnet 129

scholarly contention has recently rearisen over the editing of
Shakespeare's *Sonnets* that focuses conveniently a complex of
perennial problems, not only affecting the editing of Shakespeare
or any other author but also adumbrating vaster questions of
historical understanding. In his useful, important, and exhaustive
edition with commentary on the *Sonnets*, Stephen Booth takes
vigorous issue with a well-known essay by Robert Graves and
Laura Riding, "A Study in Original Punctuation and Spelling."
This essay, published in its original form over fifty years ago, argues
against the modernization of Shakespeare by comparing the original and reedited texts of a single sonnet, 129, "Th'expense of
Spirit in a waste of shame." By explicating the allegedly richer,
more open, more polysemous quarto version and by showing the
reductive flatness imposed by modernization, Graves and Riding
call into question what they call the "perversely stupid" habits of
most modern editors. Professor Booth, no mean polemicist himself, labels this essay "an exercise in irresponsible editorial restraint" and devotes more than five large pages to disposing of its
arguments. His basic position is that "an editor distorts the sonnet
more for a modern reader by maintaining the 1609 text than he
would if he modernized its spelling and punctuation."[1]

No one can deny the enduring importance of this contention between, on the one hand, two practicing poets writing a
long time ago as radical critics beyond the pale of the scholarly
guild and, on the other hand, a gifted contemporary member of
the guild, not lacking in professional independence and even
irreverence, but in this dispute adopting something close to a hard-
line conservative position. But in describing Booth as the con-

servative one may already falsify the issue, since Graves and Riding would argue that they are the true conservatives, preserving Shakespeare's original words and meaning against the tendentious contaminators of the intervening centuries. Perhaps one useful step toward resolving the quarrel would be to ask which side has the better right to be called conservative in the best, most positive sense.

Clearly this inexhaustible question will not be settled simply by an appeal to sonnet 129, but a glance at the two versions competing for our attention could be instructive. Booth provides both the quarto text and, facing it throughout, a compromise modernization that represents what he calls a "mid-point" between the punctuation and spelling of the original and modern directive adaptations.

> Th'expence of Spirit in a waste of shame
> Is lust in action, and till action, lust   2
> Is periurd, murdrous, blouddy full of blame,
> Sauage, extreame, rude, cruell, not to trust,   4
> Inioy'd no sooner but dispised straight,
> Past reason hunted, and no sooner had   6
> Past reason hated as a swollowed bayt,
> On purpose layd to make the taker mad.   8
> Made in pursut and in possession so,
> Had, having, and in quest, to have extreame,   10
> A blisse in proofe and proud and very wo,
> Before a ioy proposd behind a dreame,   12
>   All this the world well knowes yet none knowes well,
>   To shun the heaven that leads men to this hell.   14

> Th'expense of spirit in a waste of shame
> Is lust in action, and till action lust   2
> Is perjured, murd'rous, bloody, full of blame,
> Savage, extreme, rude, cruel, not to trust,   4
> Enjoyed no sooner but despisèd straight,
> Past reason hunted, and no sooner had,   6
> Past reason hated as a swallowed bait,
> On purpose laid to make the taker mad;   8
> Mad in pursuit, and in possession so,
> Had, having, and in quest to have, extreme,   10

A bliss in proof, and proved, a very woe,
Before, a joy proposed, behind, a dream.   12
   All this the world well knows, yet none knows well
   To shun the heav'n that leads men to this hell.   14

What are the main differences? Booth supplies a comma after "blouddy" in line 3 and another at the end of line 6 where the quarto has nothing; at the end of line 8 he substitutes a semicolon for the quarto's period; together with virtually all editors he emends the first word of line 9 from "Made" to "Mad," adds a comma after "pursuit" in line 9, and shifts the third comma in line 10. In lines 11 and 12 the surgery is radical: in 11 two commas are added and "a" is substituted for "and"; in 12 three commas are added and a period at the end replaces the quarto's only comma. Finally in line 13, a comma is shifted from the end to the middle. The spelling is modernized, with apostrophes inserted in "murdrous" and "heaven." If this text does represent a midpoint in editorial tact, we're left to wonder what further changes are possible, but in fact the text from *The Oxford Book of English Verse* quoted by Graves and Riding is still more freely repunctuated.

   This is not the occasion to analyze thoroughly the semantic transformations, some subtle and some obtrusive, effected by the modern version. But if one stands back and contemplates the two texts as a set, a few impressions emerge immediately. The revised version is undeniably more accessible. Assuming with Booth that the Jacobean reader found few obstacles to reading the poem and that the modern reader should be assisted to enjoy a similar facility so far as possible, then unquestionably the revised version does extend us that assistance. It smoothes over almost all the superficial perplexities in this poem of anguish and despair, this terrible sonnet. For example, it attaches the third quatrain to the first two, thus allowing all three to form one coherent sentence, rather than attaching the third quatrain to the couplet as the quarto does, a little mysteriously. The new version helps us to understand the first word of line 9, which here simply echoes the last word of the previous line—"mad"; in the quarto version one's eye has to move further back in line 8 to the verb "to make" and then understand "Made" in the next line as an altered form of it. "Mad" clearly assists the reader, as does the substitution of "a" for "and"; the line in its old version *could* mean, as Graves and Riding point out, that lust is both bliss and woe at once, both "in proof" and "provd," during its gratification and afterward. But that meaning has to be worked for. The revised line 12 imposes a reassuring tidiness on the puzzling original, where we have to struggle to see how lust could be a joy which is "proposed," envisioned, behind a dream. Again the original *could* make sense, but not easily. Throughout, the modern version supplies us with the *facilior lectio,* and if that is what it takes for our reading to approach the Jacobeans', then undoubtedly the quarto text can only be regarded as unsuitable. "In 129," writes Booth, "modern punctuation gains 'sheer facility in reading' and denies a modern reader nothing that Shakespeare's contemporaries would have perceived."[2]

Surely for better or worse the modernization does more than that. It really acts as a shield for the modern reader, a shield extended to protect him from the problematic contingencies of the original. It protects him from worrying whether the punctuation in front of him corresponds to Shakespeare's actual intent or only his compositor's—whether in fact it corresponds to any knowledgeable intent rather than an ignorant man's caprice. The altered text does certainly correspond to a knowledgeable intent, its editor's, and in this certainty we take comfort. We're protected as well from the strenuous effort of groping unassisted for those shifting, floating, ambiguous relations of clause to clause, phrase to phrase, that constitute one of the outstanding rhetorical features of the *Sonnets* and which Booth himself stresses. Thus in the altered text we don't have to grope for the elusive, possibly nonexistent connection between the third quatrain and the couplet that would justify their separation by a mere comma after line 12. But should we really have this protection? Do we truly want it? Don't we ultimately want, or shouldn't we want, the actual mysterious artifact history has handed down to us with all its built-in puzzlements and uncertainties? Some of these surely the Jacobean reader wrestled with also. What *did* he do with that "Made" in line 9? Why should we be spared his perplexities if his experience is the norm we're expected to approach?

Most decisively and significantly the altered text shields us from that curious Renaissance sense of grammar that fails to isolate a self-contained sentence from its successor. Take one of the most assertive and distinct and self-enclosed affirmations in the *Sonnets:* "Let me not to the marriage of true mindes / Admit impediments." That affirmation is denied in the quarto the full stop it deserves according to our logic: ". . . Admit impediments, love is not love . . ." Here at least the practice is too common to blame only on the compositor, and even if it were the compositor's alone, we have no reason to believe that it troubled the Jacobean reader. We are forced to recognize that the sense of syntactic closure, the sense of declarative completeness, the very status of the affirmation during the Jacobean period, violate our grammar and our logic. This troubling recognition would also be spared us if we confined our reading to the altered text. Even if it were true that modern punctuation denies us nothing a Jacobean would have *perceived,* it does deny us something crucial about the presuppositions he brought to the printed page: it denies us something about his mind-set. Modernization in this respect is less conservative because it fails to preserve an important element of Shakespeare's semiotic world. It not only conceals the mysteries, the contingencies, the authentic riddles, truly present for us in the original; it conceals those offenses to our logic that historical distance will always impose.

That distance makes itself felt equally in the puzzles posed by individual words. In sonnet 129 the opening phrase immediately presents a kind of hermeneutic hurdle. The expression "expence of Spirit" sustains the fundamental metaphor of the sequence linking economics with emotion and sexuality. The constant concern with thrift and profligacy organizes the *Sonnets,* and there is nothing a priori in this figural pattern that is necessarily inaccessible to a twentieth-century reader. The metaphor begins to lose us only when the economic implications of "expence" are taken literally at the physiological level. The sexual act is really impoverishing only if one holds the medieval and Renaissance belief that it shortens a man's life. If, in place of the restorative, therapeutic release our post-Freudian society perceives, one attributes to sex a literal expenditure of vitality, then the struggle between the sexes takes on a crude economic reality, and we begin to understand the linkage made by the Wyf of Bath. She ends her tale by praying for "housebondes meeke, yonge, and fressh abedde" while calling down a plague on "olde and angry niggardes of dispence."[3] In sonnets 1–126 of Shakespeare's sequence, the bourgeois poet speaks for the values of husbandry, as befits his class, in order prudently to correct the failures of this art assigned to that social class of "unthrifts" which includes the friend. In sonnet 129 the young man's profligacy is less at issue than, one presumes, the bourgeois speaker's among others. The phrase "th'expence of Spirit" means several things, including the implication that the speaker has been *unclassed* by lust, that he is now guilty of that aristocratic waste he had attempted in so many preceding poems to moderate. In yielding to lust he is yielding to a literally self-destructive extravagance, which heretofore he has followed tradition in charging to his social superiors.[4] This biological as well as sociological undoing of the self, implicit in Shakespeare's word "expence," remains an abstraction for us even if we catch its resonance. We might begin to recapture that reference to personal ontology by taking seriously the lost implications of such words as "dissolute" and "dissipated,"

Modernized spelling also helps to conceal the different status of the word itself in a prelexicographical culture. The quarto calls attention to the word "Spirit" by capitalizing it, a stress modern editors tend to drop. The word is not easily defined in any case. Glosses for "Spirit" suggested by Booth and other editors include "physical vigor," "mental energy," "spiritual essence," "life force," "bodily fluid," "penis erectus," and "the subtle vapor supposed to be contained in the heart and needed for generation." This gives seven distinct glosses which the modern reader experiences as a supersaturated plethora of competing meanings. But it is unlikely that the prelexicographical reader felt this kind of division and subdivision; it is more likely that he or she read the word "Spirit" as a multifaceted unity we can only try to imagine. The polyvalent word before the era of dictionaries could not simply be felt as the sum of an indefinite series of parallel definitions; it must have been apprehended as a veined monolith. It was not yet reducible to a vertical list of semidiscrete equivalents. It must have remained somehow a simultaneous whole which nonetheless presented multiple aspects to be perceived as context indicated. Not only the lost meanings of a word but the very process of their fusion within a single signifier eludes us.

One peculiarly elusive word appears at the openings of lines 2 and 3. One of the most deceptive signifiers in the code of any remote text is the copula: deceptive because to the naked eye it looks to be the most unchanging and the most transparent of all parts of speech. But in fact the copula, underlying implicitly or explicitly most metaphorization and predication, is the part of speech most sensitive to historically shifting intuitions of relationship and reality. It is rooted in each culture's, each era's, metaphysical and epistemological assumptions—not necessarily the assumptions spelled out discursively but those silently shared and invoked in poetry as in ordinary speech. Fully to understand the force of a copula in a given text is to understand a good deal of the text and the semiotic universe that nourished it.

Shakespeare's sonnet 129 is largely controlled by those two copulas appearing at the openings of the second and third lines. The second of these is the more important, since so much of what follows depends on it; it is also the more mysterious. To begin to understand the force of "Is" in line 3, we have to decide whether its subject, "lust," the last word in line 2, is passion working within a given individual; or rather the lustful individual himself; or rather a partially allegorized Lust, a sort of personification out of Spenser; or rather the experience of gratification. If we read "this hell," the last words of the sonnet, to summarize all that has been predicated about lust, then we have to extend the meaning of that word to the object of male desire, since the word "hell" in subsequent sonnets will clearly acquire a specific anatomical reference.[5] "Lust" thus has four or five potential meanings that fade in and out or reinforce each other a little confusingly as the reader moves through the series of participles, nouns, and clauses that maintain the predication apparently through line 12. All the rich, disturbing intricacy of meaning hangs upon that "Is." Is lust "murderous" because it destroys the individual who feels it, or is he led to feel murderous toward the person he desires? Or toward himself? Is lust "cruell" toward other feelings and traits, virtues and vices, in a kind of shadowy psychomachia, or toward human beings? Are we dimly invited to half-imagine some hypostatized embodiment, some furious naked "salvage man" spotted with gore, both hunted and hated? How does that potential predication jibe with lust as bliss and woe in line 11? There the "salvage man" disappears and lust "is" the feelings stemming from the end of its quest.

Is it possible for so many alternative predications to be jammed into one uncertain copula? As we read we have to keep revising or recombining our notions of just how the signifier "lust" is, can be, something. We strain to grasp the mysterious equations implied in that deceptively innocent bridge. Only if we are puzzled by it will we begin to unravel its secrets. Booth's argument against distortion obscures the need for puzzlement. We need to register the actual warping, which from our perspective is there, before we can set out to deal with it. The distortion in the case of the copula is particularly insidious because modernization leaves it untouched.

"No editor," Booth writes, "is likely to succeed perfectly in accommodating a modern reader and a Renaissance text to one another, but that is no reason to do nothing."[6] The question is what one *can* do if one measures the full distance between the two. To do what Booth and most editors do risks a sham accommodation with the past which in fact increases our estrangement from it. How does the editor avoid that trap? To begin to answer this question satisfactorily one really needs a theory of understanding; one has to ask how a reader would evade the trap. One has to bracket the editorial problem and consider the larger problems of hermeneutic theory; one has to reflect on the process of understanding any remote text. The growing body of hermeneutic speculation is by no means irrelevant to the practical decisions of editors, just as the consequences of their decisions are not irrelevant to theory. The crucial question focused by Booth's polemic is not whether we want original or altered texts—both are necessary for different purposes—but rather how and to what degree a modern reader's experience might resemble that of the text's first readers.

No linguist would dissent from Sapir's formulation.

> Language moves down time in a current of its own making. It has a drift. . . . Nothing is perfectly static. Every word, every grammatical element, every locution, every sound and accent is a slowly changing configuration, moulded by the invisible and impersonal drift that is the life of language.[7]

This drift was first discovered for the modern world by Dante and the philologists of the Italian Renaissance. Lorenzo Valla insisted on the central dilemma of anachronistic reading with all the energy of his ferocious intelligence. Changing referents require changing terms: *nova res novum vocabulum flagitat.* But referents and words change at varying rates of speed. Language ideally requires a continuity which neither words nor things possess.

The fact of historical estrangement, historical solitude, is doubtless most fully grasped by those like Valla who spend their careers contending with it. The pathos of estrangement has never been evoked more beautifully than by one of the heroes of modern philology, Wilamowitz.

> The tradition yields us only ruins. The more closely we test and examine them, the more clearly we see how ruinous they are; and out of ruins no whole can be built. The tradition is dead; our task is to revivify life that has passed away. We know that ghosts cannot speak until they have drunk blood; and the spirits which we evoke demand the blood of our hearts. We give it to them gladly; but if they then abide our question, something from us has entered into them.[8]

A little of ourselves will always enter into the ghosts we force to speak. If, as Heidegger suggests, we are what we understand to be, then what we understand to be will already be a part of us. The conversation with our classics will always be partial; we can never altogether escape interpretive anachronism. "Which of your Hesterdays Mean Ye to Morra?": that Joycean song haunts the historian of meanings. It haunted Theodore

Adorno: "Nothing more is given to philosophy than fleeting, disappearing traces in the riddle-figures of that which exists and their astonishing entwinings."[9] We can love from the past only that which we have begun by misunderstanding and continue to understand gropingly. Perhaps this is why we love the shard, the ruin, the blurred hieroglyph, as we love those broken, discolored, weather-beaten statues, hieratic and withdrawn, standing at the portal of a cathedral.

One can approach the central hermeneutic problem through the experience of the classroom. The teacher is compelled by his role to perform a kind of activity analogous to textual modernization. He is obliged to translate, to find contemporary equivalents and glosses for his students in order to make a remote text "accessible." He can only present a literary work to them in their terms or in terms they can follow. In doing this the teacher has literally no choice. But if he is at all self-conscious, he knows that his glosses and his explanations are subtly or palpably inaccurate. How will he gloss the word "Spirit" at the opening of sonnet 129? He has no means of conveying the different feeling for syntactic closure of the English Renaissance. And what happens in the classroom is only a heightened imitation of what happens to the solitary reader in his study; he too inevitably translates into his own dialect. He appropriates, anachronizes, no matter how deep his historical consciousness. If we read sonnet 129 in its quarto version, we try to organize its apparent disorder and soften its offenses to our mind-set. To begin to read any unfamiliar text is to try to make it less strange, make it new. In Norman N. Holland's Freudian vocabulary, the act of reading involves "a kind of fusion or introjection based on oral wishes to incorporate."[10]

The act of appropriation has been described more than once in hermeneutic theory. Hans-Georg Gadamer calls it *Aneignung,* and Paul Ricoeur uses the French word *appropriation.* In the thought of each it has a positive resonance; ideally for each it leads to self-knowledge. For Ricoeur appropriation occurs when "the interpretation of a text is completed by the self-interpretation of a subject who henceforth understands himself better or differ-

ently or even begins to understand himself."[11] Gadamer quotes
with approval Hegel's statement that *Aneignung*—appropriation
or assimilation—"is the fundamental fact of being alive." But his
own hermeneutics invests the term with a somewhat different
significance. Gadamer's analysis of the entire process of understanding is very rich and sometimes profound. His perception of
its historicity, its "situatedness," his critique of nineteenth-century
historicism, his analysis of the mutual questioning between reader
and text, his quest for a dialogue across time—these and other
contributions to hermeneutic thought are welcome and valuable.
But other elements of his theory raise doubts about its viability as
a whole system.

According to Gadamer, understanding begins when
something other, something outside, addresses us. Something,
such as a text from the past, asserts its own validity, which is
distant from our own. In responding to this stimulus we are led
properly to an awareness of our own prejudices and can correct
our own preunderstandings through a circular process which is
not vicious but productive. The proper goal of the hermeneutic
encounter for Gadamer is a blending or fusion of horizons, a
horizontverschmelzung. This occurs when the interpreter widens his
own horizon of experience to include that of the text, reaches an
intuitive understanding of the questions the text poses and answers through the common medium of language; he thus enlarges
his own personal horizon, perceives it afresh, and gains insight
into both worlds now blended into one. This experience is possible
because both interpreter and text belong to a single continuous
tradition.

> Historical consciousness is aware of its own otherness and hence
> distinguishes the horizon of tradition from its own. On the other
> hand, it is itself . . . only something laid over a continuing tradition,
> and hence it immmediately recombines what it has distinguished
> in order, in the unity of the historical horizon that it thus acquires,
> to become again one with itself.[12]

This act of combining followed by a reassuring return
to selfhood is so smooth because the tradition for Gadamer is in

fact so "continuing"; it seems to be free of all revolts, gaps, leaps, and disjunctures. The concept of tradition becomes an instrument to tame, sweeten, and abstract history, which now appears purely unbroken and unalienating. It is true that Gadamer speaks of a tension between the two horizons. But functionally this tension counts for less than the blending mediation. Distance in time, Gadamer writes, is "not a yawning abyss, but is filled with the continuity of custom and tradition, in the light of which all that is handed down presents itself to us." Elsewhere he speaks of tradition as "an unbroken stream."[13] But tradition as we know it may not be a healing, sacred river but a polluting Love Canal which carries dangerous flotsam. Tradition as a stream has many tributaries, falls, and blockages. It runs less smoothly than this account suggests, and the history of interpretation as we know it reveals the defenses interpreters have had to raise against the threat of tradition.

What if the tension between horizons proves to be intolerable? Allegoresis developed partly as one defense against unwelcome meanings suspected in past texts; we in our day have abandoned allegoresis for a more economical defense, ironization. If a given text, say More's *Utopia*, asserts too emphatically its estrangement from us, we shield ourselves by reading it ironically. Frank Kermode has recently shown the affinities of interpretation not with a fresh openness but with an enclosing institutionalism, with a group of insiders reluctant to open their gateway and reveal their arcane knowledge.[14] Graves and Riding, we remember, wrote very consciously as outsiders against one form of institutional protectionism.

The actual status of the original text emerges from Gadamer's formulation a little blurred.

> The true historical object is not an object at all, but the unity of the one [the object] and the other [true historial thinking taking account of its own historicality], a relationship in which exist both the reality of history and the reality of historical understanding.[15]

If the true object is not an object, then it is difficult to see how it can form half of a higher unity. For Gadamer the text has no existence independent of the tradition in which it is understood; in effect he denies the text an original historical situatedness such as he claims for the interpreter. This denial calls into question the equality of the dialogue as well as the tension between horizons. Essentially the text is robbed of its own particular horizon. The supposed dialogue lacks symmetry because only the interpreter's governing assumptions are called into play, not those of the text. The context of each work is not its original, living semiotic matrix but rather a series of posthumous readings. Gadamer in his own way wants to protect us from our solitude. The resulting concept of appropriation fails to isolate its potential self-deception. His account of understanding blurs a little the central problem of interpretation: language changes, modes of experience change, texts become estranged, and yet the contact with texts in their authentic otherness would provide precious knowledge and self-knowledge, would save us from a hermeneutic narcissism Gadamer himself is eager to avoid.

My own plea would be for a moment in the process of understanding which no hermeneutics has authorized. I would ask for a moment which deliberately tries to frustrate appropriation, which tries to restore the work to its own world of meanings perceived in all their distant strangeness. Simply to draw the work to ourselves, willfully, voraciously, is to dim that clarification which contact with otherness does truly bring. Let us for a moment refuse to appropriate; let us try, however unsuccessfully, to return the work to its own mysterious alienation. Instead of clutching it too quickly, we should recognize its isolation and vulnerability, recognize what deceives our expectations, offends our proprieties, refuses dialogue, will not abide our questions. We need to measure without blinking the pathos of estrangement, the ruptures of history, the blockages of tradition.[16]

It is true that this act of distancing the work is itself subject to the distortions of our historicial moment. But if our distortions are to be progressively corrected, they will not be affected by a bland tradition but by perceived interruptions of tradition. Let us try for a moment to overcome that force which Heidegger calls "averageness" (Durchschnittlichkeit) and which, he says, smoothly suppresses every kind of spiritual priority. "Overnight," he writes, "everything that is primordial gets glossed over as something that has long been well known. . . Every secret loses its force."[17] Let us try to recover that sense of the work's forceful secrecy. Let us for a moment refuse to understand.

The response to that moment can take one of two directions. One alternative would be to find a freedom in this impasse, call the rupture radical and total, and play with the flotsam of the past as context-free, neutral counters to be juggled at will. This response would free the interpreter from any responsibility to a vestige of original meaning, which, according to Jacques Derrida, will undergo a loss inherent in the character of all utterances. One can then appropriate with a vengeance, liberated from all constraints; one might even hope with Derrida to take a kind of Nietzschean joy in an endless innocent game of free associations. The one thing excluded from such play would of course be the stimulus of contact as well as the risk; there could be no dangerous impact which would challenge and conceivably clarify. The work interpreted would be an inkblot test in which the interpreter would reveal over and over only his own obsessions without understanding them, lacking any transcendental key to make sense of his private musings. Derrida's own discussions of texts by Plato, Descartes, Leibniz, Rousseau, Hegel, and others do not in fact play with them freely and "innocently," but tend rather to subject these texts to precise and often brilliant analysis which assumes personal time-bound authorship.[18] Everyone doubtless has a right to his own avocations, but some will be moved to ask, as Shakespeare asks his friend: "Why dost thou spend, upon thy selfe thy beauties legacy?" For some, the pleasure of the "profitless usurer" quickly loses its charm.

The alternative to this hermeneutic play with free associations would be much more austere. This course would try to avoid that self-indulgence as it avoided the opposite mirror indulgence that denies the work's estrangement. This hermeneutic would accept estrangement as a given and then search out patiently some bridge, some passage, some common term, which might help to mitigate it. On this basis one would suspect all modernized versions and easy assimilations, one would settle for less than full understanding, but one would accept a responsibility for a partial interpretive correspondence to an intrinsic meaning or complex of meanings. One would think not of appropriating but of working out a reading appropriate to those intrinsic meanings. One would conceive of a text coming to us bearing its own intentionality—not the intentionality of its creator but simply its own patent design for a certain kind of use. A chair exists to be sat on; a text exists to be read and read *appropriately*, within certain limits of potential response. It carries with it coded directions or provocations to the mind, and certain types of mental responses befit a given text more closely than others. The task of the reader is to ascertain the experience or the activity most perfectly corresponding to the text's coded instigations.

In the case of a remote text—and no formula can specify how remote is "remote"—the directions or instigations will always be blurred, but one accepts a need to begin deciphering them. In the case of a mathematical equation one can think of the directions to the mind as *commands* to perform certain operations; in the case of a poem one can think of the directions rather as *orientations*. To interpret, Ricoeur writes suggestively, is to set out toward the *orient* of the text. To think of interpreting as an appropriate response to coded but blurred directions is not to limit the potential wealth of suggestion of a literary work, but it is to rule out the expense of spirit in self-indulgent anachronism. The wealth of significance has to stem from the work's concrete historial situation as we can best divine it.[19] If it does this, then we may gain a small accretion of self-knowledge. In the case of Shakespeare's sonnets, this would include—what can be gathered from most Renaissance poems—the limiting regularity, the hypertrophy of logic in our assumtpions about words and syntax; in the case of sonnet 129, this might include an altered view of the pallid, therapeutic sexuality of our post-Freudian era, Eliot's "natural, life-giving, cheery automatism,"[20] which is not of course to be found in Freud. But these crude indications of acquired self-consciousness badly approximate the gradual, profound growth of understanding whereby we slowly and fumblingly come to situate ourselves in history.[21]

The first, simple, and difficult act of reading is to see

the remote text as truly remote. To begin to measure its removal from us, to intuit its privacy and specificity, to make out the density of its aura, one has to restore it to its original silence. The text comes to us as a shard, out of its own quietude and distance; by disencumbering it of its secular impediments, by stripping it of its false modernity, we release it to withdraw from us back into its own universe of meanings, cruelly and beautifully back where we can gauge its strangeness. In that strangeness begins true knowledge, the true partial knowledge that history allows us. We can begin to read only after granting the text the seclusion and the particularity of its unique inflection.

10

Pitiful Thrivers:
Failed Husbandry in the *Sonnets*

Sonnet 125 of Shakespeare's collection ("Wer't ought to me I bore the canopy") is the penultimate poem in the series addressed to the male friend. It is the last complete sonnet in this series, and in comparison with its somewhat slighter successor, 126, it appears to offer a more substantial, dense, and conclusive instrument of retrospection. It opens by distinguishing the poet from those who court his friend's love by means of external gestures, "dwellers on forme and favor," but who see their calculations fail and are condemned to admire the young man from a distance: "pittiful thrivors in their gazing spent." The poet's own devotion, he claims, consists purely of uncalculated internal gestures and it leads to a genuine, unmediated exchange.

> Noe, let me be obsequious in thy heart,
> And take thou my oblacion, poore but free,
> Which is not mixt with seconds, knows no art,
> But mutuall render onely me for thee.[1]

The couplet dismisses a "subbornd Informer," a slanderer who might accuse the poet himself of dwelling on form. But despite this calumny, the affirmation of the "mutuall render" between the two men acquires in the context of the whole collection a peculiar resonance. It can be regarded as a culminating moment in the twisting history of their relationship, and our understanding of the outcome of the "plot" in sonnets 1–126 depends in part on our interpretation of this phrase. Contrariwise, fully to grasp the implications of the phrase and the sonnet requires consideration of all that precedes, and even to some degree what follows. An informed reading will necessitate a long swing backward before returning to 125.

Within its immediate context, this is the third of three successive sonnets affirming that the poet's love for his friend is untouched by external accidents. This succession (123–25) needs to be read in the light of an earlier group (109–12) alluding to the poet's shameful and scandalous conduct and another group (117–21) alluding to the poet's apparent neglect and betrayal of the friend. Thus, if one attributes validity to the quarto sequence, the three protests of uncalculating devotion follow almost directly an experience of partial rupture, and they attempt to cement a reconciliation which has been to some degree in doubt.

But from a wider perspective, sonnet 125 is responding to problems raised from the very opening of the collection. Its resolution of pure exchange could be said to respond to the anxiety of cosmic and existential economics that haunts the sonnets and that marks their opening line: "From fairest creatures we desire increase." The paronomasia which links the two nouns translates phonetically the poet's obsessive concern with metaphorical wealth, profit, worth, value, expense, "store," "content." The "pittiful thrivors" of 125 take their place in a line of disappointed or misguided would-be thrivers distributed throughout the work. The "mutuall render," if in fact it is successful, would thus bring to a happy conclusion a quest for an adequate economic system which would avoid the "'wast or ruining" and the excessive "rent" which burden those in 125 who vainly spend themselves. Up to the climactic reciprocity at the close of that sonnet, the sequence to the young man has provided very little by way of stable exchange systems.

The first of the pitiful thrivers is the onanistic friend as he appears in the opening seventeen "procreation sonnets." By refusing to marry and to beget children, he "makst wast in niggarding" (1); he becomes a "profitles userer" "having traffike with [him] selfe alone" (4). The procreation sonnets display with particular brilliance Shakespeare's ability to manipulate words which in his language belonged both to the economic and the sexual/biological semantic fields: among others, "increase," "use," "spend," "free," "live," "dear," "house," "usury," "endowed," along with their cognates. The umbrella-pun which cov-

ers them all and which establishes a semantic node for the whole
collection lies in still another word: "husbandry."

> For where is she so faire whose un-eard wombe
> Disdaines the tillage of thy husbandry? (3)

The *ad hoc* meaning of "marriage" joins the traditional meanings
of "thrift," "estate management," "agriculture," and, by means
of a conventional metaphor, coition as ploughing. When the pun
returns ten sonnets later, the dominant meaning will emerge as
management.

> Who lets so faire a house fall to decay,
> Which husbandry in honour might uphold,
> Against the stormy gusts of winters day
> And barren rage of deaths eternall cold? (13)

"House" means both the friend's body (the *banhus*, "bonehouse,"
of the Anglo-Saxon kenning) and the family line. The bourgeois
poet accuses the aristocratic friend of a dereliction of those re-
sponsibilities incumbent on the landowning class. The apparent
implication is that through marriage the friend could "live" (4),
could make a profit by perpetuating his family.

But if, in the procreation sonnets, thriving seems ostensibly within the young man's grasp, one must recognize nonetheless the disproportionate force of the thwarting power, the
"barren rage of deaths eternall cold." Procreation progressively
comes to appear as a desperate defense, a final maneuver against
a principle which is ultimately irresistible.

> And nothing gainst Times sieth [scythe] can make defence
> Save breed to brave him, when he takes thee hence. (12)

The recurrent terror of "winters wragged hand" (6), particularly
notable in this opening group, comes to cast doubt on the viability
of marriage. Or rather, in view of the threatening "barenes everywhere" (5), husbandry emerges as a universal, existential concern
that transcends the addressee's marital status. It even becomes a
concern of the poetry we are reading, which alternately promises
to "ingraft" the friend anew in the war with Time (15) only to
describe itself as "barren" in the sequel (16). The friend, "making

a famine where aboundance lies" (1), may after all be closer to the governing principle of the world, in which case the poet and his poetry are left in a confusing limbo.

Thus a terrible fear of cosmic destitution overshadows the husbandry of the procreation sonnets, a fear in excess of the announced argument, not easily circumscribed, rendering the bourgeois desire for "store" more urgent, eccentric, and obsessive. In the main body of the sonnets to the young man (18–126), this fear continues to find frequent expression, but it is also localized much more explicitly in the poet's feelings about himself. The poetry reflects a sense of inner depletion, emptiness, poverty, which the friend is asked or stated to fill up; elsewhere it reflects a nakedness which the friend is asked to clothe. Sometimes the language evoking the friend's role might suggest literal patronage; elsewhere it might suggest a literal filling up through sex; but each of these literalizations taken alone would reduce the quality of the expressed need. The sense of depletion is more radical and more diffused, and it is inseparable from feelings of worthlessness and deprivation. Sonnet 29 ("When in disgrace with Fortune . . .") represents the speaker

> Wishing me like to one more rich in hope,
> Featur'd like him, like him with friends possest,
> Desiring this mans art, and that mans skope,
> With what I most inioy contented least.

The language faintly underscores the economic character of this despondency. Friends, if they existed, would be possessed. "Rich in hope" means both "endowed with hope" and "rich in prospect." "Inioy" here means "possess" as well as "take pleasure in" (Booth), thus justifying a secondary reading of "contented least": "poorest in whatever I own of worth." This privation is only relieved by thoughts of the friend: "thy sweet love remembred . . . welth brings," and this transfer is dramatized by the imagistic wealth of the lark simile interrupting the rhetorical bareness of the octave.

In the following sonnet 30 ("When to the sessions . . ."), the poet laments the deaths of precious friends, moans the expense of many a vanished sight, pays anew "the sad account of fore-bemoned mone," until with remembrance of his friend "all losses are restord, and sorrowes end." In 26 ("Lord of my love . . ."), the poet sends his naked poetry as an offering to his liege lord, hoping that the friend will dress the drab language in "some good conceipt of thine," will "[put] apparel on my tottered loving." Dressing the tottered (tattered) loving might mean making the poet more eloquent or more rich or more accomplished as a lover, but the nakedness seems finally to transcend rhetoric or money or seductiveness. In 38 ("How can my Muse . . ."), the friend is once again filling a void.

> How can my Muse want subiect to invent
> While thou dost breath that poor'st into my verse
> Thine own sweet argument?

The friend plays the masculine role, pouring his worth into the otherwise barren verse, leaving the poet with the travail of giving birth but rightly taking credit for any success: "The paine be mine, but thine shal be the praise." In this economic system, all value seems to reside in the friend, or in *thoughts* of the friend, and the poet seems to be a leaky vessel constantly in need of replenishing, his personal and linguistic poverty never definitively abolished.

This system, however, rests on a shaky basis. The worth of the friend may reside after all in the poet's own fancy, as at least one passage may be understood to suggest.

> So then I am not lame, poore, nor dispisd,
> Whilst that this shadow doth such substance give,
> That I in thy abundance am suffic'd. (37)

The substance of abundance may actually derive from the shadow of projection. This doubt becomes more plausible as fears of betrayal mount:

> Thou best of deerest, and mine onely care,
> Art left the prey of every vulgar theefe (48)

and as the fears are realized in the young man's affair with the poet's mistress (40–42): "Both finde each other, and I loose both twaine" (42). In other sonnets apparently free of jealousy, a threat to the friend's worth looms from the cosmic mutability already evoked in the procreation sonnets, and now an alternative economic system situates the source of value in the poetry of the sonnets. The poetry, elsewhere naked, becomes in these poems an artifact that successfully resists time and death, assures eternal life to the one it celebrates, distills his truth for the ages, acts as a perpetuating force against "mortall rage" (64). In the sonnets which affirm this source of value, the young man is represented as a potential victim, helpless against the cosmic principle of destruction, passive, disarmed, doomed without the saving power of "my verse." Verse preserves, engrafts, refurbishes; it seems informed with a masculine force the friend lacks. He remains in this system the beneficiary of a gift his worth draws to itself, but this worth is not otherwise active. "Where alack shall times best Iewell from times chest lie hid?" (65). The young man's excellence is a plunderable commodity, as it is elsewhere perishable; inert as a precious stone, it belongs to the world of basic elements in flux, "increasing store with losse, and losse with store" (64). The alleged source of genuine "store" in this class of sonnets is the poetry.

Yet it is noteworthy that the affirmations of this linguistic power tend to appear in the couplets of their sonnets (15, 18, 19, 54, 60, 63, 65; exceptions are 55 and 81). The couplets moreover tend to lack the energy of the negative vision in the twelve lines that precede them. The final affirmation in its flaccidity tends to refute itself; the *turn* fails to reverse the rhetorical momentum adequately, as the language loses its wealth and its potency while asserting them.

> His beautie shall in these blacke lines be seene,
> And they shall live, and he in them still greene. (63)

> O none, unlesse this miracle have might,
> That in black inck my love may still shine bright. (65)

The turn toward restoration can be read as a desperate bourgeois maneuver, struggling to shore up the cosmic economy against the mutability which instigates true verbal power. The poetry arguably fails to celebrate, refurbish, the worth of the young man. The worth remains abstract, faceless, blurred, even when it is not tainted.

Thus we are left with two distinct sources of alleged value, the friend and the poetry, each the basis for a rudimentary economic system, each vulnerable to skepticism. The presence of each system tends to destabilize the other by casting doubt on the kind of value it attempts to establish. To cite the poetic convention behind each system does not adequately deal with its constituent presence in this work. At stake in this conflict of systems is the status and force of the poetic word, which alternately shares its maker's hollowness and serves his (narcissistic?) fantasies of power. The one system, the one relationship, which is *not* to be found before the last sonnets to the friend is equal, direct, un-mediated reciprocity. Reciprocity is unattainable partly because of the poet's social inferiority and, so to speak, his felt "human" inferiority, because the friend frequently appears in thought, fan-tasy, or memory rather than in the flesh, because the adulatory style intermittently gives way to suspicion, resentment, fear, anger (33–35, 40–42, 57–58, 67, 69, etc.) that militate negatively against equality, because the friend as an individual remains a "shadow," undescribed, voiceless, hazy, dehumanized by the very superlatives he attracts, and because the poetry, however unclear its status, is repeatedly presented as the binding agent of media-tion, an essential go-between. It is not clear whether *any* of the sonnets is to be read as a spoken address, a dramatic monologue, rather than as a written communication. Many of them refer to themselves *as* written, refer to paper, ink, pens, and to poetic style. They may occasionally affirm a closeness between poet and friend, but their very existence suggests a distance which has to be crossed. We are never allowed to envision unambiguously the poet in the presence of his friend, as we are in love poems by Wyatt, Sidney, Spenser, and Donne.

The conflicting representations of the poetry's power (potent or weak?), its gender (male or female?), its durability (perennial or transient?), together with its mediating function between the two men raise questions about what might be called its rhetorical economics. The poetry is distinguished by its super-

charged figurative density, its inexhaustible ramifications of suggestion, its insidious metaphoric multiplications, a superfetation
which might have been accumulated to avoid at all cost the alleged
danger of nakedness. The poetry could be working to refute its
own self-accusations of dearth and repetition.

> Why is my verse so barren of new pride?
> So far from variation or quicke change? . . .
> So all my best is dressing old words new,
> Spending again what is already spent. (76)

As though to adorn the monotony, every rift is loaded with ore,
to the degree that the rhetorical density can be read as an extraordinary effort to exorcise that stylistic poverty the poetry imputes
to itself. The poet may feel himself to be depleted, but he evidently
owns enough wit to spend it extravagantly. Yet this very super-
charging of language tends to heighten a certain impression of
linguistic slippage. Metaphors are mixed, replaced by others, recalled, jostled, interfused, inverted, disguised, dangled, eroded, in
ways which blur meanings as they are enriched.

> Nativity once in the maine of light,
> Crawles to maturity, wherewith being crown'd,
> Crooked eclipses gainst his glory fight,
> And time that gave, doth now his gift confound. (60)

The enriching of metaphor, a putative demonstration of the poet's
real potency, is indistinguishable from a mutability of metaphor,
a fragmentation which might be said to demonstrate instability.
By this reading the process of verbal enrichment would coincide
with a process of deterioration; indeed the enrichment might be
perceived as leading to the slippage, "increasing store with losse,
and losse with store." The poetry would then come to resemble a
pail of the Danaides, and the questions regarding the poet's potency would remain open.

     That poetic potency is related here to sexual potency
is made clear beyond cavil by the rival poet group (78–80, 82–
86). The other poet is a rival both for patronage and for sexual
favors, and his rhetorical brilliance (or bombast) is associated with
his glittering seductiveness. Thus the poetic speaker is doubly

threatened by "the proud full saile of his great verse, bound for the prize of (al to precious) you" (86). The revealing word here is *proud,* which meant "lecherous" as well as "stately" and "ostentatious." Cognate forms have already appeared in 80, which constitutes a tissue of sexual double meanings and interweaves poetic competition inextricably with erotic.

> O how I faint when I of you do write,
> Knowing a better spirit doth use your name,
> And in the praise thereof spends all his might,
> To make me toung-tide speaking of your fame.
> But since your worth (wide as the Ocean is)
> The humble as the proudest saile doth beare,
> My sawcie barke (inferior farre to his)
> On your broad maine doth wilfully appeare.
> Your shallowest helpe will hold me up a floate,
> Whilst he upon your soundlesse deepe doth ride,
> Or (being wrackt) I am a worthlesse bote,
> He of tall building, and of goodly pride.
>   Then If he thrive and I be cast away,
>   The worst was this, my love was my decay.

So many words have sexual meanings ("use," "spends," "proudest," "saucy," "wilfully," "ride," "pride"—by attraction, "tall building") that the reader is tempted to interpret the sonnet primarily in erotic terms. But it opens with a contrast of the rivals as writers before shifting in lines 11–12 to a presumptive contrast of physical endowments. It is true that the analogy of the possibly promiscuous love object with the ocean will return more crudely and unambiguously in the dark lady group (134). But if language is presented in 80 as a means to seduction, seduction on the other hand may consist simply of verbal overpowering. "Love" and poetic language are linked so closely that the primary meaning of the final clause would seem to be "my inadequate verse has led to my rejection." The contrast of the rivals underscores what the speaker will shortly call his *penury,* a word which brings together his financial, poetic, and sexual shortcomings but which leaves uncertain what is figure and what ground. At any rate the rival, however we regard his challenge, introduces a complicating factor in the economics of the sonnets, by appearing to "thrive" (l. 13) while the speaker is ruined. In spending more, verbally, sartorially, and sexually, he may get more. Yet in the end he and his new patron will be revealed as devalued, the one by the vulgarity of his praise and the other by the vulgarity of the pleasure he takes in it. They are pitiful thrivers both. So at least the poet suggests, and he follows the rival poet group with a temporary kiss-off, not without sarcasm.

> Farewell thou art too deare for my possessing,
> And like enough thou knowst thy estimate. (87)

Farewell also to the theme of poetry's immortalizing power: with two brief exceptions (100, 107), it will disappear from the collection.

The rival poet group is of interest because it confirms the implicit linkage between monetary, verbal, and sexual "pride," and because it complicates the linkage between these forms of power and deeper, vaguer intrinsic "worth." The group is equally of interest because it throws up, almost incidentally, a revealing formulation of the sonnets' essential vulnerability, a formulation which will prove useful when we return to our starting point in sonnet 125.

> Who is it that sayes most, which can say more,
> Then this rich praise, that you alone, are you,
> In whose confine immured is the store,
> Which should example where your equall grew,
> Leane penurie within that Pen doth dwell,
> That to his subiect lends not some small glory,
> But he that writes of you, if he can tell,
> That you are you, so dignifies his story.
> Let him but coppy what in you is writ. (84)

The pen is penurious which can't add to its subject, but a praiser of the friend is subject to this penury, since in him "are locked up all the qualities needed to provide an equal example."[2] The friend's alleged excellence is such that no metaphors are available, no imagistic equivalent is possible, and the authentic praiser will limit himself to pure representation ("Let him but coppy . . ."). Only by representing accurately, achieving a perfect counterpart of the young man, will the poet overcome penury, "making his stile admired every where."

But this last solution, in its context, proves to be unsatisfactory on several grounds. First it fails to escape epideictic drabness, by the poet's own showing. It leaves the poetry "barren of new pride," spending again the respent, "keep[ing] invention in a noted weed" (76). Second, he who is to be copied proves to be less of a Platonic idea than a changeable and fallible human; for that revelation we need go no further than the couplet of this sonnet (84), with its malicious glance at the rival's demeaning flattery.

> You to your beautious blessings adde a curse.
> Being fond on praise, which makes your praises worse.

A certain pathology of praise can infect both parties. But the third and most momentous reason why the copy solution fails is that pure representation in language is not of this world. Poetry depends on figuration, but precise figural adequation is unattainable. What is said with ostensible hyperbole in the opening quatrain—that no "example" can serve as "equall" to the young man—is universally true. To attempt not to add to one's subject may court penury, as sonnet 84 argues, but the real failure lies in the necessity of accepting addition, of employing "compounds strange" (76), as the sonnets most decidedly do and as all poetry does. Poetry as representation will always be vulnerable, because in its shifting mass of meanings it can never copy with absolute precision and because that which is copied changes, gains and loses value. The economics of copying reserves its own pitfalls for aspirant thrivers; the pen is bound to be penurious.

Sonnet 105 betrays a similar vulnerability.

> Let not my love be cal'd Idolatrie,
> Nor my beloved as an Idoll show,
> Since all alike my songs and praises be
> To one, of one, still such, and ever so.
> Kinde is my love to day, to morrow kinde,
> Still constant in a wondrous excellence,

> Therefore my verse to constancie confin'de,
> One thing expressing, leaves out difference.
> Faire, kinde, and true, is all my argument,
> Faire, kinde and true, varrying to other words,
> And in this change is my invention spent,
> Three theams in one, which wondrous scope affords.
>   Faire, kinde, and true, have often liv'd alone.
>   Which three till now, never kept seate in one.

This appears to be another apology for an allegedly plain style. (I follow Ingram and Redpath in interpreting "Since" in line 3 as introducing the reason for the accusation, not its defense; the latter begins in line 5.) Although the poet claims to hew single-mindedly to a unique theme with the same constant language, he cannot, he says, be accused of idolatry because the friend, in his inalterable generosity, deserves no less. The poetry "leaves out difference," spending its invention by varying three words in others. One might argue that *some* difference is already present in this variation. But there are differences in the word "difference" itself, as one learns from a glance at Booth's paragraph on the word; among its relevant meanings are "variety," "anything else," "disagreement," "hostility." *Constant* means both "invariable" and "faithful"; *kinde* means both "generous" and "true to his own nature"; *spent*, that ubiquitous word, means both "used" and "exhausted." The sonnets escape the charge of idolatry not because the man they celebrate remains correspondingly unchanging (he is nothing if not inconstant, in both senses) but because they fail to express one thing and systematically admit difference. They alternately valorize and deplore a plain stylistic constancy which they cannot achieve.

The problem of "difference" like the related problem of accurate representation is pertinent to the affirmation of mutuality which concludes the long section of sonnets to the young man. Before we reach that affirmation, we hear of derelictions on both sides, derelictions grave enough to undermine the fragile economic systems in force earlier. The falsity of the friend, a mansion of vices (95), produces a policy of husbandry the precise reverse of that recommended in the procreation sonnets; now it is those who remain aloof from others like a stone who "husband natures ritches from expence" (94). The poet for his part has made himself a motley to the view, "sold cheap what is most deare" (110), blemished himself and his love. We have already noted the waning of poetry's asserted power as an immortalizing agent. As the sonnets spiral downward in a vortex of betrayal, counterbetrayal, and justifications not untouched with sophistry, we look for an economic alternative to mere self-deception, that "alcumie . . . creating every bad a perfect best" (114). Something like this alternative can be glimpsed briefly in 120, where the mutuality of suffering and dishonor might produce mutual guilt in compassion and lead to an exchange of quasi-Christian redemption.

> But that your trespasse now becomes a fee,
> Mine ransoms yours, and yours must ransome mee.

This glimpse of reciprocity in shared weakness fades, however, and leads to that group of three (123–25) with which we began, a group essentially protesting the poet's freedom from self-interest and the enduring purity of his feelings, which will never flag and can dispense with ostentatious demonstrations. The last of this group culminates in the proffered "mutual render" between poet and friend, before the very last poem to the friend, 126, returns to the theme of time and anticipates Nature's final, mortal settling of accounts: "her *Quietus* is to render thee."

A skeptical reading of these concluding gambits would represent them as repressing artificially the pain and guilt which have already surfaced and which will surface even more harshly in the dark lady group to follow. In their context these protests of fidelity, which "nor growes with heat, nor drownes with showres" (124), could be regarded as attempts to mask the real bankruptcy of the relationship. The negative stress of 123–25, lingering over that change (123), "policy" (124), form (125), the poet abjures, might well be read as symptomatic of a bad conscience whose spokesman would be the (internal) accusatory informer of 125. This repressive character of the final sonnets could plausibly be linked to their return to a relatively aureate style after the burst of directness earlier (as in 120—"y'have past a hell of Time"). This *suspicion* of the excessive protest does hang over the concluding group, deepened by their conspicuous discontinuity with their context. Yet a purely cynical reading would strain out that element of real wishing which is also present. The reader can recognize the implausibility of the asserted constancy while regarding the struggle to hope, the conative pathos, with respect.

The crucial sonnet in this group is 125, since it seems to offer at last the possibility of a stable existential economics, a definitive end to penury, a compensation for the expense of living and feeling, even though it does this like its predecessors in large part by exclusion.

> Wer't ought to me I bore the canopy,
> With my extern the outward honoring,
> Or layd great bases for eternity,
> Which proves more short then wast or ruining?   4
> Have I not seene dwellers on forme and favor
> Lose all, and more by paying too much rent
> For compound sweet; Forgoing simple savor,
> Pittiful thrivors in their gazing spent.   8
> Noe, let me be obsequious in thy heart,
> And take thou my oblacion, poore but free,
> Which is not mixt with seconds, knows no art,
> But mutuall render onely me for thee.   12
>   Hence, thou subbornd *Informer*, a trew soule
>   When most impeacht, stands least in thy controule.

Lines 1–12 are ostensibly responding to the calumny of the un-identified informer of line 13, a calumny whose content we can determine only through its refutation. This consists in a repudiation of what might be called affective formalism, external gestures of dutifulness like the carrying of a canopy of state over a monarch's head. Suitors who employ such external gestures may believe that they prepare in this way for an everlasting intimacy with him whose favor they court, but the intimacy "paradoxically turns out to be briefer than the time required to run through an estate by extravagance" (Ingram and Redpath). We have still another example of failed husbandry, combining formalism with the kind of decadent sophistication which would prefer cloying, elaborate sauces ("compound sweet") to the familiar taste of homely fare.

"Forme" (l. 5) brings together the young man's physical figure, the ceremonial of line 1, exaggerated courtesy, hollow gestures of servility, and the craft which produces "compound sweet," artificial confections of any sort, but which is allegedly absent from the poet's oblation. "Compound sweet" recalls the poetic "compounds strange" of 76, which the poet there reproached himself for omitting from his own verse. This suggests that dwellers on form are also ambitious poets whose style is overwrought. The image of the projected manor house in line 3 is faintly sustained by "ruining" in 4, "dwellers" in 5, "rent" in 6, and the possible allusion to compound and simple interest in 7. This version of negative formalism ends with the loaded word "spent" in 8, in which so much meaning has sedimented throughout the work; here it means "bankrupted," "exhausted," "failed," ironically "summed up" in reliance on visual externals, and doubtless also "drained of semen," as the suitors' sexual designs are reduced to voyeurism. Unsuccessful entrepreneurs, with only the groundworks built of their mansion of love, the failure of their misguided, formalist generosity is symbolized by the suitors' symbolic distance from their prize, observable but not touchable.

Lines 9–12 supply the poet's redemptive version of erotic ceremonial, which substitutes the Eucharistic oblation for the canopied court procession. In this secularized sacrament, the dutiful ("obsequious") poet freely makes an offering intended to manifest the inwardness and simplicity of his own devotion, knowing, or thinking that he knows, that his oblation will win him that unmediated, inner reciprocity which is his goal. The oblation which "knows no art," free from the charge of formalism, is that poetry which, as in 105, is confined to constancy, "to one, of one, still such, and ever so." Just as in 105 it "leaves out difference," in 125 it "is not mixt with seconds." Yet ironically and pathetically, the word *oblacion is* mixed with a transcendent Second, the deity of the Communion service, so that the metaphor can only be regarded as a very strange, and somewhat ambiguous, compound indeed. The use of the sacramental term leaves the reader uncertain just how much weight to accord it and, by introducing the unbridgeable hierarchy of human and divine, would seem to annul in advance the pure reciprocity of the "mutuall render." To deny the operation of art requires art, and this art will prohibit the reciprocal affective mutuality toward which the whole work has seemed to want to move.

To compose poetry is expensive, just as loving is expensive, and the unformulated implication of the work as a whole seems to be that expense is never truly recuperated. The increase we desire from fairest creatures never materializes. Spending leaves one spent, and it fails to buy immediacy; it places a residue of compound feeling and compound language between lover and beloved. Here in 125 the very word *seconds* is a compound. It means primarily "merchandise of inferior quality," but it associates itself with the "compound sweet" and thus with that formalist craft from which the oblation is supposedly pure. By banning "seconds" from his poetry, the poet introduces a "second," which is to say a metaphor, and one which is complicated with still more implications. Language is condemned to be compound; poetry *is* art; it shapes and forms and distorts; it introduces inequalities, like the inequality between an offering and an exchange, or the inequality between a secular offering and the sacramental body of Christ.

Thus neither a "pure" offering (Booth discerns this "second" meaning in the word *poore*) nor a pure mutuality is possible in a relationship which depends on the word; still less is it possible when the word, as here, is always presented as written. In a curious sonnet which immediately precedes the group 123–25, the poet reports that he has given away a gift he had received from the friend. This gift had been a notebook, "tables." It is unclear whether the notebook contained writing by the friend or memorials of the relationship by the poet or had been so intended by the giver but been allowed to remain blank. The stress in any case falls on the superior retentiveness of the poet's mind and heart, in contrast to the limits of the "tables."

> That poore retention could not so much hold,
> Nor need I tallies thy deare love to skore. (122)

To dispose of the notebook which contained or might have contained a written record suggests a deep dissatisfaction with language as a mediating instrument. The verb "to skore," to keep a tally, is used contemptuously, as though to insinuate that writing involves a petty arithmetic of feeling. What is striking is that the writing before us has done precisely that, has supplied us with the tallies of an intimate cost accounting. The phrase in 122 may be scornful, and yet both inside and outside the poetic fiction, the language of the poetry is all we have, keeping the score and keeping an ambiguous distance open between the tarnished lovers. As that space widens, the poet begins to look like the dwellers on form and favor, spent in his gazing across a distance. He and perhaps the friend as well become pitiful thrivers, barred from the absolute immediacy at least one of them yearns for, because poetry can never be idolatrously one and can never find the metaphor, the "example," which knows no difference. The poet's real enemy is not the "informer" as slanderer, but the voice within himself through whose forming action feeling comes into being.

In the sonnets to the dark lady that follow, poetic language is thematized less prominently; the poet's sense of inner poverty modulates to self-contempt; the physiological meanings of such words as "expense" and "will" are foregrounded. The mistress, who has "robd others beds revenues of their rents" (142), is perhaps the one thriver in the work who is not pitiful. Her role is antithetical to the young man's of the procreation sonnets; she is a "usurer that put'st forth all to use" (134) and her wealth is like the ocean's.

> The sea all water, yet receives raine still,
> And in aboundance addeth to his store,
> So thou beeing rich in *Will* adde to thy *Will,*
> One will of mine to make thy large *Will* more.

But this inflationary economy leads to a depreciation of all values, and the only feasible policy apparently lies in a Christian husbandry.

> Why so large cost having so short a lease,
> Dost thou upon thy fading mansion spend? . . .
> Buy tearmes divine in selling houres of drosse:
> Within be fed, without be rich no more. (146)

By the close of the sequence, however, the poet does not seem to have adopted this policy. In his disgust with sexuality and his own revolting entrapment in it, the poet tries systematically to subvert his own authority as poet and his perception of metaphoric congruence.

> O Me! what eyes hath love put in my head,
> Which have no correspondence with true sight. (148)

Language is systematically vulgarized, "abhored," and in the last regular sonnet to the mistress (152), the coherence of the poetic consciousness and the integrity of the poetic statement are simultaneously denied, as though the poetry had no legitimate source.

> For I have sworne thee faire; more periurde eye,
> To swere against the truth so foule a lie.

The "eye" is perjured, but also the "I" and the "aye," the capacity to affirm. "Loves eye is not so true as all mens: no" (148). It is as though the pitiless obscenity, love-denying and love-blaspheming, had to expose the *pudenda* of language to register the meanness of the seamy loyalties and tawdry bargains.

The sonnets can be read to the end as attempts to cope with progressively powerful and painful forms of cost and expense. The bourgeois desire to balance cosmic and human budgets seems to be thwarted by a radical flaw in the universe, in emotion, in value, and in language. This flaw is already acted out at the beginning by the onanistic friend who "feed'st thy lights flame with selfe substantiall fewell" (1). In sonnet 73, the metaphoric fire lies in its ashes as on a deathbed, "consum'd with that which it was nurrisht by." This becomes, in the terrible sonnet 129, "a blisse in proofe and proud and very wo," a line always, unnecessarily, emended. The vulnerability of the sonnets lies in their ceaselessly resistant reflection of this flaw, their stubborn reliance on economies incapable of correcting it, their use of language so wealthy, so charged with "difference," as to be erosive. The vulnerability of the sonnets might be said to resemble that nameless flaw that afflicts their speaker, but in their case the flaw is not ultimately disastrous. They are not consumed by the extravagant husbandry that produced them. Their effort to resist, to compensate, to register, in spite of slippage balances their loss with store. They leave us with the awesome cost, and reward, of their conative contention. The vulnerability is inseparable from the striving that leads us to them: the ''poet's'' expense and Shakespeare's expense.

11

Ben Jonson
and the Centered Self

"DEEST QUOD DUCERET ORBEM" reads the motto of Ben Jon-son's famous *impresa* with the broken compass. After the fashion of *imprese*, it contains a kind of transparent enigma, to be solved in this case by the reading of its author's canon. For the *orbis*—circle, sphere, symbol of harmony and perfection—becomes familiar to the student of Jonson as one of his great unifying images. In a sense, almost everything Jonson wrote attempts in one way or another to complete the broken circle, or expose the ugliness of its incompletion. We have had a study of the circle in the European imagination,[1] and another of the circle in seventeenth-century England,[2] both valuable explorations of this image's evocative range. But as both studies teach us, even geometric images can be plastic—must be so, insofar as they are animated by the imagination, and their cultural contexts can never fully define their suggestiveness. One criterion of the major artist is the process by which traditional symbols acquire in his work an individual resonance even as they illuminate retrospectively their tradition.

In the case of an artist like Jonson, the imagery of circularity is one means of intuiting, beneath the turbulent richness and vehement variety of his work, its underlying coherence. But it is also a token of his massive artistic independence. In Jonson, the associations of the circle—as metaphysical , political, and moral ideal, as proportion and equilibrium, as cosmos, realm, society, estate, marriage, harmonious soul—are doubled by the associations of a center: governor, participant, house, inner self, identity, or, when the outer circle is broken, lonely critic and self-reliant solitary. Center and circle become symbols, not only of harmony and completeness but of stability, repose, fixation, duration, and the incompleted circle, uncentered and misshapen, comes to symbolize a flux or a mobility, grotesquely or dazzlingly fluid. Most of the works in Jonson's large canon—including the tragedies and comedies, verse and prose—can be categorized broadly in their relation to an implicit or explicit center. That is to say, one can describe an image or character or situation as durable, as center-oriented and centripetal (I shall use these terms more or less synonymously), or one can describe them as moving free, as disoriented and centrifugal, in quest of transformation. To sketch these categories is to seem to suggest absolute poles, ethically positive and negative. But although much of Jonson's writing encourages that suggestion, it does not lack its tensions, its ambivalences, its subtle shifts of emphasis. If the categories are not themselves transformed, they show up as altered under the varying artistic light.

The great storehouse of Jonson's centripetal images is the series of masques which assert, almost by definition, the existence of an order. The succession of antimasque to masque, of crudity and disorder to beauty and order, demonstrates over and over the basic harmony of the cosmos and the realm. If the charm of the antimasque, in its picturesque gaucherie, exceeded for some spectators the more solemn appeal of what followed, this frivolous superiority did not affect the authorized affirmations of the conclusion. In *The Masque of Beauty*, the allegorical figure Perfectio appears on the stage "in a vesture of pure Golde, a wreath of Gold upon her head. About her bodie the Zodiacke, with the Signes: In her hand a Compasse of golde, drawing a circle" and in a marginal note Jonson explains of the zodiac: "Both that, and the Compasse are known ensigns of perfection."[3] These circles of perfection determine the choreography of many masques and, so to speak, the poetic choreography of many more, adding concentric denotations to the limpid verbal patterns.

The circles of the masques have reference first of all to the central figure of the king, literally seated in the center of the

hall and directly facing the stage area. The king, associated repeatedly with the sun, is himself a symbolic orb—fixed, life-giving,
dependable:

> That in his owne true circle, still doth runne;
> And holds his course, as certayne as the sunne; (7:353)

a source of radiance and order:

> Now looke and see in yonder throne,
> How all those beames are cast from one.
>   This is that Orbe so bright,
> Has kept your wonder so awake;
> Whence you as from a mirrour take
>   The Suns reflected light.
> Read him as you would doe the booke
> Of all perfection, and but looke
>   What his proportions be;
> No measure that is thence contriv'd,
> Or any motion thence deriv'd,
>   But is pure harmonie. (7:523–24)

The king's presence opposite the masquing stage (where the actors
can point and bow to him) represents a kind of metaphysical
principle which the dancers attempt to embody.[4] Thus Reason
will address the dancers of *Hymenaei*:

> Thanke his grace
> That hath so glorified the place:
> And as, in circle, you depart
> Link'd hand in hand; So, heart in heart,
> May all those bodies still remayne
> Whom he (with so much sacred payne)
> No lesse hath bound within his realmes
> Then they are with the Oceans streames. (7:225)

Here the orb of the king's presence and the circles of the dance
are associated with the community of the realm, the island encir-
cled by Ocean.[5]

The occasion for this particular masque was a court
wedding, and Jonson employs the choreographic circle to symbolize most obviously the band of matrimony. At the climax of

the final dance, the masquers form a circle, from the center of which Reason explicates the symbolism:

> Here stay, and let your sports be crown'd:
> The perfect'st figure is the round.
> Nor fell you in it by adventer,
> When Reason was your guide, and center.
> This, this that beauteous Ceston is
> Of lovers many-colour'd blisse.
> Come Hymen, make an inner ring,
> And let the sacrificers sing. (7:224)

But the masque does not limit the significance of its intricate symmetries to its occasion. The last quotation suggests that the harmony of marriage depends upon that inner principle of restraint and equilibrium embodied by the figure named Reason. Earlier in the performance, an immense sphere has been discovered onstage, "a microcosme or globe (figuring Man)," whose passions and humors Reason succeeds in subduing.[6] The ideal circle of perfection thus makes its claims upon the human soul, as upon king, realm, marriage, dance, cosmos, and principle.

The concept of an inner moral equilibrium also informs most of Jonson's verse, but there the achievement of circular harmony is considerably more precarious. The facile affirmations of the masques are intended for spectacle rather than drama, but in the verse (as in the drama) the effort to close the circle is restored to the bitter clash of the historical world. In the epigrams, epistles, and encomiastic tributes, the judgment is shrewder, the voice caustic, the moral combat uncertain. The brilliant sarcasm of the destructive pieces legitimizes the integrity of the compliments; taken together, they demonstrate the finesse of an observer neither sycophantic nor misanthropic, on whom nothing is lost, capable of fervid as well as witty discriminations. From most of the poems, we hear less asserted of the larger spheres of perfection, metaphysical or political, and more of the stable, if beleaguered, human center.

Several of the personal tributes in *The Forrest* come to rest at their conclusions upon an image of rooted stability, typically situated in an actual residence, a house or estate, a dwelling—

with all the accreted meaning Jonson brings to the verb. Thus the compliment to Sir Robert Wroth:

> Thy peace is made; and, when man's state is well,
> 'Tis better, if he there can dwell; (7:99)

and again the closing lines of "To Penshurst":

> Now, Penshurst, they that will proportion thee
> With other edifices, when they see
> Those proud, ambitious heaps, and nothing else,
> May say, their lords have built, but thy lord dwells. (8:96)

Both of these poems come to suggest that the act of dwelling at home with dignity, style, and integrity, as their respective subjects are said to do, involves a kind of inner homing, a capacity to come to rest within. Thus the reader is not quite sure where to find the literal meaning when he reaches the last quatrain of the poem which follows the two just quoted. This poem, entitled "To the World. A Farewell for a Gentlewoman, Vertuous and Noble," concludes as follows:

> Nor for my peace will I goe farre,
> As wanderers doe, that still doe rome,
> But make my strengths, such as they are,
> Here in my bosome, and at home. (8:102)

To make one's strengths at home may mean to lead a retired life, but it means as well to find that home in one's own bosom. Jonson will praise the same centered strength when he addresses an individual who is outwardly quite unlike the gentlewoman—the polymath John Selden:

> you that have beene
> Ever at home: yet, have all Countries seene:
> And like a Compasse keeping one foot still
> Upon your Center, doe your Circle fill
> Of generall knowledge. (8:159)

Virtually all the heroes and heroines (the terms are not misapplied) of the verse seem to possess this quality of fixed stability.

The grandiose spherical perfections of the masques are

not, to be sure, altogether missing from the lyrics. The marriage
of England and Scotland under James is celebrated in imagery
reminiscent of the more stylized genre:

> The world the temple was, the priest a king,
> The spoused paire two realmes, the sea the ring; (8:28)

as well as the visionary ideal of poetry:

> I saw a Beauty from the Sea to rise,
> That all Earth look'd on, and that earth, all Eyes!
> It cast a beame as when the chear-full Sun
> Is fayre got up, and day some houres begun!
> And fill'd an Orbe as circular, as heaven! (8:396)

But on the whole the circles of the lyric verse shrink toward their
center, toward the Stoic individual soul, self-contained, balanced,
at peace with itself even in isolation.

> He that is round within himselfe, and streight,
> Need seeke no other strength, no other height;
> Fortune upon him breakes her selfe, if ill,
> And what would hurt his vertue makes it still. . . .
> Be alwayes to thy gather'd selfe the same. (8:63)

This intuition of the *gathered* self, whatever its antecedents in the
Roman moralists, is profoundly Jonsonian, more personal and
more spontaneous than the inclusive ideals of cosmos and realm.
It is of a piece with the emotional reserve which Edmund Wilson
misrepresents as coldness. It is by definition exclusive:

> Well, with mine owne frail Pitcher, what to doe
> I have decreed; keepe it from waves, and presse;
> Lest it be justled, crack'd, made nought, or lesse:
> Live to that point I will, for which I am man,
> And dwell as in my Center, as I can. (8:219)

As Jonson aged and watched the centrifugal forces in his society
acquire increasing power, this sense of the beleaguered central self
became more insistent and more poignant. This is certainly the
sense of the moving poem from which I have just quoted ("To
One that asked to be Sealed of the Tribe of Ben"), as it is of *The*

New Inne, one of the so-called "dotages," where the ultimate victory of the valiant man is "Out of the tumult of so many errors, / To feel, with contemplation, mine own quiet" (6:474). What depths of mastered suffering are betrayed by the proud serenity of this arrogant and beautiful phrase!

From the beginning the verse portrays with vivid scorn the ugliness of the uncentered, ungathered selves, whose disorientation always seems related to some principle of discontinuity. The self which is not at home paints, feigns, invents, gossips, *alters* its manner and passion as whim or necessity dictates. The dramatic life of the satirical poems and passages lies in their confrontations. They may confront simply the disoriented self in its whirling flux with the poet's alert and steady eye—and then we wait for the whiplash phrase which stings and tells. Or they may confront the social frenzy with some centered figure who holds out:

> You . . . keepe an even, and unalter'd gaite;
> Not looking by, or backe (like those, that waite
> Times, and occasions, to start forth, and seeme)
> Which though the turning world may dis-esteeme,
> Because that studies spectacles, and showes,
> And after varyed, as fresh objects goes,
> Giddie with change, and therefore cannot see
> Right, the right way: yet must your comfort bee
> Your conscience, and not wonder, if none askes
> For truthes complexion, where they all weare masks. (8:118)

In the verse as in the masques, the circular values of virtue tend in their constancy to be transcribed by nouns and adjectives:

> Her Sweetnesse, Softnesse, her fair Curtesie,
> Her wary guards, her wise simplicitie,
> Were like a ring of Vertues, 'bout her set
> And pietie the Center, where all met. (8:270)

> All offices were done
> By him, so ample, full, and round,
> In weight, in measure, number, sound,
> As though his age imperfect might appeare,
> His life was of Humanitie the Spheare— (7:244)

but the hideous antics of vice, because variable, must depend on a livelier poetry of verbs:

> Be at their Visits, see 'hem squemish, sick . . .
> And then, leape mad on a neat Pickardill;
> As if a Brize were gotten i' their tayle,
> And firke, and jerke, and for the Coach-man raile . . .
> And laugh, and measure thighes, then squeak, spring, itch,
> Doe all the tricks of a saut Lady Bitch. (8:164)

Jonson seems to see his centered figures moving perpetually through this purgatory of the Protean, still at rest when active, just as the vicious are unstable even when torpid. He reports on the one hand the paradox of Sir Voluptuous Beast married, who metamorphoses his innocent wife into the serial objects of his past desire: "In varied shapes, which for his lust shee takes." The married lecher is still in a sense adulterous. But Jonson registers too the opposing paradox of a William Roe, who will return from a voyage with his "first thoughts":

> There, may all thy ends,
> As the beginnings here, prove purely sweet,
> And perfect in a circle alwayes meet.
> So, when we, blest with thy returne, shall see
> Thy selfe, with thy first thoughts, brought home by thee,
> We each to other may this voyce enspire;
> This is that good Aeneas, past through fire,
> Through seas, stormes, tempests: and imbarqu'd for hell,
> Came back untouch'd. This man hath travail'd well.
>
> (8:81)

He travels well who in a sense never travels (or travails) at all, who circumscribes hell with his courage and whose mind knows no exile, keeping one foot still upon his center, compasslike, and lives through tempest, here in his bosom and at home.

II

The equilibrated energy of the centered self is most amply demonstrated by Jonson's *Timber*. The stress in that work falls on the faculty of judgment, and in fact it demonstrates this faculty at work, choosing among authors and passages, discriminating conduct and style.

> Opinion is a light, vain, crude, and imperfect thing, settled in the imagination, but never arriving at the understanding, there to obtain the tincture of reason.
>
> (8:564)

The passages gathered in *Timber* are exercises of the reasonable understanding. A sentence like the one quoted seems to place the imagination in an outer layer of consciousness, where the centrifugal "opinion" can momentarily alight. The understanding is further within, at the psychic center of gravity, impervious to the flights of the butterfly-caprice. All of *Timber*, whether or not "original" in the vulgar sense, seems to issue from this center of gravity.

The shrewd and sane judgment of the prose is unwittingly parodied in *Catiline* by the figure of Cicero, a ponderous center of Roman gravity indeed. In *Sejanus*, the tenacious indignation of the upright Lucius Arruntius is more recognizably human, but his unrelieved railing falls short of the composure of the gathered self. This ideal seems rather to be approached by the minor character Lepidus, whose moral strategy amid the dangerous political disintegration remains home-centered:

> the plaine, and passive fortitude,
> To suffer, and be silent; never stretch
> These armes, against the torrent; live at home,
> With my owne thoughts, and innocence about me,
> Not tempting the wolves jawes: these are my artes.
>
> (4:428)

Lepidus is slightly ambiguous because his decision figuratively to "live at home" contrasts with the zealous sense of political responsibility which motivates Arruntius and the other Germanicans. Lepidus is represented as naive, but it is the Germanicans who are destroyed. In the "violent change, and whirle" of Tiberian Rome, all patterns of centripetal order are gone; even Fortune's wheel seems in the closing speeches to lead only downward, and the single remaining sphere is the adulterous liaison of Livia and Sejanus:

> Then Livia triumphs in her proper spheare,
> When shee, and her Sejanus shall divide
> The name of Caesar. . . .
> And the scarce-seene Tiberius borrowes all
> His little light from us, whose folded armes
> Shall make one perfect orbe. (4:376)

The comedies as well—far less distant from Jonson's tragedies than is the case with Shakespeare—are mainly concerned with a centrifugal world, and again in them the circles are often ironic. Thus, in *The Staple of News*, the servants of Lady Pecunia all need to be bribed, without exception or competition, by the visitor who would reach their mistress:

> We know our places here, wee mingle not
> One in anothers sphere, but all more orderly,
> In our owne orbes; yet wee are all Concentricks.
> (6:308)

And in *Poetaster*, the banished Ovid laments his exile with an ironic lack of centered self-reliance:

> Banisht the court? Let me be banisht life;
> Since the chiefe end of life is there concluded . . .
> And as her sacred spheare doth comprehend
> Ten thousand times so much, as so much place
> In any part of all the empire else;
> So every body, mooving in her sphaere,
> Containes ten thousand times as much in him,
> As any other, her choice orbe excludes. (4:285)

In the comedies, moreover, where the embodiments of a moral judgment appear only fitfully, it is much harder to locate a sense of a center. Perhaps the closest dramatic equivalent to the gathered self, living "at home," is the literal house, putative center of bourgeois dramatic existence. The weakness of the house as refuge or protective fortress seems to mirror the weakness of a centerless society.

Weak Jonson's houses certainly are, when it is necessary to exclude the potential marauder. There is in fact a recurrent pattern of domestic invasion, beginning with *The Case is Altered,* where the miser Jaques de Prie is obsessed with fear that an intruder will break in to pilfer his hidden gold. His fears are indeed realized, and we learn as well that he has himself pilfered both his gold and his daughter from a former master.[7] In *Sejanus,* it is Agrippina's house which is invaded by a pair of the tyrant's spies and an *agent provocateur,* to trap fatally the outspoken Sabinus. In *Catiline,* where the hope for political order is a little less desperate, Cicero succeeds in thwarting the conspirators' plot to murder him at home. But his escape is narrow. His luck is better than the hapless Morose's (of *Epicoene*), caricature of the centered self, whose hatred of noise leads him to "devise a roome, with double walls, and treble seelings; the windores close shut, and calk'd; and there he lives by candlelight" (5:170). It is Morose's special torment to be visited on his wedding day by a houseful of young city sparks, posturing fools, and pretentious women of fashion. "The sea breaks in upon me!" he cries at the high tide of the invasion. His double walls are of no avail. That Morose's humor does indeed represent a deliberate caricature of the centered self is made clear by one of his speeches:

> My father, in my education, was wont to advise mee, that I should alwayes collect, and contayne my mind, not suffring it to flow loosely; that I should looke to what things were necessary to the carriage of my life, and what not: embracing the one, and eschewing the other. In short that I should endeare myself to rest, and avoid turmoile: which now is growne to be another nature to me. (5:258)

Here we follow the process which wrenches the norm into the grotesque. And the cost is the frustration of barriers against the world which are always inadequate.

This pattern of domestic invasion has to be noticed, I think, when one considers those other comedies where a husband tries, more or less unsuccessfully, to protest his wife from adulterous advances. The fear of cuckoldry on the part of Kitely (in *Every Man in his Humor*) is unjustified but nonetheless acute. Corvino's fear (in *Volpone*) is equally acute until the commercial element intrudes. Fitzdottrell's intermittent anxiety (in *The Devil is an Ass*) over his wife is abundantly justified by the wiles of her suitor, and perhaps one is justified in adding to the list the plots of the witch Maudlin (in *The Sad Shepherd*) to undermine Robin Hood's marriage by assuming the form of Marian. Still another variant is the staged incursion of the disguised Surly (in *The Alchemist*) to make off with Dame Pliant. The obvious *fabliau* comedy of these episodes has to be included in the broader pattern of domestic invasion. The havoc caused by the various invasions measures the defenselessness of characters who depend for their protection on bricks and mortar. The mischief in *The Alchemist* occurs because the master of the house is literally away from home. In other plays the absence is figurative rather than actual, but the mischief is approximately equal.

In the disoriented world of Jonson's comedies, the most nearly successful characters seem to be the chameleons, the Shifts and Brainworms and Faces who refuse to be centered, who are comfortable with the metamorphoses society invites. A kind of witty complicity emerges occasionally from Jonson's treatment of his disguisers, to suggest that he was taken by their arts in spite of himself. Thus Carlo Buffone describes the transformations of Puntaruolo (in *Every Man out of his Humor*) with a sarcasm very nearly lyrical:

> These be our nimble-spirited Catsos, that have their evasions at pleasure . . . no sooner started, but they'll leap from one thing to another, like a squirrel, heigh: dance! and do tricks in their discourse, from fire to water, from water to air, from air to earth, as if their tongues did but e'en lick the four elements over, and away. (3:460)[8]

So Picklock (in *The Devil is an Ass*) will proudly describe his Protean changeability:

> Tut, I am Vertumnus,
> On every change, or chance, upon occasion,
> A true Chamaelion, I can color for't.
> I move upon my axell, like a turne-pike,
> Fit my face to the parties, and become,
> Streight, one of them. (3:327)

We are of course meant to see this pride as ironically misplaced, but such is not the case of Brainworm in *Every Man in his Humor,* whose skill in manipulating disguises seems to win justified approbation. Thus when at the conclusion Brainworm exclaims, "This has been the day of my metamorphosis," he is rather admired than scolded. The human value of his whirlwind role-changing seems to counterbalance the more familiar value of the elder Knowell's advice to his nephew: "I'd ha' you sober, and contayne yourself" (3:306). Perhaps this early play betrays a genuine tension in Jonson's moral sympathies which the "authorized" morality of the verse and later plays tends to becloud. There is indeed scattered evidence to suggest a strain of half-repressed envy for the homeless and centrifugal spirit. *Volpone* seems to me the greatest, though not the only, work to deal with that strain and make it into art.

III

The subject of *Volpone* is Protean man, man without core and principle and substance. It is an anatomy of metamorphosis, the exaltations and nightmares of our psychic discontinuities. It is one of the greatest essays we possess on the ontology of selfhood.[9] For *Volpone* asks us to consider the infinite, exhilarating, and vicious freedom to alter the self at will once the ideal of moral constancy has been abandoned. If you do not choose to be, then, by an irresistible logic, you choose to change, and in view of the world we are called upon to inhabit, perhaps the more frequently one changes, the better. Machiavelli wrote: "He is happy whose mode of procedure accords with the needs of the times. . . . If one could change one's nature with time and circumstances, fortune would never change." Volpone demonstrates the ultimate hectic development of Machiavelli's shifty pragmatism, and raises it from a political maxim to a moral, even a metaphysical, state of being.

This metaphysical dimension is introduced almost at

the outset, in the cynical show performed by Volpone's dwarf and hermaphrodite. The history of Androgyno's transformation through history by means of metempsychosis, a process which exposes his soul to all the most debasing conditions of human and even bestial existence—this history announces and parodies the series of disguises and transformations assumed by the citizens of Jonson's fictive Venice. Androgyno's soul was once contained in the body of Pythagoras, "that juggler divine," and went on, "fast and loose," to enter other bodies. The human jugglers of the play themselves operate on the basis of a fast and loose soul.

The will to multiply the self animates the long speech by Volpone which appears at the exact middle of the play and which gives that will what might be called its classic statement. The speech is ostensibly intended to advance the seduction of Celia, but as Volpone is progressively carried away by his fantasy, his intoxication has less and less to do with the bewildered woman he seems to address. What his speech really betrays is his secret heart's desire:

> Whil'st, we, in changed shapes, act Ovids tales,
> Thou, like Europa now, and I like Jove,
> Then I like Mars, and thou like Erycine,
> So, of the rest, till we have quite run through
> And weary'd all the fables of the gods.
> Then will I have thee in more moderne formes,
> Attired like some sprightly dame of France,
> Brave Tuscan lady, or proud Spanish beauty;
> Sometimes, unto the Persian Sophies wife;
> Or the grand-Signiors mistresse; and, for change,
> To one of our most art-full courtizans,
> Or some quick Negro, or cold Russian;
> And I will meet thee, in as many shapes:
> Where we may, so, trans-fuse our wandring soules,
> Out at our lippes, and score up summes of pleasures.
>
> (5:84)

The passion behind this extraordinary speech involves more than the histrionic art; it aims at the perpetual transformation of the self. Thus the various disguises which Volpone assumes—invalid, mountebank, corpse, *commendatore*—have to be regarded as tentative experiments toward that multiplication, to the point that the very term *disguise* comes to seem inadequate.

The role of corpse is that least suited to the many-selved man, and the stroke is suggestive which imbues Volpone with a fear of paralysis. His worst moment before the end comes when he must lie immobile in court to counterfeit a dying invalid:

> I ne're was in dislike with my disguise,
> Till this fled moment; here, 'twas good, in private,
> But, in your publike, *Cave*, whil'st I breathe.
> 'Fore god, my left legge 'gan to have the crampe;
> And I apprehended, straight, some power had strooke me
> With a dead palsey: well, I must be merry,
> And shake it off. (5:108)

It is no accident that the language of this soliloquy is echoed in Volpone's sentence:

> Since the most was gotten by imposture,
> By feigning lame, gout, palsy, and such diseases,
> Thou art to lie in prison, crampt with irons,
> Till thou bee'st sicke and lame indeed. (5:135)

This terrible punishment contains the profundity of a Dantesque *contrapasso*. The sinful thirst for perpetual metamorphosis calls for the immobility of bed and chain.

Volpone's passion for transforming himself is shared, imitated, fragmented, and complemented by most of the remaining characters. It is shared most conspicuously by his parasite Mosca, whose disguises are even more supple, more volatile, more responsive to the pressure of events, and in the worldly sense, more practical:

> But your fine, elegant rascall, that can rise,
> And stoope (almost together) like an arrow;
> Shoot through the aire, as nimbly as a starre;
> Turne short, as doth a swallow; and be here,
> And there, and here, and yonder, all at once;
> Present to any humour, all occasion;
> And change a visor, swifter, than a thought!
> This is the creature, had the art borne with him.
>
> (5:66–67)

Thus runs Mosca's accurate self-appraisal, whose delight in his art must have been shared by his creator, but remains tinged nonetheless by the irony of a pitiless judgment. The irony extends a fortiori to the play with deception which occupies the two deceivers' victims. The rhetoric of Mosca's auto-congratulation is anticipated by his praise of the legal profession, and by extension of Voltore:

> I, oft, have heard him say, how he admir'd
> Men of your large profession that could speake
> To every cause, and things mere contraries,
> Till they were hoarse againe, yet all be law;
> That, with most quick agilitie, could turne,
> And re-turne; make knots, and undoe them;
> Give forked counsell. (5:34)

Voltore's quick agility to turn and return sounds like the volatility of a Mosca, a fly, a swallow who will turn short and be there and yonder all at once. Only a little slower to turn is Corvino, whose savage anger for his wife's (allegedly) compromising appearance at her window succeeds in an instant to the decision to prostitute her. Even the feeble Corbaccio, so frightening in his murderous senility, attempts to disguise the poison he proffers as a medicinal opiate, just as he disguises from himself the truth of his condition:

> faines himselfe
> Yonger, by scores of yeeres, flatters his age,
> With confident belying it. (5:40)

But the funniest example of discontinuity is Lady Wouldbe, whom Volpone calls "perpetual motion." The comedy of her inspired scene at his bedside stems from his frustration in damning the tide of her conversation. Each of his anguished attempts to silence her provides a channel to a new topic, until he recognizes his helplessness before her infinite variety. The lady indeed produces a therapeutic philosophy to justify this trick of her mind and tongue to ramify without end:

> And, as we find our passions doe rebell,
> Encounter 'hem with reason; or divert 'hem,
> By giving scope unto some other humour

> Of lesser danger: as, in politique bodies,
> There's nothing, more, doth over-whelme the judgement,
> And clouds the understanding, then too much
> Settling, and fixing, and (as't were) subsiding
> Upon one object. (5:74)

The lady's notion is that sticking to the subject is positively dangerous to the indisposed soul. Her speech provides a rationale, at her own trivial verbal level, for the perpetual motion which the more sinister Venetians also embody in their fashion. There is a special joke here for the student of Jonson, for what is this "settling and fixing, and, as 'twere, subsiding" of the judgment but that very gathering of the self which we know the playwright to have admired above all? It was an audacious and delightful thought to insert this allusion to the play's missing center into the incoherent chatter of an absurd bluestocking.[10]

The disguises and role-playing of the main plot are repeated in the subplot chiefly by the character of Peregrine, who in Act Five poses successively as a newsbearer and merchant, while giving out that the real Peregrine is actually a spy. But the more interesting character for our purposes is Sir Politic Wouldbe. We know from the verse that Jonson admired only those travelers who, in a symbolic sense, remained at home—as the Englishman Sir Pol conspicuously refuses to do. His opening lines, with their fatuous cosmopolitanism, already damn him: "Sir, to a wise man, all the world's his soile. / It is not Italie, nor France, nor Europe, / That must bound me, if my fates calle me forth" (5:45). His rootlessness, his homelessness, in the Jonsonian sense, are underscored again by the Polonius wisdom of his travel philosophy:

> And then, for your religion, professe none;
> But wonder, at the diversitie of all;
> And, for your part, protest, were there no other
> But simply the lawes o' th' land, you could content you.
> Nic: Machiavel, and monsieur Bodine, both,
> Were of this minde. (5:90)

Sir Politic's cultural relativism is his own equivalent to Volpone's fantasy of Protean eroticism, to Mosca's calculated visor-changing, to Lady Wouldbe's theory of diversion. He is an eternal traveler in the deepest sense, with his chameleon's willingness to do as the Romans and take on the moral coloring of his surroundings. His tongue repeats what its owner hears, like the tongue of the parrot his name suggests. The tortoiseshell in which he finally hides suggests a creature without a stable home base, and this is indeed the symbolic interpretation Sir Pol himself makes of his own exile: "And I, to shunne, this place, and clime for ever; / Creeping, with house, on backe" (5:121).

Set against all these figures of transiency stands the figure of Celia, who represents—more effectively than her associate Bonario—whatever principle of constancy the play contains. In her chief dramatic scene, her role is simply to hold firm under pressure, and she fulfills it. She is the one important character who is immobile and centripetal, and Jonson underlines this distinction by framing her drama in terms of immurement. We first hear of her as guarded and imprisoned by her fearful husband, and this imprisonment is intensified after she drops her handkerchief to Scoto-Volpone.

> I'le chalke a line: o're which, if thou but chance
> To set thy desp'rate foot; more hell, more horror,
> More wilde remorceless rage shall seize on thee,
> Then on a conjurer, that, had heedlesse left
> His circles safetie, ere his devill was laid. (5:61)

Celia must remain at the center of a circle drawn by her husband, who fails to recognize the greater strength of her own inner centrality. This recognition is implicitly reached by the judges who, at the play's end, deliver her from her immurement and return her, a free agent, to her father's house. This enfranchisement contrasts not only with the forced paralysis of Volpone, but with the other sentences as well: Mosca is to live "perpetual prisoner" in the galleys, Corbaccio will be confined to a monastery, and Corvino pilloried. So many ways of denying the febrile thirst for transformation.

Throughout the play, the basic instrument of transformation was to have been gold. It is wrong, I think, to consider wealth as the ultimate goal of *Volpone's* various scoundrels. Wealth is rather the great transformer, the means of metamorphosis:

> Why, your gold . . . transformes
> The most deformed, and restores 'hem lovely,
> As't were the strange poeticall girdle. Jove
> Could not invent, t' himselfe, a shroud more subtile,
> To passe Acrisius guardes. It is the thing
> Makes all the world her grace, her youth, her beauty.
> (5:112)

The cruel lesson of the play is that gold fails to confer that infinite mobility its lovers covet, but rather reduces them to the status of fixed, subhuman grotesques. To multiply the self is to reduce the self—to fox, crow, fly, vulture, and tortoise. That art which turns back on nature by denying natural constancies ruins both nature and itself.

The very opening lines of *Volpone* invoke a pair of alternative circles.

> Good morning to the day; and, next, my gold:
> Open the shrine, that I may see my saint.
> Haile the worlds soule, and mine. . . .
> That, lying here, amongst my other hoords,
> Shew'st like a flame, by night, or like the day
> Strooke out of chaos, when all darkenesse fled
> Unto the center. O, thou sonne of Sol,
> (But brighter then thy father) let me kisse,
> With adoration, thee. (5:24–25)

The gold piece, an illusory sun, occupies the place of king, soul, *anima mundi*, God. The travesty of worship is augmented by the scriptural misquotation. On the day of creation, according to Scripture, darkness did not fly to the center but to the outer chaos beyond the firmament. Volpone's blunder gives away his basic misapprehension. His moral strategy depends on centrifugal assumptions, on the labyrinthine flux of a world without order. But he betrays in fact merely the benighted darkness of his own center.

IV

The issue at stake in Jonson's comedies was not irrelevant to the crisis of what might be termed Renaissance anthropology. I have argued elsewhere[11] that the sixteenth century witnessed the climax of a many-sided debate over the flexibility of the human self. The high Renaissance on the continent appeared intermittently to promise both a lateral mobility, a wider choice of roles and experience, and a vertical mobility, an opening toward something like transcendence of the human condition. To abridge summarily a very complex history, one can say that the vertical mobility came to be recognized as chimerical, but that the lateral mobility was permanently and progressively conquered for the modern world. In England, more tardy and conservative than the Continent, these new perspectives were regarded more cautiously, but they did not fail gradually to be recognized. Shakespeare, in comedies and tragedies alike, punishes the character who is stubbornly immobile, to reward the character who adapts and shifts. But Jonson's drama, more truly conservative, reflects as we have seen the horror of a self too often shifted, a self which risks the loss of an inner poise. It reflects this horror even as it portrays, more brilliantly than Shakespeare, the whirlwind virtuosos of such multiplication. *Volpone* portrays virtuosos of basically lateral transformations. His other supreme artists, the scoundrels of *The Alchemist,* tend to play rather with vertical transformation—or, to use the play's own jargon, with "sublimation."

The sublimation presents itself ostensibly to the various characters—the trio of rogues included—as basically financial, but, just as in *Volpone,* gold becomes a counter and a metaphor for an ulterior good which varies with the individual. They all want to be raised—socially, sexually, religiously, metaphysically; they all hunger for the transmuting miracle of their respective alchemies. The one apparent exception is Surly, who announces explicitly his uniqueness: "Your stone cannot transmute me." No one of the other major characters possesses the judgment to say that, and it is of ironic significance that Surly himself will return two acts later transmuted by disguise. Once in the house, his righteous anger modulates into cupidity for Dame Pliant's fortune, and he demonstrates that he is in fact no more impervious to the stone than are the objects of his contempt. No Ciceros and no Celias here; the impulse to sublimation is well-nigh universal.

Like trickster, like victim—both share the same dreams upon the stone. This of course is the meaning of the opening quarrel, which shows each mountebank furious at the other's ingratitude for having been raised to his new social elevation—a raising that is phrased even here in alchemical hocus-pocus. Face has been "translated" by Subtle, who has

> Rais'd thee from broomes, and dust, and watring pots,
> Sublim'd thee, and exalted thee, and fix'd thee
> I' the third region, call'd our state of grace.
> Wrought thee to spirit, to quintessence, with paines
> Would twise have won me the philosophers worke.
>
> (5:297)

So Subtle, in Face's version, has thanks to him acquired a new incarnation.

> Why! who
> Am I, my mungrill? Who am I?

shouts Face at the outset, and the mongrel magician snarls:

> I'll tell you.
> Since you know not your selfe. (5:295)

But Subtle can only tell him who he has been, and what he is now, and Doll can remind them both pleadingly what they may hope to become.

Thus their hopes to be translated through their art reach across the gulf of deception to join the quainter dreams of their clients. The scale of ambition runs from the banal fantasies of a Drugger through the Puritans' quest to "raise their discipline" to the stupendous images of Epicure Mammon. In the sexual apotheoses of Mammon, like Volpone's, the self is endlessly renewable and his partner more variable than nature herself:[12]

> Wee'll . . . with these
> Delicate meats, set our selves high for pleasure,
> And take us downe againe, and then renew
> Our youth, and strength, with drinking the elixir,
> And so enjoy a perpetuitie
> Of life, and lust. And, thou shalt ha' thy wardrobe,
> Richer than Natures, still, to change thy selfe,
> And vary oftener, for thy pride, then shee:
> Or Art, her wise, and almost-equall servant. (5:364)

Nature indeed is the victim of all those people who choose to alter and transcend their condition; they all want, in Mammon's memorable phrase, to "firke nature up, in her owne center."

The literal center of the action, the house of Lovewit, is, until the fifth act, a usurped and thus a displaced center. The centrifugal displacement is suggested metaphorically in Mammon's opening lines:

> Come on, sir, Now you set your foot on shore
> In Novo Orbe; here's the rich Peru,
> And there within, sir, are the golden mines,
> Great Salomon's Ophir! (5:314)

Exoticism equals eroticism, and both lead away from home. The moral center of the play is also elusive, since Lovewit, when he returns, acquires a kind of complicity along with a wife and fortune. The officers of justice, unlike those of *Volpone*, remain permanently deceived. The closest approximation to a moral resolution appears in Face's valedictory to the audience:

> I put myselfe
> On you, that are my country; and this Pelfe,
> Which I have got, if you do quit me, rests
> To feast you often, and invite new ghests. (5:407)

"Country" here means "jury," but it also means *mes semblables, mes frères.* Face is asking the spectators to show their tolerant forgiveness of his shenanigans by their applause. Jonson's appreciation of the artist-scoundrel qualifies his disapproval of the centrifugal self, a little to the detriment of artistic coherence.

Bartholomew Fair, the last of Jonson's three master comedies, leads all of its bourgeois characters out of their houses to baptize them in the tonic and muddy waters of errant humanity. Away from the protective custody of their routine comforts, they wander, lose themselves, mistake the fair's disguises, pass through the ordeals it has prepared for them, and reach the chastening conclusion: "Remember you are but Adam, Flesh, and blood!" (6:139). In the midst of these comic ordeals, the identity of lost home and lost selfhood is very strong, strongest of all in the mouth of Cokes the fool:

> Dost thou know where I dwell, I pray thee? . . . Frend, doe you know who I am? or why I lye? I doe not my selfe, I'll be sworne. Doe but carry me home, and I'le please thee, I ha' money enough there, I ha' lost my selfe, and my cloake, and my hat. (6:90–91)

In the end Cokes will go to his dwelling, at the home of his kinsman the justice, but the justice will bring, so to speak, the fair home with him. He will invite, that is to say, all the rowdy and disreputable denizens of the fair to dinner, in a spirit that mingles festivity with reproof:

> JUSTICE: I invite you home, with mee to my house, to supper: I will have none feare to go along, for my intents are *Ad correctionem, non ad destructionem; ad aedificandum, non ad diruendum.* So lead on.
> COKES: Yes, and bring the Actors along, wee'll ha' the rest o' the Play at home. (6:140)

Bartholomew Fair ends with this word "home," like the "Farewell of the Vertuous Gentle-woman." But the home of the comedy is inclusive, and we glimpse—at least in this one work of mellow license—a Jonson less jealous of the centered self's prerogatives, more warmly and less ambiguously tolerant of the histrionic personality.

Perhaps there is meaning to be read in the openness of Jonson's last dramatic home—the bower of Robin Hood and Marian in *The Sad Shepherd*. In this charming, unfinished work of his old age, the last incarnation of the Protean figure, the witch Maudlin, is unambiguously repellent, but the dwelling itself is virtually unprotected by physical walls. It depends for its strength on the circular affection of man and woman: "Marian, and the gentle Robin-hood, / Who are the Crowne, and Ghirland of the Wood" (7:45). Here, in less ritualistic symbols than the wedding masques', Jonson reaches out to find the completion of his orb in the mutuality of conjugal love.[13] "Where should I be, but in my Robins armes. / The Sphere which I delight in, so to move?" (7:33).

Many late poems, as we have seen, represent a lonely shrinking inward to a harder and isolated core. But we can perhaps discern a contrary impulse reflected in the motto of the aging Jonson's *ex libris: Tanquam explorator.* Was Eliot thinking of that moving phrase when he wrote in *Little Gidding:* "Old men ought to be explorers"? In *The Sad Shepherd,* at any rate, there is a fresh urge to venture out. To be sure, the quality of an *explorator,* for Jonson, involved less of a Sir Politic Wouldbe than a William Roe, whose ends always meet his beginnings. But we can be grateful that his intuition of the centered self continued to leave room for an exuberant if discriminating curiosity. The compass, keeping still one foot upon its center, never ceased to swing its other foot wide in firm and unwearied arcs.

12

History and Anachronism

One might begin to talk about history and literature in our tradition by returning to the moment when they were first perceived to be interdependent. This occurred roughly at the opening of the early modern period; it may not be too much to say that this occurrence permitted modern history to begin. The perceptions that cultures change, that change produces what we call period style, and that period style affects writing—these perceptions first became current among the Italian Humanists of the earlier fifteenth century, and they permanently altered our conceptions of literature. As a result of these perceptions, a text became potentially datable on internal evidence, and of course many texts were so dated by Humanist philologists. But a second result was that texts could become *dated* in our modern negative sense; they could be seen to reveal a defunct period style; they could become "out of date." My subject is the connection between these two related properties: the text's revelation of its date and the text's destiny to be dated. Both properties are present in the idea of *anachronism*, which can be defined as a clash of period styles or mentalities. (The term *style* here has to be understood in the widest possible sense.) I want to look at this theme first in the period that discovered it and then move to other periods and cultures.

Petrarch late in life received from the emperor Charles IV a query concerning the authenticity of two letters purportedly written by Julius Caesar and Nero. Petrarch responded with a furious jeremiad exposing the fraudulence of the two fakes by means of stylistic and historical analysis (*Seniles* 16.5). Thus Petrarch anticipated the achievements of later Humanists by demonstrating an anachronistic gap between the letters' fictive date and their much later date of composition. The term *anachronism* did not exist in Petrarch's vocabulary; the middle Greek word *anachronismos,* deriving from a verb meaning to be late in time, produced a derivative in the Italian language only in the later sixteenth century, in French and English only in the seventeenth. But the concept of a chronological misplacement was already there in nucleus in Petrarch's letter, and it would become an important issue in Renaissance literary criticism. In fact, its prominence in Renaissance criticism is remarkable because it is one of the few concerns of that era which are not anticipated in some degree by ancient criticism.

It is true that the ancient Alexandrian school, and notably Aristarchus, was sensitive to the error of anachronistic *reading.* Aristarchus opposed those critics of Homer who objected to a princess like Nausicaa doing the laundry; he pointed out that folkways had changed over the centuries and that social change made these objections inappropriate. There is a brief anticipation of this insight toward the end of Aristotle's *Poetics* (1461a). Aristarchus also insisted that the meaning of a Homeric word be accorded its original, time-specific meaning. But this attention to reading was not commonly carried over by the ancients to anachronistic writing. Horace does refer briefly and negatively to the metaphoric mingling of Chian and Falernian wines, by which he seems to mean Greek and Roman styles. But the overwhelming preponderance of ancient theory ignores the potential risk of this mingling, and stresses the value of syncretic assimilation. The two most popular ancient metaphors for the imitation of models— digestion and mellification—valorize this syncretism. Seneca, who uses both metaphors, is representative when he calls for "many arts, many precepts, models from many eras." Umberto Eco has analyzed the confusions and inconsistencies of one ancient author as in effect a failure to control anachronism. Aulus Gellius' discussion of colors is incoherent, writes Eco, because he was exposed to the influence of so many cultures, and thus fails "to arrange the material which he takes from the writers of different epochs into strict fields."[1] This remark might suggest that late Latin syncretism needed a theoretical sophistication that it lacked.

When we turn to Renaissance writers, we find their

sensitivity to the risk of anachronism far more developed, and here again it was Petrarch who first formulated the risk with authority and supplied it with the metaphor that his successors would echo most often. Petrarch writes that he prefers his own modest style to another, more pretentious one (he's probably thinking of Cicero), just as he prefers his own gown to another, more elegant and ornamented. A writer, he says, cannot change garments like an actor and would be laughed at if he tried (*Familiares* 22.2). This establishes the sartorial analogy that would dominate Renaissance discussion and suggests the danger of ridicule attendant on anachronistic writing. To cite one passage out of dozens available, Pietro Aretino made the following remark about superannuated literary styles: "Our ears are weary of hearing [old-fashioned expressions], and to read these phrases in books makes one laugh as much as seeing a knight on the piazza in battledress bedecked with gold spangles . . . so that he seems either demented or in fancy dress. And yet in other times these were the clothes worn by Duke Borso and the great soldier Bartolomeo Colleoni!"[2] Here the superannuated writer is exposed to the nightmare embarrassment of wearing the wrong clothes in public.[3] In the quarrel over Ciceronianism that raged over the Continent during the earlier sixteenth century, each side accused the other of anachronism. The issue was somewhat less pressing in Renaissance England, but we do find Samuel Daniel reflecting an alertness to it. Perhaps anachronism was such a bogey to so many Renaissance writers because so many were playing with imported classical styles imposed on inherited native styles.

A scholar interested in this problem quickly discovers that distinctions have to be made, that some sort of typology is necessary, and I want now to suggest a set of categories that I have found useful. One can distinguish first of all a *naive* category of anachronism produced by a culture lacking a strong historical sense, a culture such as the European Middle Ages. Jupiter as emperor, Mars as knight, Chaucer's reference to Amphiaraus, one of the seven against Thebes, as a bishop, Gavin Douglas' reference to maenads as "nuns of Bacchus"—these are examples of naive anachronism, and they are not in themselves, surely, artistic blemishes. They help to compose the texture of a work without pretensions to historical control, and they accommodate the available knowledge to the available means. They may appear in such a work as Chaucer's *Troilus,* which as a whole is anything but naive. That category of innocent anachronism can be contrasted with a second, *abusive* type, the product of a culture struggling for historical awareness but in given cases adapting crudely, tactlessly, without attention to context. The habit of the strict Ciceronian to refer to the Christian God as "Jupiter Optimus Maximus" is abusive because the writer wants to repress history, not out of ignorance but out of a misconceived, rigid, and inappropriate decorum. Or at a deeper level, abusive anachronism stems from a failure of historical imagination and assimilation, a failure to create a coherent itinerary from an understood past to a vital emergent present. Each scholar can supply his own titles for this category; I would think of Petrarch's *Bucolicum carmen* or Ronsard's *Franciade.*

This category can be distinguished from a third which also emerges from a culture struggling to control history—what we might call *serendipitous* anachronism. Here an example from the visual arts is at hand: Brunelleschi, incorrectly believing the Florentine baptistery to be ancient, used some of its Romanesque elements to design a neoclassic masterpiece, the Pazzi chapel. All of these categories, stemming from ignorance or repressing or felicitously misunderstanding the nature of change, can be distinguished from a fourth category, which confronts and uses the conflict of period styles self-consciously and creatively to dramatize the itinerary, the diachronic passage out of the remote past into the emergent present. It is this last type of controlled and *creative* anachronism which seems to me to operate in the richest and most rewarding works of the Humanist Renaissance, from *The Praise of Folly* to *Paradise Lost.*

To these four categories—naive, abusive, serendipitous, creative—a fifth of a somewhat different order needs to be added, a category that transcends Renaissance poetics altogether and leads to a perennial drama of all complex cultures. This might be called *pathetic* or even *tragic* anachronism, and I want to devote the rest of this paper to it. It pervades our tradition, but again in the thought of the Renaissance we can find peculiarly expressive and poignant formulations of its force. Castiglione, arguing in *The Book of the Courtier* for the perpetuation of noble old words, represents them as beleaguered and threatened by temporal change. "It seems almost impious," he writes, "to endeavor . . . to destroy and, as it were, bury alive those which have already survived many centuries and have defended themselves with the shield of usage against the envy of time, and have kept their dignity and splendor when, by way of the wars and ruins of Italy, changes have come about in the language, in buildings, dress, and customs." Later in the same book he compares the birth and death of words to the blossoming and withering of flowers, repeating a topos from Horace; words, he writes, enjoy for a while "grace and dignity, until they are gradually consumed by the envious jaws of time, when they too go to their death; because in the end, we and all our things are mortal."[4] In both these passages the mutability of language stands synecdochically for the mutability of human life and all human works. All dignity (*dignità*—a word that recurs in both passages), all *grazia*, all *splendore*, are subject to arbitrary vogue, to those inevitable changes and declines perceived as affecting not only language but also architecture, dress, manners, artifacts—all the works of man, and individual men and women as well. Needless to say, Castiglione was not the first to hold this view, and in the second passage quoted he may have been deliberately echoing a passage from Dante; nonetheless this conception of doomed survival acquires a special resonance in his book, which mourns repeatedly the disappearance of a gracious human institution, a ducal court, and its most prominent members.

The Book of the Courtier thus glances at a kind of anachronism that is universal in complex societies; all of us and all the things we wear and make and build and write, our rituals and styles and folkways, are condemned to anachronism insofar as we and they endure into an estranging future. When a building goes up, it is shaped by a period style, and as it continues to stand in a changing city, it will be perceived as representative of its date and its style. It may possibly continue to be admired, but as time passes it will be progressively isolated; it will suffer a kind of loneliness;

sooner or later its utility will be called into question. It will be tolerated, if at all, as a relic, as a landmark or timemark. Pathetic anachronism derives from the destiny of all enduring human products, including texts, since all products come into being bearing the marks of their historical moment and then, if they last, are regarded as alien during a later moment because of these marks. Things that survive are "dated," and in the negative implications of that term lies the potentiality for pathos. Language itself *dates*, and the wandering, the drifting, of the written word has been a theme of Western thought from Plato to Derrida. If culture contains this drifting within certain limits, it also serves to institutionalize period style. And human beings like words can themselves become outmoded relics. Doctor Johnson's preface to his *Dictionary* offers a synecdoche similar to Castiglione's. Johnson's somber elegy for the English language, "resigned to the tyranny of time and fashion, and exposed to the corruptions of ignorance, and caprices of innovation"—this elegy represents degeneration as "incident to words, as to their authors," and again later refers to "a natural tendency to degeneration" in tongues and governments.[5] We need not accept Johnson's equation of change with degeneration to recognize the legitimate tragedy of survival. From this perspective, anachronism ceases to be a local and occasional phenomenon; it becomes a universal fate.

If literary texts like buildings and objects are dated, then we can ask whether and how a text deals with its own datedness, the pathos of its potential future estrangement. I have already suggested one solution in speaking of "creative anachronism," which involves a deliberate dramatization of historical passage, bringing a concrete present into relation with a specific past and playing with the distance between them. To represent change through creative imitation, to dramatize in art a survival of the past into an altered present, would seem to provide a text with a certain resilience in confronting its own survival. Against this solution which insists on historicity can be set a pseudo-classical solution that implicitly denies history, that wants to transcend it by attaining a sublime timelessness. That solution of a false neoclassicism seems in fact the most vulnerable to ultimate estrangement. Saul Morson writes that "a text or genre will be vulnerable to parody . . . to the extent that it ignores or claims to transcend its own originating context; parody is most readily invited by an utterance that claims transhistorical authority."[6] A text that somehow acknowledges its historicity self-consciously would seem better fitted to survive its potential estrangement than a text that represses history.

I have discussed elsewhere the ways in which creative anachronism, creative imitation, enacts a successful survival or rebirth.[7] Here I want rather to discuss a complementary technique of dealing with the threat of superannuation, a technique that confronts the problem of pathetic survival. One way to study the historical consciousness of an era, a writer, a literary text, is to look at the role of the character or voice perceived as superannuated. The text that presents such a character will seem to turn aggressively against the past. Superannuation invites irony; by presenting the superannuated figure ironically (even when this figure is the poetic speaker), the text ostensibly detaches itself from that figure's archaic perspective and asserts its own relative modernity, points to the greater width of its own horizon. The text refuses to subject itself to this figure's limitations of understanding; it takes a step into an emergent present that the superannuated are incapable of taking. And yet in those texts that merit our interest, this gesture of detachment is not taken without misgivings, since the outmoded character will incarnate to some degree the past that has nourished the writer and his work, a past that he repudiates at his peril. The superannuated character will typically attract ambivalence, the ambivalence of all historical change, and this divided awareness will affect the posture of the text toward its own historicity.

We can find this awareness in the literature, if not the criticism, of classical antiquity. It is not, to be sure, present in Homer; the figure of Nestor in both Homeric poems is not presented as superannuated, and this fact tells us something about Homer's sense of history. Homer can be contrasted in this respect to Aeschylus, whose Eumenides find themselves outmoded by a

new praxis of justice at Athens, and are slowly persuaded to
recognize, though without pathos, the claims of this modern le-
gality. There may be a touch of the obsolescent tinge in geing Sophocles'
Ajax. But what is literally the *locus classicus* of this drama in our
tradition can be found in the central work of Western culture, the
Aeneid.

Book III of the *Aeneid* describes the temporary reunion
of the wandering Trojans with Andromache and her second husband, Helenus, at Buthrotum on the Adriatic. As Aeneas comes
upon her, she is making an offering to an empty tomb consecrated
to Hector, vainly calling for his spirit to issue from a duplicate
grave. She stands near a stream which Virgil calls a "false Simois,"
referring to the river at Troy ("falsi Simoëntis"). Everything in fact
in this little community has the character of a miniature replica;
Buthrotum is a little Troy, which one enters through simulated
Scaean gates; a dry riverbed has to serve as the Xanthus, another
river that crosses the Trojan plain. Andromache, hysterical in her
monomania, lives with her companions in a prison house of
memory, as empty as the tomb at which she prays. The *Aeneid*, as
David Quint has recently shown, is about the value of not remem-
bering;[8] forgetfulness for the future Aeneas will become an iron
necessity. And yet Andromache's anachronistic fidelity retains a
forlorn dignity, and Aeneas' tears as he leaves correspond to a
valid envy. The *Aeneid* displays an awareness of tragic anachronism
that Virgil's culture did not formulate discursively, and as the
central classic of Western civilization it inscribed this awareness,
this ambivalent sympathy, upon our whole tradition. It authorized
the regret that stems from turning one's back, as the poem as a
whole turns its back. Andromache and Helenus are signs for the
dominance of that Homeric past from which Roman epic struggles
to free itself, but not without misgivings, and these misgivings
have remained to define our intercourse with our past.

Virgil himself assumes the pathos of the anachronistic
survivor as a character in Dante's *Commedia*. This pathos is present
from Virgil's first appearance but it becomes acute in the *Purgatorio*.
As he attempts to lead his companion up the mountain, his status

is slightly altered. He has never been there before; he doesn't know the way; he's obliged to ask directions; and more than once he postpones a full response to Dante's questions until the appearance of Beatrice. In the earthly paradise at the summit, he follows Dante for the first time. The reader's and Dante's last glimpse of him occurs during the elaborate pageant of the Christian faith, when the pilgrim turns full of wonder to his guide who responds with a face equally bewildered, literally "burdened with stupefaction," "carca di stupor." A moment later he will disappear. The Virgil drama ends with that gaze of stupefied bewilderment measuring the pagan's anachronistic distance from a superseding reality. One could say that the drama ends with a recognition scene, in which the character registers clearly the degree of his exclusion and his obsolescence. By means of this recognition scene, Dante the poet measures the diachronic distance his poem has moved from its own source and original authority, its *maestro* and *autore*. Dante implicitly situates his own poem in history and refers indirectly to its artistic and spiritual itinerary. He had courted anachronism as a Christian poet who took Virgil as his model, and he deals with that threat by thematizing the distance Virgil remains behind. In its long survival into an estranging future, his poem is less dated for us because it incorporates a diachronic passage.

In thinking about the treatment of the superannuated character in literary texts, one question we can ask is whether that character is allowed a recognition scene like Virgil's, is allowed or condemned to confront his or her anachronistic pathos, or whether on the other hand he or she is shielded from it as Andromache is. Don Quixote on his deathbed, having recovered to universal sorrow what he calls his sanity, resists all efforts to restore him to illusion and quotes the proverb: "In last year's nests there are no birds this year," a proverb that might be taken to imply that both the chivalric novel and its champion have no place in the present. We seem to discern a faint recognition scene. Shakespeare allows his John of Gaunt, uncle of Richard II, a glimmer of recognition as the old man, an hour before his death, pronounces an elegy on *his* England, "this blessed plot, this earth, this realm . . . now bound in with shame, with inky blots and rotten parchment bonds." Gaunt correctly links his own imminent death with the passing of that medieval realm which knew no inky blots. But it is the fate of Hotspur one play later *not* to recognize this anachronism, and in that failure of recognition lies precisely Hotspur's charming inadequacy, his completeness and integrity as a relic of a perishing ideology. Shakespeare underscores that failure in such a way as to provide his audience with the recognition he denied Hotspur, and in doing this he protects his play from rigidity; he leaves it open to the relativity and flexibility of history. The demonstration of Hotspur's blindness distances the play from its own medieval past, including a theater less alert to history. This theater has emerged as Hotspur did not emerge, was too perfected to emerge.

Literary texts seem distinguishable in terms of their treatment of anachronistic pathos, treatment which cannot help being self-referential, since the text must situate itself in relation to that past represented as outmoded. The visible vulnerability of the superannuated character makes manifest the less visible vulnerability of the text, which is always dated by the historicity of its signifiers. The self-referential gesture is perhaps most obvious in lyric poetry, since the superannuated character there is likely to be the poet or his or her spokesman. The last poem Yeats wrote was called "The Black Tower": it was composed just before his death, and it evokes with a kind of bitter homage the quixotic vigil of beleaguered warriors, their king almost certainly dead, holding out hopelessly to honor an oath, nothing more than skeletons standing in the tower which is their tomb to defend it against besiegers. The poem alternates a voice speaking for the warriors with the voice of an observer dismissing them as "old bones."

> Those banners come to bribe or threaten,
> Or whisper that a man's a fool
> Who, when his own right king's forgotten,
> Cares what king sets up his rule.
> If he died long ago
> Why do you dread us so?

There in the tomb drops the faint moonlight,
But winds come up from the shore:
They shake when the winds roar,
Old bones upon the mountain shake

The tower's old cook that must climb and clamber
Catching small birds in the dew of the morn
When we hale men lie stretched in slumber
Swears that he hears the king's great horn.
But he's a lying hound:
Stand we on guard oath-bound!

There in the tomb the dark grows blacker,
But winds come up from the shore:
They shake when the winds roar,
Old bones upon the mountain shake.

This is Yeats' epitaph for himself and his few friends, skeletal relics defending withered codes of integrity in an age of timeservers. There is irony toward these old bones whose words are the sounds of their shaking in the wind, soldiers dead at their post who may merely fantasize the hostile banners they think beleaguer them. In that irony lies Yeats' recognition, his knowledge that fidelity will appear to the superseding world as folly. His poem is clairvoyant toward his own outdated quixotism but harsher toward the modern age that dismisses his rigidity. For the anachronistic man and woman, history will always seem to present a fall. "The Black Tower" acknowledges this and yet maintains that *its* fall has occurred. In all of the works I cited before Yeats', the dominant discourse of the work is set over against the discourse of the survivor. But "The Black Tower" detaches itself more sharply from the modern observer, so that the discourse of Yeats' poetry as a body is aligned with the forlorn outlook of the warriors. In effect he is already ironically predicting or announcing his poetry's anachronistic eccentricity in the Europe of the thirties and beyond, so that the prediction of anachronism becomes implicitly a critique of the debased present and future.

     This same alignment is present in a famous poem by Baudelaire, "Le Cygne," which returns to the Virgilian figure of Andromache to convey the poet's sense of exile in a changing, modernized city. Andromache's nostalgia is assimilated to the speaker's as he muses pensively on the disappearance of a cluttered but picturesque area of old Paris where dilapidated shacks, piles of barrels and roughhewn stone, random bric-a-brac overgrown with weeds, had bordered on a menagerie. As he walks through the new Place du Carrousel which has replaced all that tawdry urban litter, the poet discovers himself as an exile in time.

> Le vieux Paris n'est plus (la forme d'une ville
> Change plus vite, hélas! que le coeur d'un mortel).

The poem becomes a lament for the ghostly city present in the poet's memory, a lost city that clashes anachronistically and allegorically with the more orderly, modern metropolis going up about him. His poem is full of images of exile and loss, like the image that supplies the title, the clumsy and pathetic swan escaped from the old menagerie. Baudelaire's poem, like Yeats', refuses to detach itself from the obsolescent and forces us to read its rhetoric as of a piece with that cluttered, ramshackle dilapidation now being abolished. The dignity of the poem invests the dilapidation with a certain charm, but there is no effort to minimize its mean disorder. On whichever side the textual discourse aligns itself, a fundamental ambivalence remains. And by invoking Andromache in its opening lines ("Andromaque, je pense à vous"), the poem seems to assert a certain continuity of anachronistic pathos transcending change.

Baudelaire's and Yeats' poems affirm in their different ways qualified convictions of lost value. But in the many characters of nineteenth-century fiction presented as superannuated, this conviction is subjected to complex crosscurrents. Part of the brilliance in Stendhal's portrait of the Marquis de la Mole lies in the subtle hints of the marquis's self-perception. He is never given an explicit recognition scene within the pages of the novel, and yet the alert reader understands that the marquis is without illusions, that he goes through the operatic motions of political intrigue, perpetuates the rituals of the *ancien régime,* with clear eyes and tacit scorn. In the person of the marquis, *Le Rouge et le noir* pays a kind of tribute to the vestigial dignity of an outmoded class, a class whose values leave unmistakable traces on the text itself. The novel was completed only a few months before the revolution of 1830; its publication more or less coincided with events that it anticipated and that would determine the conditions of its own short-term survival. The novel could predict them without altogether celebrating them, and in its contempt for bourgeois vulgarity, in its gestures of intermittent sympathy toward the best of a doomed caste, it rendered itself deliberately a kind of instant anachronism. The Marquis de la Mole incarnates its anachronistic velleities toward the past.

This ambivalence is still more obtrusive and indeed openly thematized in Turgenev's *Fathers and Children*, where the struggle of the generations pits the so-called nihilist Bazarov and his disciple Kirsanov against Kirsanov's father and uncle. By the end of the novel this struggle will pit Bazarov literally against the uncle Pavel Petrovitch in a duel from which the older man is carried away wounded. But well before that the father, Nikolai, and Pavel engage in a conversation that constitutes for one of them, but only for one, a recognition of his inevitable superannuation.

> "So that," began Pavel Petrovitch, "so that's what our young men of this generation are! They are like that—our successors!"
>
> "Our successors!" repeated Nikolai Petrovitch, with a dejected smile. . . ." Do you know what I was reminded of, brother? I once had a dispute with our poor mother; she stormed, and wouldn't listen to me. At last I said to her, 'Of course, you can't understand me; we belong,' I said, 'to two different generations.' She was dreadfully offended, while I thought, 'There's no help for it. It's a bitter pill, but she has to swallow it.' You see, now, our turn has come, and our successors can say to us, 'You are not of our generation; swallow your pill.' "
>
> "You are beyond everything in your generosity and modesty," replied Pavel Petrovitch. "I'm convinced, on the contrary, that you and I are far more in the right than these young gentlemen, though we do perhaps express ourselves in old-fashioned language, *vieilli*, and have not the same insolent conceit."[9]

This little exchange epitomizes the dual perspective that Turgenev as novelist maintains throughout his novel. The anxiety of Nikolai Petrovitch, the ineffectual, amiable, and sentimental landowner, is also Turgenev's anxiety as he looks ahead to the survival of his art in a society of Bazarovs, effectual and unsentimental Philistines. He is known to have felt a personal kinship with his character Nikolai Petrovitch, whose gentle, melancholy, groping irresolution parodies the irresolution of the novel that contains him.

After the conversation quoted, Nikolai takes a walk in his arbor, muses on his position, and recognizes the growing distance between his son and himself. He feels that the younger men are both further from the right and yet somehow superior to his generation, and he wonders if this superiority doesn't lie in their showing fewer traces of slave ownership. This reluctant generosity tinged with feelings of exclusion presents a simplified but not unfaithful version of the novel's own tangled ambivalences toward a future less unjust but less tolerant. The alternative to this generosity is the cold contempt of the brother Pavel, relic of a world of outmoded gallantries, an "antique survival" as Bazarov calls him, in his own word *vieilli*. Pavel's contempt is a reaction based on sterile loyalties, and it leads directly, as the novel indicates, to spiritual death. But Bazarov also meets death, a literal death of the body, as though the era he adumbrates were not yet ready to begin. Nikolai Petrovitch lives on and is appointed a mediator to administer the emancipation reforms, but, predictably, succeeds in pleasing none of the classes he is called upon to reconcile. He is condemned to the discontents of the mediator, which are the discontents of the novel, its honesty a source of division and its generosity tinged by fear. *Fathers and Children* is one extended recognition, striving for a lucidity which does not truly liberate but simply permits an ambiguous, uneasy survival.

Turgenev's work can be compared with another ambitious study of historical turmoil which appeared ten years after it, Dostoevsky's *The Devils*. The later novel begins and nearly ends with that most memorable superannuated character, Stepan Trofimovitch Verkhovensky, charming, pathetic, useless, and guilty, a character whom Dostoevsky described as "the cornerstone of everything" in the book. Stepan Trofimovitch incarnates and parodies the past out of which his creator's thought and art have grown and against which they define themselves. A soft-minded liberal of the forties, dilettante atheist, middle-class socialist, confused antinationalist, he is the tutor of Stravrogin, absentee father of the revolutionary leader Piotr, former owner of the convict and murderer Fedka, whom he had callously sold into the army to pay a debt. Stepan in his apparent helplessness has functioned as a kind of origin for the demonic present that frightens and repels him. He is an unwitting source of evil, and his anachronistic relation to the revolutionary generation he has helped to produce lies partly in his ignorance of consequences, his aestheticism of politics.

Stepan is a caricature of the novelist's early liberalism, and his inadequacies are pitilessly revealed; yet despite his compulsive French, his frequent bouts of tears, his social parasitism, his abandonment of his son, his absurd poem, his alternating terror and melodramatic bravado—despite or because of these things, he appeals to the reader's pity as do few other characters in the novel's populous world. In Stepan Trofimovitch we can study Dostoevsky's effort to redeem a past of guilty innocence, and what is unique in *this* superannuated character is the final conversion which exorcises his own demons and clears the air symbolically for a future the novelist and reader need not fear. It is Stepan who formulates at the end the scriptural metaphor of exorcism that underlies the plot and which opens up a future purged of madness. It is Stepan who, at the moment of his recognition scene, is made to express the redemptive truth which is the work's only response to insane malignancy.

> *"Nous sommes tous malheureux mais il faut les pardonner tous. Pardonnons,* Lise, and let us be free for ever. To be quit of the world and be completely free. *Il faut pardonner, pardonner, et pardonner. . . .* Now I've torn myself in half; left behind a mad visionary who dreamed of soaring to the sky. *Vingt-deux ans,* here. A shattered, frozen old man."[10]

In Stepan's symbolic return to the Russian folk and to the perennially sane Russian reality, in his drifting toward Christian faith just before his death, Dostoevsky contrives a ritual cleansing of national defilement and an uprooting of the sources of evil. Stepan's life can be read as a historical allegory that purifies the future for belief and for writing.

This redemptive death of a superannuated character opposes itself to the more common destiny of a tragic death, such as the disappearance of Michael Henchard in Hardy's *Mayor of Casterbridge*. Henchard embodies a prescientific, pretechnological, defeated relation to the earth, a relation that Hardy links to the Old Testament, that is the matter of his fiction and that is superseded by the shallow skill of the new man Farfrae. All these various examples suggest that the superannuated or anachronistic character can be regarded as a complex sign for that past out of which emerges the writer's work together with his culture. This character is a highly stylized sign, often a distorted or reductive sign, of that past, but he or she plays nonetheless a privileged role in the work because his or her destiny is bound up with the work's own presumptive destiny as no other character's is.

Perhaps the most endearing anachronism of modern fiction is Marcel's grandmother in Proust. It is true that the grandmother, as Auden remarked, is one of the few successful portraits of a saint in literature, but she is accorded nonetheless the comedy as well as the pathos of her superannuation. The comedy even tinges that quality which most renders her saintlike, her loving and profound generosity.

> We could no longer keep count in the family . . . of all the armchairs she had presented to married couples, young and old, which on a first attempt to sit down on them had at once collapsed beneath the weight of their recipient. But my grandmother would have thought it sordid to concern herself too closely with the solidity of any piece of furniture in which could still be discerned a flourish, a smile, a brave conceit of the past. And even what in such pieces supplied a material need, since it did so in a manner to which we are no longer accustomed, was as charming to her as one of those old forms of speech in which we can still see traces of a metaphor whose fine point has been worn away by the rough usage of our modern tongue. In precisely the same way the pastoral novels of George Sand, which she was giving me for my birthday, were

regular lumber-rooms of antique furniture. . . . And my grandmother had bought them in preference to other books, just as she
would have preferred to take a house that had a gothic dovecot, or
some other such piece of antiquity as would have a pleasant effect
on the mind, filling it with a nostalgic longing for impossible journeys through time.[11]

Here in this last phrase we can detect the link between the grandmother and the work in which she lives, since the novel in all its
vastness is concerned, less idiosyncratically but even more obses-
sively, with impossible journeys through time, "impossibles voy-
ages dans le temps." The grandmother anticipates and gently
parodies her grandson's quest; she embodies the touching, quixotic, and absurd futility that attends most enterprises like his, and
that his novel must somehow transcend if it is not to collapse like
one of her armchairs. The narrator's posture facing backward
replicates the posture of the woman he is looking back toward,
and if she is granted no recognition scene, he himself experiences
more than one.

An exemplary instance is his return to the Bois de
Boulogne, which as a child he had loved to visit in order to admire
the radiant elegance of Odette Swann and the subordinate elegance of the world in which she moved. This return, in the closing
pages of *Du côté de chez Swann,* reveals to the narrator the anachronism of his own expectations, for instead of Odette's victoria he
finds only motor cars, instead of her lovely gowns he finds ugly
Greco-Saxon tunics, instead of gentlemen's gray "tile" hats he
finds men strolling bareheaded. Faced with irrational disappoint-
ment, he recognizes, as his grandmother had not, "how paradoxical it is to seek in reality for the pictures that are stored in one's
memory" and that "remembrance of a particular form is but regret
for a particular moment." This recognition frees him from the
quixotism of her nostalgia, whose naiveté is his starting point. The
recognition will enable him later to write a great novel, but it will
also ensure that the novel's drama of temporality will be subjective. For unlike the novels by Stendhal, Turgenev, and Dostoevsky,
A la recherche du temps perdu in effect dehistoricizes time by locating
its power within the private sensibility. The replacement of the

victoria by the motor car is relatively insignificant; the intense conflict is located not in the particular form of history but in the particular moment of memory. Thus the grandmother's real naiveté lies not in her outmoded tastes but in her wish to comfort her nostalgia with mere objects.

Proust's subjectivity has helped to shape thought about time in our century, but it has not defused the tension stemming from objective change and actual anachronization. We meet the age-old ambivalence in Thomas Mann's Serenus Zeitblom and in Angus Wilson's "Darling Dodos"; in America it colors the work of Eudora Welty, John Cheever, and Robert Lowell. And increasingly in the twentieth century, this ambivalence tinges the representations of an entire superannuated society, as in Chekhov's *Cherry Orchard,* Shaw's *Heartbreak House,* the novels of Faulkner, or Renoir's film *La règle du jeu* with its ominous refrain, "C'est une race qui se perd."

Western writers tend to displace the threat of becoming vestigial to their characters or their poetic personae, thus attempting to affirm their control, manifest their awareness, reduce their vulnerability. To recognize as a writer the drama of the survivor is to invest one's work with a little more plasticity, to distinguish writing from the rigidity of ritual. To stage a tragedy of anachronism is perhaps the most effective way of exorcising it, just as for the critic, perhaps, speaking about obsolescence is a defense against becoming obsolescent. Our literature seems fated to dramatize its historical misgivings with merciless persistence, comically and cruelly returning to relics that are reproachful, inescapable, and emblematic.

Notes

Introduction

1. Samuel Daniel, "A Defence of Ryme," in G. Gregory Smith, ed., *Elizabethan Critical Essays*, 2:363 (Oxford: Oxford University Press, 1959).

2. Rainer Maria Rilke, *Duino Elegies*, J. B. Leishman and Stephen Spender, tr. (New York: Norton, 1939), p. 53. The German text reads: "die unsägliche Stelle, wo sich das reine Zuwenig / unbegreiflich verwandelt—, umspringt / in jenes leere Zuviel" (ll. 84–86, p. 52).

3. De Man's discussion of the intricate relationships between rhetoric and grammar appears in the first chapter of his *Allegories of Reading* (New Haven: Yale University Press, 1979), pp. 6ff. On p. 130 he writes that "Nietzsche contemptuously dismisses the popular meaning of rhetoric as eloquence and concentrates instead on the complex and philosophically challenging epistemology of the tropes." This "privileging figure over persuasion" de Man sees as "a typically post-Romantic gesture," although he personally appears to dissociate himself from it. The tendency to privilege the one over the other is indeed still alive and well; despite de Man's disclaimer one can trace a hierarchization in his own distinction between the "popular" and the "philosophically challenging."

4. Charles d'Orléans, *Poésies*, Pierre Champion, ed. (Paris: Champion, 1956), 2:477.

5. Thomas Nashe, *Selected Works*, Stanley Wells, ed. (London: Arnold, 1964), p. 138.

6. Friedrich Nietzsche, *The Use and Abuse of History*, A. Collins, tr. (Indianapolis: Bobbs-Merrill, 1957), p. 21. Quoted by Thomas M. Greene, *The Light in Troy: Imitation and Discovery in Renaissance Poetry* (New Haven: Yale University Press, 1982), p. 35.

7. Ludovico Ariosto, *Opere minori*, Cesare Segre, ed. (Milan: Ricciardi, n.d.), p. 568.

8. Walt Whitman, *Leaves of Grass* (New York: Modern Library, n.d.), p. 408.

1. Erasmus' "Festina lente": Vulnerabilities of the Humanist Text

1. English translations of passages from the *Adagia* are taken from *The "Adages" of Erasmus*, M. M. Phillips, tr. (Cambridge: Cambridge University Press, 1964). The passage quoted above appears on p. 180. Future references will be indicated parenthetically

after each quotation. On the one or two occasions where I have not followed Phillips' translation, no parenthetical reference is supplied. Comments by Phillips quoted below are taken from her long introduction to her translations.

For the Latin text of the "Festina lente" essay, I have used Erasmus von Rotterdam, *Ausgewählte Schriften*, vol. 7, edited with facing German translation by Theresia Payr (Darmstadt: Wissenschaftliche Buchgesellschaft, 1972). Payr's text follows the Leyden edition of 1703. I have also consulted several editions of the *Adagia* published during Erasmus' lifetime.

2. *Parallels (Parabolae sive similia)*, R. A. B. Mynors, tr., vol. 23 of the *Collected Works of Erasmus* (Toronto: University of Toronto Press, 1978), pp. 131, 130.

3. *The Enchiridion of Erasmus*, Raymond Himelick, tr. (Bloomington: Indiana University Press, 1963), pp. 49, 54.

4. "Quid sit paroemia," *Adagiorum Chiliades* (Venice: Aldus Manutius, 1508), p. 1r.

5. This expression is not an adage cited by Erasmus. Its author was one Furius Antias, a Roman poet who appears to have flourished ca. 100 B.C. The phrase happens to be extant because it was quoted by Aulus Gellius (*Attic Nights*, XVIII, ii, 4).

6. Terence Cave, *The Cornucopian Text: Problems of Writing in the French Renaissance* (Oxford: Clarendon Press, 1979), p. 111.

2. Petrarch *Viator*

1. Quotations from the *Familiares* are based on the Latin text of the critical edition by Vittorio Rossi and Umberto Bosco, *Le Familiari*, 4 vols. (Florence: Sansoni, 1933–1942). Translations are mine unless otherwise attributed. The passage quoted is from Book XIV, letter 1. Future references will be supplied parenthetically after each quotation.

2. Quotations from Petrarch's vernacular poetry are taken from Francesco Petrarca, *Opere*, Emilio Bigi, ed. (Milan: Mursia, 1968). Translations are from *Petrarch's Lyric Poems*, Robert M. Durling, tr. and ed. (Cambridge: Harvard University Press, 1976). I have placed in brackets in a subsequent quotation the one alteration I have made in Durling's renderings.

3. English quotations from the *Secretum* are taken (with minimal variations) from *Petrarch's Secret*, William H. Draper, tr. (London: Chatto and Windus, 1911). The passage quoted appears on pp. 114–15. The Latin original can be found in *Opere*, p. 618.

4. The motif of the right-hand path recurs frequently in Petrarch's work. See *Petrarch's Secret*, p. 128 (*Opere*, p. 630), with its quotation from the *Aeneid*, VI.540–43. See also *Familiares* XII.3. Bigi's note to *Canzoniere* 264 cites eclogue IX and *Epistolae metricae* I.14.

5. Francesco Petrarca, *Opere latine*, Antonietta Bufano, ed., 2 vols. (Turin: U.T.E.T., 1975), 1:772–74.

6. Quotations from this work in both languages are taken from *Petrarch's "Bucolicum carmen"*, Thomas G. Bergin, tr. (New Haven: Yale University Press, 1974).

7. Latin text in Francesco Petrarca, *Invective contra medicum*, Pier Giorgio Ricci, ed. (Rome: Le Monnier, 1950), p. 89.

8. Latin text in Francesco Petrarca, *Sine nomine,*Ugo Dotti, ed. and tr. (Bari: Laterza, 1974), letter 17, p. 180.

9. The pursuit of glory is represented in the *Secretum* as a journey. "We travel many ways to the same end, and, believe me, though you have left the road worn by feet of the crowd, you still direct your feet by a side-path towards this same ambition that you say you have thought scorn of; it is repose, solitude, a total disregard of human affairs, yes, and your own activities also, which just at present take you along that chosen path, but the end and object is glory." *Petrarch's Secret,* p. 74; Latin text in *Opere,* p. 582.

10. *Invective,* p. 30.

11. Latin text from *Opere,* p. 972. English version based on *Petrarch: A Humanist among Princes,* edited and translated (in part) by David Thompson (New York: Harper and Row, 1971), p. 1. Thompson's translation of this letter revises *Petrarch: The First Modern Scholar,* J. H. Robinson and H. W. Rolfe, eds. (New York: Putnam, 1898).

12. Francesco Petrarca, *Prose,* G. Martellotti and others, eds. (Milan: Ricciardi, 1955), p. 222.

13. "Magnas res equare sermonibus et verbis arte contextis animi faciem latentis ostendere, is demum, puto, supremus eloquentie finis est, cui dum humana mens inhiat, sepe calle medio victa subsistit."

14. Ernst Cassirer and others, eds., *The Renaissance Philosophy of Man* (Chicago: University of Chicago Press, 1961), p. 40. Latin text in *Opere,* p. 734.

15. The "Praefatio" in which this phrase appears is not included in most manuscripts or in the Ricci edition. It can be found in the *Opera* published in four volumes at Basel in 1581, 2:1087.

16. Francesco Petrarca, *Rime, trionfi, e poesie latine,* F. Neri and others, eds. (Milan: Ricciardi, 1951), p. 734.

17. Thompson, ed. *Petrarch,* p. 75. Latin text in *Epistolae de rebus familiaribus et variae,* Giuseppe Fracassetti, ed., 3 vols. (Florence: Le Monnier, 1859–1863), 2:432.

18. *Sine nomine,* letter 18, p. 200 ("Quisquis limen illud introiit, confestim suus esse desiit"); letter 15, p. 158. English quotations from *Petrarch's Book without a Name,* Norman P. Zacour, tr. (Toronto: Pontifical Institute of Medieval Studies, 1973), pp. 109, 91.

19. English quotations are taken from *Petrarch's Africa,* Thomas G. Bergin and Alice S. Wilson, tr. (New Haven: Yale University Press, 1977). The passage quoted appears in Book I, lines 20–24. The first reference in each footnote to a quotation from this poem will indicate the book and line numbers in Bergin and Wilson. The Latin quotations are taken from the critical edition by Nicola Festa (Florence: Sansoni, 1926).

20. When in Book VIII the Carthaginian envoys lead away their prisoners recovered from Rome, the latter are compared to the souls freed by Christ at the harrowing of hell, with an apology for the offense to decorum.

> Indulge me if I dare here to equate
> the earthly with the heavenly, man's things
> with the eternal, and the trivial
> with the sublime. (VIII.1417)
>
> Liceat terrestria celo
> Equare, eternis mortalia, maxima parvis. (VIII.999)

The word *parvis,* running counter to so much in the poem, signals the gulf dividing the poet's loyalties. One must also wonder what precisely the simile allows one to make of that Roman republic which the prisoners are leaving and for which so much blood is bravely shed. Earlier, the personification of this republic is shown kneeling before the throne of God, praying for victory, at the battle of Zama and ending with a plea for future generations.

> Even though
> you spare not me, forgive my progeny
> whom a new faith, mayhap, in years to come
> will make more pleasing in your sight. (VII.879)

> Si michi non parcis, populis ignosce nepotum,
> Quos nova religio faciet tibi forsan amicos. (VII.657)

If pagans, not yet enlightened by revelation, risk destruction by a Christian God, something of the risk must attach itself to the Christian poet who celebrates their history.

21. "Gallica qui vario complebit rura pavore / Et fluvios atri violabit sanguinis unda" (II.221). This passage anticipates the charge leveled against Hannibal that he "pollutes ["turpas"] lakes, rivers, pools and lands and seas with gore" (VI.347). Latin text VI.267.

22. II.356–57; "gladiis perrumpere sacra / Fas erit" (II.272).

23. "Cum sepe ad certam legiones currere mortem / Viderimus" (III.632).

24. As a young man in Rome he breaks in to the house of the potential traitor Metellus (IV.266ff.; IV.195ff.); later at the battle of Cartagena he "pierced through the armored ranks and fought his way into the city's heart" (IV.385–86). "Non menia crebis / Turribus . . . / Scandentem muros perque omnia tela ruentem / Sustinere ducem" (IV.279–85).

25. Quoted by Bergin and Wilson, *Petrarch's Africa*, p. xi.

26. It is ironically relevant that the circulation of the Mago passage, the only lines from the poem released during Petrarch's lifetime, led to malicious criticism on the part of some readers and thence produced a furious letter from the poet to Boccaccio *(Seniles,* II.1), revealing very plainly his sensitivity to public exposure.

27. To tell this story, Petrarch writes, would be to sully the Muses (IX.584–85): "patiarque nec unquam / Carmine tam mesto sacras maculare Sorores" (IX.419).

28. " . . . seque ipse fatebitur ultro / Plus nulli debere viro" (IX.262).

29. "Quid tot valuere rapine? / Raptor raptorem spoliat" (VIII.28).

30. I have altered slightly the rendering of Bergin and Wilson.

3. *Il Cortegiano* and the Choice of a Game

1. Quotations in English from Castiglione are drawn from the translation by Charles S. Singleton (Garden City: Anchor Books, 1959). Quotations in Italian are taken from the edition by Bruno Maier (Turin: U.T.E.T., 1964). The references in parentheses indicate first the book and then the chapter in which the quoted passage appears.

2. These examples are taken from Thomas Frederick Crane, *Italian Social Customs of the Sixteenth Century* (New Haven: Yale University Press, 1920), p. 10.

3. Jacques Ehrmann, "Homo Ludens Revisited," *Yale French Studies* (1968), no. 41, pp. 31–57.

4. Contained in Eugenio Garin, ed., *Prosatori Latini del Quattrocento*, pp. 44–98. (Milan and Naples: Ricciardi, n.d.).

5. Hannah Arendt, *The Human Condition* (Chicago: University of Chicago Press, 1970), p. 198.

6. D. W. Winnicott, *Playing and Reality* (New York: Basic Books, 1971), p. 102.

4. The End of Discourse in Machiavelli's *Prince*

1. Quotations in Italian from *Il principe* and the *Discorsi* are taken from Niccolò Machiavelli, *Opere,* Ezio Raimondi, ed. (Milan: Mursia, 1969). This passage from the *Discorsi* appears on p. 253. Future page references to Raimondi will appear parenthetically after the quotation.

Quotations in English from *The Prince* are taken from the translation by George Bull (New York: Penguin Classics, 1980). Quotations from the *Discourses* are taken from *The Prince and the Discourses*, introduction by Max Lerner (New York: Modern Library, 1950). The passage quoted appears on p. 397. The parenthetical page references will refer to these English editions. I have however taken the liberty throughout of substituting the Italian word *virtù* for its supposed English equivalent, since the argument of this essay depends upon the reader's recognition of this term.

2. *Tutte le opere di Niccolò Machiavelli,* F. Flora and C. Cordié, eds. (Milan: Mondadori, 1950), 2:768–69. My translation.

3. Sydney Anglo, *Machiavelli: A Dissection* (London: Gollancz, 1969), p. 236.

5. The Hair of the Dog That Bit You: Rabelais' Thirst

1. Quotations from Rabelais' French text are taken from his *Oeuvres complètes,* Pierre Jourda, ed., 2 vols. (Paris: Garnier, 1962). Parenthetical volume and page numbers will refer to this edition. The passage here quoted appears in 1:288–89. English translations are taken from François Rabelais, *Gargantua and Pantagruel,* J. M. Cohen, tr. (New York: Penguin Books, 1983). The passage here quoted appears on p. 214.

2. Littré illustrates the definition "se changer en mal" with a quotation from Montaigne: "Le vin s'altere aux caves." He quotes Amyot: "sans y avoir rien de corrompu ny d'alteré." *Le Trésor de la langue française* quotes a usage from 1388: "On trouva qu'il estoit alteré d'entendement." Demerson, glossing the noun *altération* as it appears in the description of the drought ("ceste horrificque altération"), gives "dégradation des conditions naturelles de la vie." François Rabelais, *Oeuvres complètes,* Guy Demerson, ed. (Paris: Seuil, 1973), p. 223 n. 7.

3. *Oeuvres,* Demerson, ed. p. 225 n. 22.

4. Demerson suggests a pun here on *aiguillons divins,* popular exercises of piety (p. 225 n. 25). The word *lancement* contains a pun on the German word *Landsman.*

5. The idea that the pursuit of wealth causes the growth of the arts is developed

at length in Aristophanes' *Plutus*. The "Prologus" to Persius' satires refers to the *venter* as "magister artis" and evokes the inspirational power of greed for money.

6. "Dire que notre Histoire est histoire des hommes ou dire qu'elle est née et qu'elle se développe dans le cadre permanent d'un champ de tension engendré par la rareté, c'est tout un." Jean-Paul Sartre, *Critique de la raison dialectique* (Paris: Gallimard, 1960), p. 202. Already in *L'Etre et le néant*, as Fredric Jameson points out, "the very origin of action . . . was found in the structure of the human being as *lack*, as ontological privation, attempting to satisfy itself, to fulfill itself, and thereby to arrive at some definitive state of being." *Marxism and Form* (Princeton: Princeton University Press, 1971), p. 232.

7. Marsilio Ficino, *The Letters of Marsilio Ficino*, translated by members of the language department of the School of Economic Science, London (London: Shepheard-Walwyn, 1978), 2:79–80. The Latin text can be found in the *Opera omnia* of Ficino (Turin: Bottega d'Erasmo, 1959), 1:749. I owe this reference to Paul Oskar Kristeller. Kristeller argues in an essay that the unquenchable thirst which only increases with drinking, attributed to a certain Adovardo by Lorenzo de' Medici in the second capitolo of his *Simposio*, parodies the Neoplatonic thirst for the divine. See "Lorenzo de' Medici platonico" in Kristeller's *Studies in Renaissance Thought and Letters* (Rome: Edizioni di Storia e Letterature, 1956), pp. 213–19, especially p. 219.

8. I have discussed at greater length Rabelais' treatment of these problems in "The Unity of the *Tiers Livre*," an essay forthcoming in the *Acta* of the Colloque International François Rabelais held at Tours in September 1984.

9. "Le brevaige contenu dedans la couppe de Tantalus representé par figure entre les saiges Brachmanes" (1:402) ("that within the cup of Tantalus, which the Brahmin sages represented figuratively" [286]) will send the instructed reader to the *Life of Apollonius of Tyana* by Flavius Philostratus, where Tantalus is represented as a symbol of joy rather than frustration. Here the force of the learned allusion works against the force of the common reader's "naive" response. This instance could be cited as an example of the interpretive traps presented by Rabelais' text and by Humanist allusion in general. The greater the obscurity of the allusion, whether in the sixteenth or twentieth century, the more recondite the appeal to a small elitist audience capable of identifying the unspecified work and author, then the higher the probability of hermeneutic miscalculation.

6. Rescue from the Abyss: Scève's Dizain 378

1. This is clear in the case of Valéry's *Charmes*, where "Aurore" and its follower, "Au platane," stand in a sharply dialogic relation to the final poem, "Palme."

2. "Rhetoric seeks to discover the means of coming as near such success as the circumstances of each particular case allow." Aristotle, *Rhetoric*, 1355b, W. Rhys Roberts, tr. For the enthymeme's dependence on the contingent, the probable, and the fallible, see 1357a-b, 1396a, 1402b.

3. All quotations from Scève are taken from *The "Délie" of Maurice Scève*, I. D. McFarlane, ed. All translations are mine. (Cambridge: Cambridge University Press, 1966).

4. McFarlane in a note to 378 suggests that the return to consciousness renders

the speaker *unprotected,* since he had previously been in a trance and thus immune from death. This reading assumes that "plus" should be read "ne . . . plus." Aside from the doubtfulness of that assumption, the interpretation is surely refuted by the statement that the Esprit has been perishing while asleep. Coleman's discussion can be found in her *Maurice Scève: Poet of Love* (Cambridge: Cambridge University Press, 1975), pp. 157ff.

5. I have discussed the iterative present tense in "Styles of Experience in Scève's *Délie,*" *Yale French Studies,* no. 47, pp. 68–69, and in *The Light in Troy: Imitation and Discovery in Renaissance Poetry* (New Haven: Yale University Press, 1982), pp. 119–26.

7. Dangerous Parleys—Montaigne's *Essais* I:5 and 6

1. French text from *Essais: Reproduction photographique de l'édition originale de 1580.* Daniel Martin, ed. 2 vols. (Geneva: Slatkine; Paris: Champion, 1976), I:20–22. English translations are taken from the edition of Donald Frame, *The Complete Works of Montaigne* (Stanford: Stanford University Press, 1957).

2. *Essais,* pp. 22–23.

3. *Ibid,* pp. 23–24.

4. *Ibid,* pp. 26–27.

5. All succeeding quotations from Montaigne are taken from the edition of P. Villey, reedited by V. L. Saulnier, *Les Essais de Montaigne: Edition conforme au texte de l'exemplaire de Bordeaux* (Paris: PUF, 1978). Parenthetical references are to the page numbers of this edition.

6. For useful discussions of the inside/outside polarity in Montaigne, see Richard L. Regosin, *The Matter of My Book: Montaigne's "Essais" as the Book of the Self* (Berkeley and Los Angeles: University of California Press, 1977), especially pp. 82–90; and Jules Brody, *"De mesnager sa volonté* (III:10): Lecture philologique d'un essai," in R. C. La Charité, ed. *O un Amy! Essays on Montaigne in Honor of Donald M. Frame,* pp. 34–71. (Lexington, Ky.: French Forum, 1977).

7. The image of the wild beast withdrawn to its den sends us back to the aphorism of Lysander in I:5, where the crafty commander is told to supplement the lion's skin with the fox's. Trickery with language is foxy; pressumably reliance on pure valor requires no speech, involves no engagement, places no strain on individual integrity, remains leonine.

8. I have altered slightly Frame's translation.

9. Terence Cave, *The Cornucopian Text: Problems of Writing in the French Renaissance* (Oxford: Clarendon Press, 1979), p. 299.

10. Cave, *Cornucopian Text,* p. 318.

11. *Ibid.,* p. 298.

12. I have again altered slightly Frame's translation.

8. *Love's Labour's Lost:* The Grace of Society

1. Quotations from *Love's Labour's Lost* are from the New Variorum Edition, H. H. Furness, ed. (Philadelphia: Lippincott, 1904).

2.   BEROWNE: O if the streets were paved with thine eyes,
Her feet were much too dainty for such tread.
DUMAINE: O vile, then as she goes what upward lyes?
The street should see as she walk'd over head.

(IV.iii.295–98)

3. Still another step, just preceding and accompanying the pageant, is the reconciliation of Berowne to Boyet, upon whom Berowne has vented considerable irritation during this scene in two extended speeches (354–73, 513–34). The second speech (concluding bitterly, "You leere upon me, do you? There's an eie / Wounds like a Leaden sword") is met with a surprisingly soft reply:

BOYET: Full merrily hath this brave manage, this carreere bene run. (V.ii.535–36)

That courtesy, a bit unexpectedly magnanimous and suggestive of a generosity beneath Boyet's mockery, elicits in turn Berowne's retirement from the quarrel:

Loe, he is tilting straight. Peace, I have don
(V.ii.537)

and anticipates the warmer rapprochement a few moments later:

Well said old mocker, I must needs be friends with thee.
(V.ii.609–10)

"Tilting straight" is generally taken to mean "tilting immediately"; it would make more sense if interpreted "in a straight-forward manner, without malice or irony." This interpretation would better fit Boyet's actual speech, and motivate better Berowne's retirement. In any case, the acceptance of Boyet, with his tougher and more "realistic" wit, by Berowne (and by extension his companions) is not without psychological and thematic importance.

4. To cite two critics:

"In contrast to that of the Princess, the behaviour of the men is incredibly unattractive, particularly that of Berowne. It is difficult to believe that this is the same man who spoke so eloquently a short time ago about the soft and sensible feelings of love, and promised Rosaline to mend his ways. . . . The laughter is unattractive, wild, and somehow discordant . . . and it has little resemblance to the laughter we have heard in the play before this, delicate, sophisticated, sometimes hearty. But never really unkind" (Bobbyann Roesen, *"Love's Labour's Lost," Shakespeare Quarterly* [1953], 4:422–23).

"After this defeat, and especially after Berowne's self-criticism one might expect the men to begin acting with more discretion and self-consciousness; but any such expectation proves false, for in the pageant of the Nine Worthies, which breaks in on the men's defeat, their behavior attains to a new degree of crudity" (E. M. W. Tillyard, *Shakespeare's Early Comedies* [New York: Barnes and Noble, 1965], pp. 147–48).

5. "I am a Votarie, I have vow'd to *Iaquenetta* to holde the Plough for her sweet love three yeares" (V.ii.961–62).

6. Just as death has been an abstraction, so disease has heretofore served Berowne as a source of witty imagery:

Light Wenches may prove plagues to men forsworne.
(IV.iii.404)

Write *Lord have mercie on us,* on those three,
They are infected, in their hearts it lies:
They have the plague, and caught it of your eyes.
(V.ii.466–68)

7. Walter Pater, *Appreciations* (London: Macmillan, 1913), p. 166. Pater is speaking specifically here of the style of Berowne; the larger context deals with the "foppery of delicate language" as it is toyed with throughout the play.

8. "All the wooers must learn to be patient, to wait out the full seasonal cycle which the songs represent. . . . The gaudy blossoms of Ver, the wonderful artifice of wit and wooing, are to be tried by the rigors of winter—of experience in the real world." Joseph Westlund, "Fancy and Achievement in *Love's Labour's Lost*," *Shakespeare Quarterly* (1967), 18:45.

9. The Signet edition of *Love's Labour's Lost*, John Arthos, ed. (New York and Toronto, 1965), p. 146.

10. "Sarà adunque il nostro cortegiano stimato eccellente ed in ogni cosa averà grazia, massimamente nel parlare, se fuggirà l'affetazione." Baldassare Castiglione, *Il Cortegiano, con una scelta delle opere minori*, Bruno Maier, ed. (Turin: U.T.E.T., 1955), p. 129.

11. Helge Kökeritz, *Shakespeare's Pronunciation* (New Haven: Yale University Press, 1953), p. 110.

9. Anti-Hermeneutics:
The Case of Shakespeare's Sonnet 129

1. The essay by Graves and Riding first appeared under the title "William Shakespeare and E. E. Cummings" in *A Survey of Modernist Poetry* (London: Heinemann, 1927) and in revised form was later included in Graves' *The Common Asphodel* (London: Hamilton, 1949) under the title "A Study in Original Punctuation and Spelling." The reply to Graves and Riding appears on pp. 447–52 of *Shakespeare's Sonnets*, Stephen Booth, ed. (New Haven: Yale University Press, 1980). The passages quoted appear on p. 447.

2. *Sonnets*, p. 450. Booth explains and defends his editorial policy on p. ix of his preface as follows:

"My primary purpose in the present edition is to provide a text that will give a modern reader as much as I can resurrect of a Renaissance reader's experience of the 1609 Quarto; it is, after all, the sonnets we have and not some hypothetical originals that we value. I have adopted no editorial principle beyond that of trying to adapt a modern reader—with his assumptions about idiom, spelling, and punctuation—and the 1609 text to one another . . . . Both my text and my commentary are determined by what I think a Renaissance reader would have thought as he moved from line to line and sonnet to sonnet in the Quarto. I make no major substantial emendations and few minor ones. It might therefore seem reasonable to reprint the Quarto text alone and simply comment on that, but the effects of almost four centuries are such that a modern reader faced with the Quarto text sees something that is effectively very different from what a seventeenth-century reader saw.

In modernizing spelling and punctuation I have taken each poem individually and tried to find a mid-point between following the punctuation and spelling of the Quarto text (which modern readers, accustomed to logically and semantically directive punctuation and spelling, are inclined to misinterpret) and modern directive spelling and punctuation (which often pays for its clarity by sacrificing a considerable amount of a poem's substance and energy). In each case

I have tried to find the least distorting available compromise. Sometimes no compromise is satisfactory, and I describe the probable operation of a line or quatrain in a note."

3. Lines 1258–63. See also "The Shipman's Tale," 7.170ff.

4. The considerable reality behind the nobility's reputation for extravagance is detailed in chapter 10 of Lawrence Stone's *Crisis of the Aristocracy, 1558–1641* (Oxford: Oxford University Press, Clarendon Press, 1965).

5. See, e.g., sonnet 144, line 12.

6. *Sonnets*, p. 448.

7. Edward Sapir, *Language* (New York: Harcourt, Brace and World, 1949), pp. 150, 171.

8. Ulrich von Wilamowitz-Moellendorff, *Greek Historical Writing and Apollo*, G. Murray, tr. (Oxford: Oxford University Press, 1908), p. 26.

9. T. W. Adorno, *Moments Musicaux* (1930), quoted by Susan Buck-Morss, *The Origins of Negative Dialectics* (New York: Free Press, 1977), p. 52.

10. Norman N. Holland, *The Dynamics of Literary Response* (New York: Norton, 1975), p. 104.

11. French text in Paul Ricoeur, "Qu'est-ce-qu'un texte?" in R. Bübner et al., eds., *Hermeneutik und Dialektik*, 2:194–95. (Tübingen: Mohr, 1970).

12. Hans-Georg Gadamer, *Truth and Method* (New York: Seabury Press, 1975), p. 273. German text in Gadamer, *Wahrheit und Methode* (Tübingen: Mohr, 1960), p. 290:

"Das historische Bewusstsein ist sich seiner eigenen Andersheit bewusst und hebt daher den Horizont der Überlieferung von dem eigenen Horizont ab. Andererseits aber ist es selbst nur . . . wie eine Überlagerung über einer fortwirkenden Tradition, und daher nimmt es das voneinander Abgehobene sogleich wieder zusammen, um in der Einheit des geschichtlichen Horizontes, den es sich so erwirbt, sich mit sich selbst zu vermitteln."

13. Gadamer, *Truth and Method*, pp. 264–65, 262.

14. Frank Kermode, *The Genesis of Secrecy: On the Interpretation of Narrative* (Cambridge: Harvard University Press, 1979).

15. Gadamer, *Truth and Method*, p. 267. German text in *Wahrheit und Methode*, p. 283: "Der wahre historische Gegenstand ist kein Gegenstand, sondern die Einheit dieses Einen und Anderen, ein Verhältnis, in dem die Wirklichkeit der Geschichte ebenso wie die Wirklichkeit des geschichtlichen Verstehens besteht."

16. Maurice Blanchot evokes the danger to the literary work judged to be good; it is likely to be "made useful" and exploited. The work judged to be bad on the other hand is preserved by its lack of esteem: "set aside, relegated to the inferno by libraries, burned, forgotten: but this exile, this disappearance into the heat of the fire or the tepidness of oblivion, *prolongs in a certain way the just distance of the work . . . .* The work does not endure; it is" (my italics). French text in *L'espace littéraire* (Paris: Gallimard, 1955), p. 270.

17. Martin Heidegger, *Being and Time*, J. Macquarrie and E. Robinson, tr. (New York: Harper and Row, 1962), p. 165.

18. "This structuralist thematic of broken immediacy is therefore the saddened, *negative*, nostalgic, guilty Rousseauistic side of the thinking of play, whose other side would be the Nietzschean *affirmation*, that is the joyous affirmation of the play of the world and of the innocence of becoming, the affirmation of a world of signs without fault, without truth, and without origin which is offered to an active interpretation." Jacques Derrida, *Writing and Difference*, A. Bass, tr. (Chicago: University of Chicago Press, 1978), p. 272;

French text in *L'Ecriture et la différence* (Paris: Seuil, 1967), p. 427. The very allusions to Rousseau and Nietzsche in the sentence quoted imply a knowable, traceable continuity, an identifiable determinacy inherent in the ideas of these two thinkers and resistant to the misunderstandings of history. The "immediacy" of their work would appear not to have been broken. It is unclear finally just how much Derrida concedes to history.

19. It is true, as Stanley Fish has argued, that interpretation is guided by context, but to deny the text (with Fish) *any* priority to interpretation is to be excessively rigid. The literary text when read as literature is precisely of that kind which invites a series of circular adjustments between itself and its interpretive context. This series never ends; it never fully succeeds; but a fitting interpretive context possesses a flexible capacity for revision which Fish is unwilling to recognize. The fact is that interpreters can meaningfully discuss a text, persuade one another, and revise their interpretations without surrendering an entire "set of interpretive assumptions." Revised interpretations within a single "context" are possible because a prior text does exist. See Stanley Fish, "Normal Circumstances, Literal Language, Direct Speech Acts, the Ordinary, the Everyday, the Obvious, What Goes Without Saying, and Other Special Cases,"*Critical Inquiry* (1978), 4:625–44.

20. T. S. Eliot, *Selected Essays* (London: Faber and Faber, 1956), p. 429.

21. Wolfgang Iser writes suggestively of the reading process: "The production of the meaning of literary texts . . . does not merely entail the discovery of the unformulated . . . it also entails the possibility that we may formulate ourselves and so discover what had previously seemed to elude our consciousness." *The Implied Reader* (Baltimore: Johns Hopkins Press, 1974), p. 294. But I would not agree that "the convergence of text and reader brings the literary work into existence" (p. 275). To split the text and the work is to court a potentially narcissistic subjectivism.

10. Pitiful Thrivers: Failed Husbandry in the *Sonnets*

1. All quotations from the sonnets are taken from the reproduction of the quarto text in *Shakespeare's Sonnets*, Stephen Booth, ed. (New Haven and London: Yale University Press, 1980). I have normalized the usage of *u/v*. The glosses by Booth occasionally cited are taken from the compendious notes to this edition. I also have occasion to cite glosses from the edition by W. G. Ingram and Theodore Redpath, *Shakespeare's Sonnets* (New York: Barnes and Noble, 1965).

2. *Shakespeare's Sonnets*, D. Bush and A. Harbage, eds. (Baltimore: Penguin Books, 1967).

11. Ben Jonson and the Centered Self

1. Georges Poulet, *Les Métamorphoses du cercle* (Paris: Plon, 1961). In his chapter on the circle in Renaissance literature, Poulet stresses the dynamic impulse and the tendency toward *élargissement* of the circle during this period. The present essay offers a

somewhat different aspect, without of course challenging his interpretation of those texts on which his own view is based.

2. Marjorie Nicolson, *The Breaking of the Circle* (Evanston, Ill.: Northwestern Univ. Press, 1950). The useful book by Edward B. Partridge, *The Broken Compass: A Study of the Major Comedies of Ben Jonson* (New York: Columbia Univ. Press, 1958), does not, despite its title, pursue the imagery of compass or circle to great length.

3. All references, unless otherwise identified, are to *Ben Jonson*, eds. C. H. Herford and Percy and Evelyn Simpson, (Oxford: Univ. Press, 1925–1952). Parenthetical references after quotations will give first the volume and then the page in this edition. The passage above is from 7:188.

4. See Dolora Cunningham, "The Jonsonian Masque as a Literary Form," *ELH* (1955), 22:108–24; reprinted in J. Barish, ed., *Ben Jonson: A Collection of Critical Essays* (Englewood Cliffs: Prentice-Hall, 1963), pp. 160–74.

5. A harmonious England is itself a protected circle of order in Jonson's imagination. Compare the epilogue to *Every Man out of his Humor:*

> Let forraine politie be dull as lead . . .
> And turtle-footed peace dance fayrie rings
> About her court; where, never may there come
> Suspect, or danger, but all trust, and safetie (3:599)

or this injunction to Minerva from one of the odes:

> Throwe, Holye Virgin, then,
> Thie Chrystall sheild
> About this Isle, and charme the rounde. (8:421)

6. The same imagery reappears in Jonson's subsequent wedding masque, *The Haddington Masque,* which also contains the discovery of a sphere onstage, now containing the constellations of the zodiac. The symbolism is explained by its supposed maker, Vulcan:

> It is a spheare, I' have formed round, and even,
> In due proportion to the spheare of heaven,
> With all his lines, and circles; that compose
> The perfect'st forme, and aptly doe disclose
> The heaven of marriage: which I title it. (7:258)

The commonplace repeated in both wedding masques that the sphere is the most perfect form goes back to Aristotle, *De Caelo,* II, 4. Compare Ronsard: "en la forme ronde / Gist la perfection qui toute en soy abonde." *Hymne du Ciel,* ll. 33–34.

7. This motif of breaking, entering, and stealing is repeated in a subplot involving the storming of the town of Vicenza and the subsequent kidnapping of a noble infant.

8. Compare Buffone's reply to the question how he himself does: "Faith, spending my metal, in this reeling world (here and there) as the sway of my affection carries me" (3:472).

9. Alvin Kernan, in the excellent introduction to his edition *(The Yale Ben Jonson,* New Haven and London, 1962), has rightly stressed the theatrical bent of the two principal villains. I am inclined to see these propensities as part of the larger portrayal of the centrifugal personality.

10. Perhaps there is another joke. In the speech preceding the one quoted, Lady Wouldbe refers with some scorn to English authors who steal from Guarino and Montaigne. The remark is typical of her wayward and jumbled name-dropping. But the humor lies in her own theft—or at least intended theft—from Montaigne an instant later

in the speech quoted above; for this sage advice to divert our passions to some lesser humor represents a scrambled summary of Montaigne's essay *"De la diversion"* (III:4):

> Quand les medecins ne peuvent purger le catarre, ils le divertissent et le desvoyent a une autre partie moins dangereuse. Je m'appercoy que c'est aussi la plus ordinaire recepte aux maladies de l'ame. . . . On luy faict peu choquer les maux de droit fil; on ne luy en faict ny soustenir ny rabattre l'ateinte, on la luy faict decliner et gauchir.

Essais, A. Thibaudet, ed. (Paris: Editions de la Pléiade, 1950), p. 930.

11. Thomas Greene, "The Flexibility of the Self in Renaissance Literature," Demetz, Greene, and Nelson, eds., in *The Disciplines of Criticism,* pp. 241–64 (New Haven and London: Yale University Press, 1968).

12. The infinite flexibility of women in this play is suggested not only by the name and conduct of Dame Pliant, but also by the name and conduct of Doll, whose nature changes like a literal doll's with the dresses she wears.

13. Perhaps there is meaning in this play's relegation to a madman of the cosmic imagery common in the masques. The deranged Aeglamour imagines, in his grandiose fancies, that his (supposedly) dead mistress will repair the broken circles of the cosmos:

tempring all
The jarring Spheeres, and giving to the World
Againe, his first and tunefull planetting.
O' what an age will here be of new concords! (7:45)

The more modest sphere of Robin's and Marian's love acquires a greater force but also greater isolation in the light of this baseless fantasy.

12. History and Anachronism

1. Umberto Eco, *A Theory of Semiotics* (Bloomington: Indiana University Press, 1976), p. 80.

2. Pietro Aretino, *Selected Letters,* George Bull tr. (New York: Penguin, 1976), p. 101.

3. In the *locus classicus* of Renaissance anachronistic analysis, Erasmus' *Ciceronianus,* a modern Ciceronian is said to be "as ridiculous an orator as if in tragic dress he danced in the Atellan farce; or put a yellow robe on a cat, as the saying goes; or purple upon the ape; or adorned Bacchus and Sardanapulus with the skin of a lion and the club of Hercules." Desiderius Erasmus, *Ciceronianus,* Izora Scott, tr. (New York: Columbia University Teachers College, 1972), p. 59.

4. Baldesar Castiglione, *The Book of the Courtier,* Charles S. Singleton, tr. (New York: Doubleday, 1959), pp. 5–6, 58.

5. Samuel Johnson, *The Works of Samuel Johnson* (Troy, N.Y.: Pafraets, 1903), 11:224, 234, 259.

6. Gary Saul Morson, *The Boundaries of Genre* (Austin: University of Texas Press, 1981), p. 118.

7. Thomas Greene, *The Light in Troy: Imitation and Discovery in Renaissance Poetry* (New Haven and London: Yale University Press, 1982), pp. 37ff. and *passim.* The

present essay was written in part to clarify and extend the treatment of anachronism in this book.

8. David Quint, "Painful Memories: *Aeneid* 3 and the Problems of the Past," *The Classical Journal* (1982), 78:30–38.

9. Ivan Turgenev, *Fathers and Children*, Constance Garnett, tr. (New York: Modern Library, n.d.), pp. 62–63.

10. Fyodor Dostoevsky, *The Possessed*, Constance Garnett, tr. (New York: Dell, 1961), p. 555.

11. Marcel Proust, *Swann's Way*, C. K. Scott Moncrieff, tr. (New York: Modern Library, 1956), pp. 56–57.

Index